D1602679

Key Legal Issues for Schools

The Ultimate Resource for School Business Officials

Edited by
Charles Russo

Published in partnership with the
Association of School Business Officials International

Rowman & Littlefield Education
Lanham, Maryland • Toronto • Oxford
2006

Published in partnership with the
Association of School Business Officials International

Published in the United States of America
by Rowman & Littlefield Education
A Division of Rowman & Littlefield Publishers, Inc.
A wholly owned subsidary of The Rowman & Littlefield Publishing Group,
Inc.
4501 Forbes Boulevard, Suite 200, Lanham, Maryland 20706
www.rowmaneducation.com

PO Box 317
Oxford
OX2 9RU, UK

British Library Cataloguing in Publication Information Available

Library of Congress Cataloging-in-Publication Data

Key legal issues for schools : the ultimate resource for school business officials /
[edited by] Charles Russo.
    p. cm.
  ISBN 1-57886-344-9 (hardcover : alk. paper)— ISBN 1-57886-343-0 (pbk. :
alk. paper)
  1. Educational law and legislation—United States. 2. Students—Legal status,
laws, etc.—United States. 3. School employees—Legal status, laws, etc.—
United States. I. Russo, Charles J.
  KF4119.K49 2006
  344.73'07—dc22

2005018111

⊗™ The paper used in this publication meets the minimum requirements of
American National Standard for Information Sciences—Permanence of Paper
for Printed Library Materials, ANSI/NISO Z39.48-1992.
Manufactured in the United States of America.

Contents

Acknowledgments

As with any book, there are a number of people who must be thanked. Two sets of people in two different organizations were very helpful in initiating this book. Thanks to Cindy Tursman and Tom Koerner at Rowman & Littlefield Education, as well as Dr. Anne Miller, executive director of the Association of School Business Officials International (ASBO), and Ms. Siobhan McMahon, ASBO's director of membership, marketing, and communications. Of course, it almost goes without saying that I am grateful to the authors for their valuable contributions to this book. At the University of Dayton, I would like to thank my assistant, Ms. Elizabeth Pearn, for her efforts in helping to prepare the manuscript for publication and to Ms. Cheryl Marcus for her assistance in proofreading the final text. Last, but certainly not least, I would like to express my thanks to and love for my wife Debbie for her ongoing love and support, without whom none of this work would have been completed.

Introduction

School business officials (SBOs) must, in many respects, serve as all things to all people. Put another way, SBOs must be knowledgeable about a wide range of legal, and other, issues ranging from contracts to setting policy to state bidding laws, let alone constitutional matters involving students and teachers. At the center of the many SBO duties are issues involving the law. Thus, the chapters in this edited book have been written by a diverse array of individuals with experience as educational leaders in schools or who possess significant expertise in education law.

Aware of the need to keep SBOs up to date on many issues in the ever changing world of education law, this volume is divided into two parts. More specifically, each of the chapters is designed to examine a specific area about which SBOs need information. The first section deals with issues that primarily impact on the management of schools, while the second part examines questions primarily focusing on the rights of students and teachers.

The first part of the book, covering chapters 1–7, covers policy formation, legal issues surrounding budgeting and accounting, contracting for school boards, school choice and privatization, transportation, technology, and negligence.

- Chapter 1, on policy formation, by Timothy J. Ilg and Philip E. Tieman of the University of Dayton, both former superintendents, provides advice on this important task. As important members of management teams, the authors offer insights to SBOs so that they can assume a more active role in this vital process.

- Chapter 2, by Donald R. Johnson, another former superintendent as well as a former SBO, provides a brief overview of accounting and budgeting practices that are so central to the daily work of SBOs.
- Chapter 3, by Bradley Colwell, examines another important task in the professional lives of SBOs, school board contracting.
- Chapter 4, by Frank Brown, reviews important and timely issues associated with the growing trend toward privatization in public education, discussing why SBOs should be concerned about this practice.
- Chapter 5, by Ralph D. Mawdsley, a former superintendent in a non-public school, considers one of the most far-reaching of the daily tasks of school systems, student transportation, highlighting major issues that arise on a regular basis.
- Given the growing impact that technology has on the day to day lives of SBOs and their school systems, chapter 6, by Timothy E. Morse, an assistant director of special education, provides an up-to-date examination of emerging issues in this vital area.
- The first part of the book rounds out with chapter 7, by Charles J. Russo, with a look at one of the more significant concerns of SBOs and all educational leaders, namely how to avoid liability for negligence.

The second section in the book focuses on the rights of employees and students. These chapters cover the supervision and evaluation of employees, the rights of employees and students, and issues concerning special education and students with disabilities. This part concludes with an examination of the place of legal issues surrounding aid to non-public schools and the place of prayer and religious activity in public schools.

- Chapter 8, by C. Daniel Raisch, a former superintendent, zeroes in on the important task of how educational leaders should properly supervise staff.
- Chapter 9, by Ralph D. Mawdsley, reviews the many statutory and constitutional rights of school employees.
- In a similar manner, chapter 10, by Patrick D. Pauken, examines the constitutional rights of students.

- Chapter 11, by Allan G. Osborne, a school principal and former director of special education, focuses in on the ever expanding rights of students with disabilities under the Individuals With Disabilities Education Act and other federal statutes.
- Chapter 12, by Ralph D. Mawdsley, examines perhaps the most contentious of all issues involving the Supreme Court, the place of religion in public education.

Of course, no single book can ever hope to cover the myriad of legal topics that SBOs and other educational leaders must master in their professional lives. Thus, in the event that school boards are contemplating legal actions, they and their SBOs should consult their attorney. Even so, the editor hopes that these well-written and researched chapters will serve as an up-to-date and ready source of information to help keep SBOs and other educational leaders abreast of the many changes in the ever evolving area of education law.

1

Effective Policy Formation: A New Challenge

Timothy J. Ilg and Philip E. Tieman

More than a decade of standards-based reforms has changed almost every aspect of American education policy decision-making. School boards are under increased pressure to provide all children with a quality education. Student achievement has become the ultimate measure of educational value. Increasingly, citizens and public school critics are dissatisfied with their public schools and their boards. They see boards as more interested in micro-managing school systems than providing solid policies and procedures. They do not see the boards devoting enough time to policy oversight and communication efforts to inform the public of the rationale of board policy.[1] Boards are increasingly looking inward toward central office personnel to assist them in structuring solid policies to address the myriad of problems facing school districts in the 21st century. If superintendents and school business officials are to play key roles in policy formation, they must be highly knowledgeable of board policy development procedures. Hopefully, this chapter will assist them in this important task.

School boards need assistance in facing the increased criticism of the failure of their students to make adequate progress on state standards, as they are seemingly disengaged with regard to student achievement.[2] Public school critics have demanded that school boards focus their attention on student academic achievement. Unfortunately, there is little evidence in the literature to show a direct link between board policy and its impact on student learning.[3] However, there is evidence that achievement can be influenced by coordinated board policies and their active involvement in statewide reform efforts.[4] To some extent, the fact that a board has policies on student achievement will have a positive impact by demonstrating that student learning is a priority.

Historically, boards have spent little time on one of their primary responsibilities—policy development. When boards adopt systematic approaches to policy development, they can ensure consistency between and among goals, long-range planning, resource distribution, and assessment. They can govern their districts by developing policies that specify desired ends and determine acceptable means of reaching goals.[5] In effect, boards plan their strategic direction through their policies.[6] In addition to policy-making, school boards are responsible for planning, monitoring, communicating, and advocating for the children in their communities. More specifically, boards should adopt strategic plans with clear visions and specific goals and strategies. The planning process should involve the establishment of educational standards, assessment measures, and the development of an annual budget that reflects the priority goals of the district. In monitoring the operations of their schools, boards evaluate the superintendent, adopt measures for assessing student achievement, maintain fiscal oversight, and regularly review progress reports. Communicating in an open and honest manner with the public is a crucial board responsibility. Boards must establish procedures for reporting to parents about student achievement, for reaching out to the community to seek input on community needs, and for seeking support for district efforts. Most important, boards must be advocates for the children in the community, and they must communicate their children's needs to the politicians and policy-makers at all levels.

Focusing school boards on the crucial responsibilities of policy-making, planning, monitoring, communicating, and advocating should go a long way in keeping them from becoming immersed in the daily administration of their schools. This micro-managing has been a major criticism of the school governance structure for many years.[7] The work of boards should focus on policy-making, budget adoption, contracting and evaluating the superintendent, and developing long-range plans. First and foremost, boards must be policy-makers. They must establish and regularly review policies that define their structures, rules of procedure, communication and decision-making processes, code of conduct, and other policies pertaining to district governance. They must also establish and regularly review policies that set expectations for district educational and operational functions.

Thus, this chapter discusses in detail procedures for developing board policies in a structured and focused manner.

BOARD POLICY DEVELOPMENT

Well-developed, well-articulated policies are often indicators of the attitude and commitment of school boards toward following effective management practices. Insofar as policies permeate all aspects of a district's organizational life, they represent the most powerful lever for exercising board leadership. Clear board policies will provide a board with a consistent plan for how it will operate, compelling it to stay focused on the critical challenge of providing vision and leadership for improving student achievement. On the other hand, poor policy-making, characterized by impulsive or politically expedient actions that are based on incomplete data, frequently set the stage for long-range problems. These problems will ultimately damage a board's ability to influence the achievement levels within a district.

The policies adopted by school boards are often treated as a school district's "law," since they are principles to chart courses of action. Policies provide a community, employees, and students with visible statements of a board's beliefs and practices regarding educational and management practices. Further, they are public statements through which boards can be held accountable. Although policies should be succinct and number as few as possible, they must contain everything boards have to say about values and perspectives that underlie all organizational decisions, activities, practices, budgets, and goals. Thus, boards must see the need of understanding and practicing the intricacies of policy-making as one of their most important responsibilities. Policy decision-making, at its best, will lay out a vision for strengthening the relationships between schools and communities while establishing procedures for meeting a district's needs and creating benchmarks for its own success.

Policies generally originate from legislative directives and statutes developed by federal, state, and local government units regarding school operating matters.[8] The sweeping provisions of the No Child Left Behind Act[9] have necessitated changes in long-standing practices at the local level and wholesale revisions to board policies. The National School

Boards Association (NSBA) has identified more than 45 categories of policies such as employment and hiring, assessment, student privacy, and employee liability that must be reviewed as a result of this legislation.[10] In these cases, policies will simply fulfill pass-along mandates originating at the state or federal level. State reform acts, such as Kentucky's Education Reform Act of 1990, granted far-reaching powers to the state and local school councils.[11] Although board members often view increased state involvement as an encroachment on traditional board authority, some educators see this trend as positive for school governance, since boards can focus their attention on important internal matters and policy matters. Such an approach encourages states to repeal all current regulations regarding school boards and create performance criteria for them to hold them accountable for student progress. In effect, school boards would be education policy boards only.[12]

Boards have enacted additional policies over the years in response to the expanding influence of judicial decisions on their decision-making processes. Traditionally, courts have given school boards broad latitude to act in the best interest of the public.[13] For example, the Fifth Circuit court of appeals affirmed the right of a school board in Louisiana to establish a mandatory uniform policy.[14] Previously, the Ninth Circuit upheld a finding that school officials in California did not violate the First Amendment right to free exercise of religion of a teacher in California by requiring him to teach evolution in biology classes.[15] In such controversial matters, since the courts are not always consistent in their rulings, it is imperative for boards to receive a comprehensive review of all cases before they establish policies. In another case, the Seventh Circuit affirmed that a school board in Illinois could prohibit a teacher from teaching creation science on the basis that he was not free to inject his religious beliefs into the public school curriculum.[16]

Traditionally, the development of board policies has taken place in a variety of structures. In many cases, school boards developed policy statements in response to local issues. In this way, policies are fundamentally public decisions that take shape through procedures, programs, and services. Boards should not restrict the sources from which they receive the impetus to change or establish policies. On the other hand, boards must clearly communicate to the public that policy development is their responsibility.[17]

Policy statements are usually written at the local level by school administrators or board members and are reviewed by counsel. Alternatively, many boards engage the services of professional organizations such as their state school boards association and/or private policy development companies to develop their policy manuals. No matter how boards approach policy development, they must consider the impact of policy on their employees and, more particularly, on administrators who are responsible for its implementation.

In light of the far-reaching impact of board policy, boards and educational leaders would be wise to consider the following recommendations as a means of developing and maintaining current policies:

1. School boards and superintendents should include sufficient funds in their annual budgets to retain the services of professional agencies to review and revise their current policy documents and to provide, at a minimum, annual reviews and draft updates of policies on a quarterly basis. Such an agency can provide board members with sample policies, regulations, and exhibits from other districts in a state. A firm can also provide statistical data, research studies, program information, and other resources needed to make informed decisions on local issues. In addition, a professional service can ensure that a board's student handbooks and administrative guidelines reflect current board policy.

2. The general operating procedures of school boards should include annual reviews of all new and revised policies to determine whether modifications should be made on the basis of implementation experiences. The board and superintendent of schools might consider establishing a Policy Review Committee to identify issues and situations that should be considered for the annual policy review activities. In addition to board members, the committee should have at least one principal and one central office administrator such as the school business official (SBO) as permanent members. The SBO is a logical choice because of the number of policies in the typical policy manual that deal directly with activities under his or her responsibility. A typical list of such policies includes activity bus pool, annual financial audit, procedures for approving facilities' construction contracts, building codes, bus maintenance, and contracted maintenance

services. Such a committee should systematically review one-third of a district's policy manual each year and make recommendations to the board for revisions. In this review process, a committee should evaluate the effectiveness of the new or revised policies based on pre-established criteria. The following questions should be helpful in judging the quality of a policy:

- Does the policy give clear direction to the superintendent and staff?
- Is the policy required by a law, regulation, or judicial mandate?
- Does the policy state clearly to whom it is directed or for whom it was developed?
- Is the policy comprehensive enough to provide flexibility in the rules that will be developed to assist in its implementation?
- Is the policy practical? Can the policy be administered without undue burden on the staff? Does the policy address the criteria that will be used to evaluate implementation?
- Is there an operational or governance need for the policy?
- Is the issue important enough to warrant a new policy? Is policy development the appropriate response?

3. A Policy Development Committee should be formed to develop new policies and to revise existing ones which may be necessary outside of the annual review process. The committee should carefully analyze the circumstances that created the need for a new policy before forwarding any new policy to the board. The process for identifying the need for a new policy should be broad enough to include major stakeholders in the community, such as parents, students, staff, and community members. Once the need is confirmed, committee members should isolate the key issues and collect as much data as possible. Information should include federal, state, and local laws, state department of education mandates, negotiated agreements, job descriptions, and current practices. In addition, a committee should consider what other boards have done, establish a range of possible alternatives, consider "Impact Statements," and seek consensus on an approach. Although committee members must pay special attention to the necessary aspects of legal compliance, they must main-

tain a sharpened focus on the vision, direction, and purpose of school board policies for assuring public accountability for student achievement.

4. The drafts of new and revised policy statements should be reviewed by the school board's attorney for final review and editing. Other interested parties in the school community can participate in the review process as appropriate.

5. The board and superintendent should encourage consultation with interested groups and individuals in the policy-making process. The board should engage in a public discussion of policies before they are placed on an agenda for formal adoption. This could be a wonderful opportunity to pursue deliberative discussions with the public in open forums in order to foster and engage in dialogue and conversation on board policies as well as other matters of public interest. One effective technique is to circulate a proposed policy to as many people in a district as possible who will be directly affected by the new policy. Many districts post the new or revised policies and/or procedures on their websites for a 21-day public comment period. Some districts provide 60 days' notice of their intention to consider and vote on proposed policies at subsequent regular meeting. In addition, boards post proposed policies in the schools and at all central office sites. Interested parties should be required to make written rather than oral response as to the impact of a proposed policy. Of course, all statements should be carefully reviewed by boards before they take official action. Moreover, a proposed policy should be placed on a board's agenda a month before any formal vote for discussion and revision. After the first reading, the policy should be refined if needed before the second reading and adoption. The superintendent is normally responsible for redrafting policy proposals.

6. Once school boards formally adopt policies, they should inform employees and stakeholders that they have done so. Once a final version has been adopted, the policy will be effective, thus making administrative procedures also effective on that date. The superintendent and/or the designee should be prepared to distribute the policy to all staff members and post it in conspicuous areas in the schools and administrative offices as well as on the district's website. Districtwide officials are responsible for implementing policy by drafting regulations and

procedures, developing programs required by it, communicating it to all groups, and ensuring that all employees comply with the policy. The SBO plays a key role in the compliance phase because many, if not all, of the classified staff usually report to this person.

7. Board policy manuals need clearly to separate the policies from the administrative regulations and procedures. All edicts of the state, signed contracts, and board rules and regulations concerning its own procedures should be presented as board policy. The administrative regulations are the rules developed by the administration to put policy into practice. They tell how, by whom, where, and when things are to be done. As long as the administration operates within the guidelines of the general policy, it may change administrative regulations without prior board approval unless the board specifically prohibits it from doing so. Normally, boards would be wise to state clearly what they will not allow, but remain silent regarding specific staff actions. This will enable boards to set limits on the actions of the administration without micro-managing a district. Carver defines this as "executive limitations" in which a board identifies the behaviors that are unacceptable and permits the superintendent to act freely within those boundaries.[18] In general, school boards and superintendents prefer a blend of the two positions and believe they work best when there is flexibility between policy-making and administration.[19]

8. It is crucial that policy manuals are formatted in a logical and easy to maneuver fashion. In most manuals, the policies and procedures are given the same numbered sequence within the subject index in order to make it more user friendly. Typically, the document would be divided into areas of responsibility such as:

- *Educational Philosophy*. This section includes a district's philosophy, mission statement, and philosophical framework for making decisions.
- *Board Policy Function and Operations*. These include the organization of the board, procedures for policy-making, and the structure for evaluating staff and district operations.
- *Administration/Executive Function*. This includes policies associated with management responsibilities, policy implementation, and administrative goals.

- *Personnel*. This section deals with job descriptions, hiring practices, disciplinary actions, evaluations, and compensation.
- *Student Personnel*. This includes due process, attendance, discipline, and student records.
- *Educational Program*. This policy section deals with curriculum, instructional practices, textbook selection procedures, and general program responsibilities.
- *Business and Operational Function*. Of course, school business officers are highly involved in this area. Policies here include safety programs, fiscal accounting, food service, clerical, maintenance, purchasing, and budgeting.
- *School/Community Relations*. This section addresses such issues as visitation of schools, use of facilities, public information, and community involvement.

9. A board member should be responsible for keeping the policy manual up to date. Normally, a staff member is assigned responsibility to assist the board member in accomplishing the following tasks:

- Controlling access to and safeguarding the electronic files for both print and online versions of the manual.
- Updating both the print and online versions of the manual as soon as the board approves the policy.
- Ensuring that policies are not modified through the use of memos or other internal correspondence without going through the approved process.
- Encouraging employees to use the online version of the policy manual, thus reducing the number of print copies.

CONCLUSION

The practices listed above should assist school boards in carrying out their duties as policy-makers. When boards lead districts through formulating policies and evaluating their implementation, they have the most control over the organization. Such governance promotes vision and inspiration in the organizations. Many analysts agree that the role of boards of education should be governing by establishing the organization's goals, setting its policy, and planning its strategy, rather than administering the organization.[20] However, since there is no simple division between policy and administration, it is often difficult to decipher managing the organization from monitoring the organization. Tension is part of the equation when a superintendent has a role in shaping policy as well as a leadership position in a district. It is rarely possible to have a rigid separation of policy and operations.[21] Collaboration between the board and superintendent is needed to effectively ensure policy formation and implementation. When both sides have empathy for each other's roles and see the relationship as a partnership, there is effective governance in the district.[22]

Partnerships are created when both sides assist each other in carrying out their duties. For instance, administrators can assist boards in carrying out their responsibilities as policy-makers by providing them with important information. Making decisions based on policies and, ultimately, allocating resources to produce the best outcomes require dependable, comprehensive information. It should assist boards in identifying and explaining possible options and their consequences, comparing intentions with results, and providing program descriptions and resource allocation. Administrators can also help board members in obtaining information that is independent of what the staff gives them so they can make their own judgments. School business officials should play important roles in providing their boards with financial information on many important school functions. Thus, a thorough knowledge of board policy development should assist school business officials both in providing relevant information on key issues and in guiding boards toward effective policies.

NOTES

1. J. Danzberger, M. Kirst, and M. Usdan, *Governing Public Schools: New Times, New Requirements* (Washington, D.C.: Institute for Educational Leadership, 1992).

2. M. McCarthy and M. B. Cello, *Washington Elementary Schools on the Slow Track Under Standards-Based Reform: Making Standards Work* (Seattle, Wash.: Center on Reinventing Public Education, 2001).

3. D. Land, *Local School Boards Under Review: Their Role and Effectiveness in Relation to Students' Academic Achievement* (Baltimore: Center for Research on the Education of Students Placed at Risk, 2002).

4. R. Elmore, "The Role of Local School Districts in Instructional Improvement," in *Designing Coherent Education Policy*, ed. Susan H. Fuhrman (San Francisco: Jossey-Bass, 1993), 96–124.

5. J. Carver, "Toward Coherent Governance," *School Administrator* 57, no. 3 (2000): 6–10.

6. D. Belfall, *Associations in Canada: Future Impact and Influence* (Toronto: Foundation for Association Research and Education, 1995).

7. M. A. Resnick, *Effective School Governance: A Look at Today's Practice and Tomorrow's Promise* (Denver: ECS Distribution Center, 1999).

8. T. Kowalski, *The School Superintendent: Theory, Practice, and Cases* (Upper Saddle River, N.J.: Prentice-Hall, 1999).

9. No Child Left Behind Act, 20 U.S.C. 6301 et seq. (2002).

10. National School Boards Association, *The No Child Left Behind Act: Policy Guidelines for Local School Boards* (Alexandria, Va.: Author, 2002). Available at www.nsba.org/cosa/Hot_topics/nclba.htm.

11. C. Pippo, "Sweeping the Boards Clean," *Phi Delta Kappa*, March 1992, 510–511.

12. Twentieth Century Fund, *Facing the Challenge: The Report of the Twentieth Century Fund Task Force on School Governance* (New York: Author, 1992).

13. D. Conley, *Roadmap to Restructuring: Policies, Practices, and the Emerging Visions of Schooling* (Eugene: ERIC Clearinghouse on Educational Management, University of Oregon, 1993).

14. *Canady v. Bossier Parish Sch. Bd.*, 240 F.3d 437 (5th Cir., 2001).

15. *Peloza v. Capistrano United Sch. Dist.*, 37 F.3d 517 (9th Cir., 1994).

16. *Webster v. New Lenox Sch. Dist. # 122*, 917 F.2d 1004 (1990).

17. J. Carver, *Boards That Make a Difference* (San Francisco: Jossey-Bass, 1990).

18. Carver, "Toward Coherent Governance."

19. J. McCurdy, *Building Better Board-Administrator Relations* (Arlington, Va.: American Association of School Administrators, 1993).

20. D. S. Leighton and D. H. Thain, *Making Boards Work: What Directors Must Do to Make Canadian Boards Effective* (Toronto: McGraw-Hill, 1997).

21. R. D. Herman and R. D. Heimovics, *Executive Leadership in Nonprofit Organizations: New Strategies for Shaping Executive-Board Dynamics* (San Francisco: Jossey-Bass, 1991).

22. C. O. Houle, *Governing Boards: Their Nature and Nurture* (San Francisco: Jossey-Bass, 1989).

2

Accounting and Budgeting Functions

Donald R. Johnson

Many professions, through their professional organizations, develop sets of standards that denote the levels of performance that are expected of members. In 1995 the Association of School Business Officials International developed and adopted such a set of professional standards for school business administrators.[1] An integral part or feature of professional standards is the skills and knowledge base necessary for individuals to perform to the level set by the standards. Some skills permeate all standards and are necessary components of the knowledge base. One such skill is an understanding of legal considerations in the administration of accounting and budgeting functions.

STANDARDS

The Illinois State Board of Education established standards for the preparation and licensure of chief school business officials (SBOs) and used the following knowledge and performance indicators to demonstrate preparation in legal aspects.[2]

Standard 4: Legal Aspects

The competent chief school business official understands and applies the legal aspects of educational leadership.

Knowledge Indicators: The competent chief school business official:

4A. Understands the state and federal constitutional rights that apply to individuals within the public education system.

4B. Understands appropriate statutory and constitutional authority regarding the general administration of public schools.

Performance Indicator: The competent chief school business official:

4C. Analyzes and implements significant statutory and case law relative to a number of management fields, including financial resource, human resource, facility and property, information, and ancillary services (including subcontracting).

Some illustrative examples of activities that SBOs could perform in order to demonstrate that they have satisfied these requirements are:

- Develop employee discipline/corrective action examples for education support personnel.
- Research developer fees.
- Research the Drug Free Workplace Act of 1998.
- Research the legality of transfer of interest between funds.
- Review Board Regulations and their relation to state statutes.
- Analyze the pros and cons of subcontracting custodial services.

School leaders need to be aware of legal implications from involvement with any of the above or similar activities.

Individual states may have legal requirements for school leaders and/or school boards to follow in accounting principles. Chief among these requirements is whether to use the cash or accrual method of accounting for the district's money. Everett, Johnson, & Madden[3] employ the following definitions of these terms:

- Accrual Basis: The basis of accounting under which revenues are recorded when earned and expenditures are recorded as soon as they result in liabilities for benefits received, notwithstanding that the receipt of the revenue or the payment of the expenditure or in part in another accounting period.

- Cash Basis: The basis of accounting under which revenues are recorded only when actually received, and only cash disbursements are recorded as expenditures.

INTERNAL CONTROLS

School board officials, especially SBOs, need to establish and follow guidelines for the safe handling of money. Generally, these guidelines come under the heading of internal controls. There are legal implications for school leaders in establishing, monitoring, or managing internal controls. Some illustrative internal code activities are:[4]

Inventory Control

- Only authorized individuals should be able to purchase replacement inventory.
- Inventory purchases should be made only from approved vendors.
- Specific employees should be assigned responsibility for the custody of the inventory.
- Store inventories in locked locations and restrict access in such areas to a few specific individuals.
- Items that are deemed obsolete or otherwise unusable should be mutilated or destroyed so they cannot be used. The disposal should be documented.
- Maintain perpetual inventory records in both dollars and quantities for large amounts of inventory.

Petty Cash

- Maintain petty cash in a locked, secure location at all times.
- A limited number of employees should handle all petty cash transactions.
- Keep petty cash funds separate from other cash.
- Establish a maximum amount for individual disbursements from the petty cash fund.
- Never disburse petty cash unless proper, original receipts are attached.

- Review documentation periodically to determine whether any of the receipts in the fund are unusual.
- Reconcile on a regular basis by someone other than the petty cash custodian.

Property, Plant, and Equipment

- All capital purchases should require advance written approval by authorized personnel and should be included in the department's capital budget.
- Limit the number of employees authorized to approve capital purchases.
- Compare capital budgets to actual expenditures and analyze significant differences.
- Properly code all capital purchases.
- Detailed property listings should indicate the location of each asset; assign responsibility for the asset to a particular employee.
- Tag each asset with a unique identification number immediately upon receipt.
- A complete physical inventory of a department's property and equipment should be conducted whenever there is a change in the department head.
- All retirements of assets should be properly authorized prior to disposing of the items and removing them from the property and equipment listing.

Purchasing and Cash Disbursement

- Responsibility for purchase requisition approval should be separate from the purchase requisition preparation, recording, and receiving functions.
- Include the account code on all purchase requisitions.
- Never split purchases in an attempt to avoid the approval required for larger purchases by the appropriate levels of authority.
- Purchase requisitions should be signed by an authorized employee.
- The employee accepting goods should inspect and count them. Counts should agree with the purchase requisition and purchase order before payment is approved.

- Responsibility for check disbursement approval should be separate from that of other purchasing functions whenever possible.
- Review all invoices to make sure that no sales tax has been added.
- Keep blank checks locked up at all times; assign the responsibility for controlling the blank checks to a designated employee.
- Make checks payable to specific payees, never to "cash," "petty cash," or "bearer."

Revenue and Cash Receipts

- Centralize receiving of cash as much as possible.
- Deposit all cash receipts on a timely basis.
- Lock up all cash receipts prior to making the deposit.
- Prohibit employees or parents from cashing personal checks.
- Don't accept checks written for an amount greater than the amount due.
- Cross train employees to perform other financial tasks, and require these employees to rotate job duties periodically.
- Assign individual passwords to log onto the computerized accounting system to record transactions.
- All safes should be kept locked during the day.
- Bank reconciliations should be reviewed and approved by the appropriate supervisor.

OTHER

Additional accounting and budgeting areas that have implications for educational leaders include the following items:[5]

- Identifying legal requirements and procedures for acquiring insurance for school districts. This could include procedures for conducting a needs assessment for insurance purposes; different types of insurance required by schools and their characteristics; the components of an insurance contract and procedures for filing an insurance claim; and periodic appraisal, evaluation, and review procedures and requirements for insurance management.

- Understanding the elements of the personnel function. This could include issues and procedures related to hiring and assigning staff; requirements and procedures for using and maintaining personnel records; disciplinary, termination, and due process procedures; and federal, state, and local regulations governing employment practices.
- Understanding support staff performance evaluation procedures. This could include types and characteristics of methods and instruments for assessing job performance; legal and ethical procedures for communicating and disseminating evaluation results to support staff; and the use of evaluation information to improve job performance.
- Understanding rules and regulations governing employee compensation. This could include the cost impact of various compensation plans; the components of payroll procedures; and types and purpose of payroll records.
- Understanding employee benefits. This could include legal requirements for providing employee benefits; types of employee benefits and their characteristics; and the financial implications of employee benefits.
- Reviewing and applying the legal requirements for budget adoption.
- Establishing and verifying compliance with finance-related legal and contractual provisions.
- Understanding the legal constraints and methods of issuing long-term general obligation bonds, including the bond rating process and role of rating services.
- Reviewing and analyzing procedures for the bidding, selecting, evaluating, and managing of fringe benefit programs, including the legal requirements and tax consequences of fringe benefit programs using federal and state codes.
- Developing appropriate procedures for selecting and using professional services of architects, engineers, construction managers, and other professionals, and understanding their roles and responsibilities.
- Reviewing the legal and administrative responsibilities for advertising, awarding, and managing construction contracts, including contractor bankruptcy, product failure, and poor workmanship.
- Establishing policies and procedures to provide proper comprehensive insurance protection to the school district, developing the common types of protection needed, and providing basic insight into the acquisition and evaluation of insurance programs.

- Complying with federal and state statutes regarding liability limits and bond requirements.
- Complying with federal laws regarding asbestos abatement, radon gas, lead contaminants, and other potentially hazardous substances, reviewing and developing district policies regarding students and staff infected with contagious diseases, and developing guidelines for promoting health and wellness programs for staff and students.

CONCLUSION

It almost goes without saying that educational leaders who work with accounting and budgeting should adhere to a code of ethics. Moreover, some states include ethics for SBOs as part of their constitutions.[6] By adhering to professional standards, educational leaders should develop and use the skills and knowledge base necessary to have an understanding of legal considerations in the administration of accounting and budgeting functions.

NOTES

1. T. E. Glass, R. E. Everett, and D. R. Johnson, "Survey Results: Preparing School Business Administrators," *School Business Affairs* 64, no. 9 (1998): 19–23.

2. Illinois State Board of Education, www.isbe.state.il.us/profprep/pcstandard rules.htm, www.iasbo.org.

3. R. E. Everett, D. R. Johnson, and B. M. Madden, *Financial and Managerial Accounting for School Administrators* (Lanham, Md.: Scarecrow Education, 2005).

4. B. Nuehring and R. Ally, "Annual Bookkeepers Seminar: Internal Controls" (DeKalb: Illinois Association of School Business Officials, 2000).

5. Northern Illinois University, www.niu.edu/coe/lepf/coursedescriptions.

6. Texas Association of School Business Officials, www.tasbo.org/PDF/COE.pdf.

3

School Board Contracting

Bradley Colwell

School boards and their school business officials (SBOs) make hundreds of business transactions each year. This is in addition to the numerous purchase requests SBOs receive each year that are not funded. Consequently, SBOs should have an established set of guidelines to determine whether to approve a proposed transaction. These guidelines are necessary to make sure that all purchases are financially feasible and not duplicative of other employees' purchase requests. Further, SBOs should have the centralized authority to approve all school district purchases and not allow employees to make individual purchases without the knowledge of the SBO or other school administrator.[1] Should a proposal not be approved for purchase, it is essential that an employee receive feedback explaining why the request was denied. Yet, above all else, the guiding principle of a SBO should always be "what's in the best interest of students' education."

Before a school board enters into an agreement for the purchase of a product or for professional service, a SBO must review the proposed agreement to ensure it will be a legal transaction. Two questions serve as the focal point of this chapter: when is a transaction subject to the competitive bidding process, and what should be in a written contract?

THE NATURE OF COMPETITIVE BIDDING

All purchases in excess of a state's bidding threshold are subject to its competitive bid procedures. The basic concept of competitive bidding is that bids are submitted and evaluated in a fair and objective manner. This most often means that SBOs and other school officials award contracts on the basis of the lowest bids. The key benefit of bidding is that it promotes competition, thus assuring lower costs and providing equal access to all prospective bidders to supply a school district's goods and services. In addition, competitive bidding increases the efficiency and effectiveness of school district resources. The negative aspects of competitive bidding include the expense in preparing the bid documents, the extended time necessary to comply with the bidding requirements, inflexibility of the process, and the competitive disadvantage to minority business owners that may keep them from being awarded a contract.

The role of the SBO in the competitive bid process is to assist with the procurement of required goods and services while ensuring that all applicable school policies and procedures as well as applicable federal and state laws and regulations are adhered to regarding the acquisition of goods and services (see appendix A).

WHEN TO BID A CONTRACT

A fair and transparent competitive bidding process is essential to the acquisition of goods and services for public school systems. However, since a board does not have to bid every contract, it is incumbent on SBOs to be very familiar with the statutory thresholds that mandate when transactions are subject to the competitive bid process. If a transaction exceeds the statutory threshold, then a SBO should competitively bid the contract. If not, then a board can enter a contract with the vendor of its choice without having to utilize the bidding process.

SBOs must take into consideration a number of variables before concluding whether their boards should submit contracts for competitive bids. Two factors that SBOs must consider are a project's size and scope. Any large-scale project or a job with multiple phases or that will be subcontracted should likely be competitively bid. However, the most important variables when considering whether to bid a project are the legal considerations. State statutes and court cases often provide insight into what type of contracts need to be let through the competitive bidding process. Competitive bidding is usually triggered by a project's dollar amount as well as by the type of service/project involved. For example, most states mandate that school boards must bid contracts that involve the purchase of supplies, material, or work that exceeds a specified dollar amount (ranging between $7,500 and $50,000). Some states have adopted a higher minimum dollar amount for bidding contracts for capital projects that involve remodeling or renovation of an existing school facility.

School boards must also bid contracts dealing with certain types of projects, regardless of cost. For instance, statutes usually mandate the bidding of contracts for major repairs, erection of buildings, or for other structural improvements. Moreover, most states have statutory provisions that exempt contracts for certain types of services and goods from the competitive bidding requirement. These are typically contracts for services of individuals possessing a high degree of professional skill; for perishable food and beverages; for maintenance or servicing of equipment by the manufacturer or authorized service agent of that equipment; for goods or services procured from another governmental agency; for goods or services which are economically procurable from only one source, such as utility services or purchases of magazines, or funds expended in an emergency and approved by three-fourths of the board members. Even so, SBOs should never attempt to avoid state bidding requirements by dividing projects into separate contracts that reasonably should be contained in one contract.

PREPARING FOR A BID

Once a determination has been made to bid a project, SBOs must prepare the bid documents. Foremost, SBOs should seek final input from the various school district constituents that will use the product or service. This will primarily include the affected school employees (certified and noncertified), with involvement of external constituencies (including parents, taxpayers, and the business community) for larger capital projects.[2] This input will help to evaluate how the bid documents should be prepared to reflect the proposed use of the contracted service or product.[3]

SBOs should also consult with content-area experts. For instance, the board's architect and engineer should be actively involved in all aspects of preparing the bid documents for a capital project. Further, it is always prudent to have the board's attorney review bid documents to ensure legal compliance with all federal and state laws.

Concurrent with seeking constituency input, SBOs, in conjunction with their boards and district administrators, should be making final plans on project budgeting. This includes not only overall estimated costs, but costs of each phase within larger capital projects such as HVAC or plumbing. Another fiscal component to consider is what impact, if any, a funding source may have on bid documents. This may only be an issue for more expensive projects, but it is necessary to decide whether a project will be financed by selling bonds, raising property taxes, or external funding such as competitive grants, and how this may impact prospective bidders.

REQUEST FOR BIDS

Once bid documents have been prepared, school boards must comply with all procedural requirements regarding the letting of contracts. A board's failure to adhere to the statutory bidding requirements constitutes an unlawful act that may render a contract unenforceable.

Legal Notice

State laws may require school boards to advertise bids before they can award contracts. The purpose of advertising is to avoid favoritism by informing all prospective bidders of the bidding opportunity as well as to afford bidders sufficient time to submit well-considered bids. Most times this is satisfied by a legal notice in a local newspaper (usually required to run 10 days before the bid date) and/or by posting notice on a bulletin board outside a district's primary administrative office. Some states mandate that school boards send notice by mail to all businesses that have filed requests in writing that they be listed for solicitation on bids for particular items.

An advertisement generally includes a description of the scope of the work or materials involved, the time frame when bid specifications will be available for review or how they can be obtained, the time and location of where to submit bids, and when the bids will be opened. Some advertisements may include whether a pre-bid meeting will take place to answer questions about a project, as well as a statement that the board reserves the right to accept or reject all bids (see appendix B).

Bid Specifications

School boards must make certain that sufficient information is provided to ensure that all bidders can make responsive bids. This information, called bid specifications, should be an accurate and detailed description of the service or goods that is available to all prospective bidders either in hard or electronic copy.

Bid specifications should include a detailed description of the scope of the service or the materials, including quantity of the supplies, as well as if there is a desired preference for a specific brand name. In addition, the specifications may include the time frame when the work is to be completed, where the materials are to be delivered, and whether preference will be given to a local or in-state provider. It is also important to provide basic logistical information about the bidding process, such as the contact person for additional information (usually the SBO), the time period and location for submitting a bid, necessary qualifications of potential contractors, and the requirements of a bid deposit.[4]

Key provisions to be included in the bidding documents for professional services include:

- Commitment to a district's completion date without exception, or else payment of a monetary penalty such as $400 per day for each calendar day over the deadline.
- All cost overruns due to contractor error are the cost of the contractor. Only those changes contained in a "change order" are the board's responsibility.
- A provision regarding compliance with the state's Prevailing Wage Act, the Preference Act, and the Human Rights Act.
- A hold-harmless agreement and a clause for liability and Workers Compensation insurance to which the school board is named as an additional insured.

It is imperative that SBOs provide any amendments to the bid specifications to all prospective bidders or else a contract could be nullified.

AWARDING A BID

Bid Opening

All bidders must submit sealed bids on or before the date and time the bids are to be opened. Unless otherwise stated, a school board should not accept faxed or emailed bids. All bids, including alternate bids, should be opened at a public bid opening and should be read aloud. State law will specify who can open the bids, but it is usually limited to a board member or a board employee. Often, a representative for each bidder is present to hear the competing bids.

After the bids are opened, boards should determine whether the bids received are fully responsive to the bid specifications. This is done to ensure that all bidders have an equal chance to secure bids and do not prosper from not following the rules. The key legal issue in evaluating "responsiveness" is a bid's degree of variance from a bid specification. A "minor" deviation from a specification, such as an oversight of a technical bidding process that did not impact the outcome of the bid, will not require a bid's rejection. On the other hand, in most instances where bids contain "material" variances, except for mathematical or clerical errors, school boards should reject the bid and not allow the contractor to modify its bid. Material variances give bidders a substantial advantage not afforded other bidders.

A common example of bid variances is when a bid contains mistakes. School boards should be very cautious of bids that are considerably lower than other bids. This may indicate that bidders have made apparent mistakes and may later wish to rescind their bids. In this situation, the best alternative is to verify the accuracy of bids during the bid opening.

Once bids are opened, it is generally unacceptable to allow bidders to modify their bids. However, some states may allow bidders to withdraw mistaken bids before boards act on them.

After bids are opened, school boards select bidders by evaluating each bid and its bidder, then awarding contracts to the "lowest responsible bidders." Boards should inform bidders that the evaluation process may take a reasonable period of time to complete.

Lowest Responsible Bidder

State statutes and accompanying case law have provided a list of factors that school boards should consider when evaluating whether bidders are the lowest responsible bidders. Obviously, the "lowest" bidder is determined by the cost contained in the bid. However, boards must consider additional criteria in evaluating whether a bidder is "responsible," which minimally includes conformity with bid specifications, delivery terms, quality, serviceability, the financial status of the bidder, work experience, reputation, ability to perform the contractual duties, the quality of equipment to be furnished for the project, and past experience with the bidder.[5]

After considering all of the criteria, it is possible that school boards may award contracts to someone other than the lowest bidder. Since when this occurs there is a possibility of future litigation, boards must be able to support their decisions and show that they were reasonable. In sum, boards must award bids to the lowest bidders or else declare bidders irresponsible within the meaning of state statutes.

After selecting the lowest responsible bidder, school boards may attempt to enter negotiations with the successful bidder in an attempt to get more favorable terms. Even so, boards should avoid negotiating with anyone other than the lowest bidder. This often occurs when there is confusion regarding who is the low bidder or to avoid awarding the contract to the low bidder.

Rejection of Bids

School boards should reserve the right to reject any or all submitted bids because bids may come in over budget or do not confirm to bid specifications. If there is confusion over who is the lowest bidder, a board needs to examine the cause of the confusion. If the source of confusion was a lack of clarity in the bid specifications or process, then a board may wish to consider rejecting all bids, revising the specifications, and rebidding the project. Rebidding a project is not without consequence, because the bids would have already been publicly opened, and bidders would know the bids of their competitors before they submit second bids.

Bid Protest

Any actual or prospective bidders who are aggrieved in connection with the solicitation, evaluation, or award of contracts must make written requests to a board's SBO to review the transaction. The request for review must be made within a specified time (usually 3–5 working days) after notification of an award and must include the specific provisions alleged to have been violated, along with a statement of the relevant facts. The SBO will review the award and provide a written explanation of the decision to the bidder making the request. In the event that the SBO's review discovers any significant deviation from the rules, a board may change an award. However, if the SBO rejects the protest, the aggrieved bidder may appeal to the board for final action.

Most states also afford a low bidder who is not awarded a contract the opportunity to seek redress or challenge an award through the judicial system. If a bidder's challenge is successful, a court could award the contract to the low bidder and/or allow recovery of monetary damages.

REQUEST FOR PROPOSALS

Unlike requests for bids, in which the primary evaluative factor is cost, school boards can also prepare Requests for Proposals (RFPs). RFPs are a competitive bid process utilized for more complex transactions where factors other than price are used to make a final purchasing decision. Specifically, RFPs are often used when boards have not developed an exclusive method to achieve their goals and are seeking alternatives from contractors. In consultation with key school officials, SBOs should develop criteria and weighting scales that can be used to evaluate proposal submissions. These criteria should be made part of the bid specifications so that prospective bidders can submit responsive and informed proposals.[6]

CONFLICT OF INTEREST

To maintain public trust and confidence, public officials must conduct official business in the best interest of the public. In school settings, board members have a fiduciary duty to uphold the best interests of their districts when conducting official business. An increasing issue for most public bodies, including school boards, is dealing with conflicts of interest.

Conflict of interest is best described when a board member's personal interest is perceived to be different from the best interest of the school district such that a reasonable person might question whether the board member is influenced by his or her own interest. Some state laws prevent school board members from financially profiting or otherwise personally benefiting from school contracts. Most state statutes not only prohibit interested board members from voting on such contracts, but also prevent the interested board members from participating in the deliberation of awarding a contract after they have publicly disclosed the nature of the interest. However, if the award of a contract would otherwise constitute a conflict of interest, it is not resolved by a voting abstention. In addition to board members, SBOs must ensure that no school employees or other representatives receive anything of value to influence school board's votes.

THE CONTRACT

After school boards select successful bidders, they and the contractors will culminate their final agreement in the form of a written contract. SBOs should consult with their board attorneys before presenting a contract for a board's ratification. Most states provide that school boards can only approve contracts voted on in open session at public meetings.

Elements of an Enforceable Contract

The key to a good contract is to provide sufficient detail without having it become too long or full of legal jargon. All contracts should address the following areas:

- Name and contact information of the parties.
- Duration of the contract and how it can be terminated.
- Scope of the goods or services.
- Price of the project and quantity of any materials.

Minimally, other items to be considered in a contract may include the method of payment, copyright or patent ownership, a hold-harmless agreement, verification of necessary insurance, dispute resolution, adherence to state and federal laws, non-assignment of the contract to another contractor, and remedies for breach by the parties.

Federal and state laws also require that contracts with public entities contain certain provisions. These provisions are mandated to ensure nondiscriminatory practices by the parties providing the services or goods, namely discrimination based on race, sex, religion, color, national origin, or age. Public contracts usually also require the parties to have written sexual harassment policies.

In addition to non-discriminatory practices, contracting parties must agree to adhere to fair treatment of their labor force. Most states require public contractors to pay prevailing hourly wages to skilled workers as well as ensure that overtime is granted and that minimum wage is paid to all other eligible employees.

As a final matter, if selected bidders fail to provide all post-award documents mandated in the bid specifications, school boards can rescind the contracts. Such documentation might include a surety bond, confirmation of insurance coverage, or a policy against workplace harassment.

CONCLUSION

A written contract represents the end product of a legal process in which a school board and contractor agree to conduct business together. As a matter of public policy, school boards must bid contracts for certain goods or services that exceed a specified dollar amount. Most states have laws describing the bidding process and setting the minimum dollar amount when bidding is required. Statutes usually mandate the bidding of certain types of projects, such as capital improvements, but excused from this bidding requirement are contracts requiring highly specialized skills, contracts with other government agencies, or repair of goods under warranty.

School boards must let contracts to the lowest responsible bidders. Boards select the lowest responsible bidders after considering the dollar amounts of the bids, along with bidders' conformity with bid specifications and their ability to perform projects.

Throughout this process, the role of SBOs cannot be overstated. They oversee everything from initial requests from school boards for services or materials, through the bidding phase, to the award of contracts. Even then, the task of SBOs is not finished because of their obligation to monitor the performance of contractors through the duration of contracts. This will ensure that school boards receive what they paid for and that services were provided in such a way that best promotes their educational function.

APPENDIX A

Procedures for a Purchase Requisition

The following is the procedure for initiating a Purchase Requisition:

a. Submit a completed Purchase Requisition to the SBO clearly indicating the goods and services to be purchased and the estimated purchase price. The Purchase Requisition is the authorization to initiate the procurement process; it enables a Purchase Order and/or Contract to be generated.

b. Identify potential sources of supply (if known).

c. Prepare the bid document for distribution.

d. Suppliers must be given a reasonable period of time (based on the size and complexity of the proposed purchase) to provide a response.

e. Once the bids are received, the SBO reviews all bids/proposals received prior to the designated closing date and time, to ensure commercial compliance and compliance with the mandatory requirements of the bid document.

f. Based solely on the evaluation criteria, the successful bidder is selected. All documentation is to be returned to the district office and should clearly indicate the successful bidder as well as the items to be purchased.

g. The SBO notifies the successful Supplier/Contractor and issues the Contract/Agreement and/or Purchase Order.

h. No goods and services are to be provided to the school district until a fully executed Contract/Agreement and/or Purchase Order is in place.

APPENDIX B

Legal Notice for Local Newspaper

The Wumperton School District is accepting bids for a new school bus. Bid specifications can be picked up at the superintendent's office located 555 Clocktower Drive, Atlanta, GA 55222. Specifications can be picked up Monday through Friday from 8:00 A.M. to 4:00 P.M. There will be a pre-bid meeting on May 6, 2005, at 10:00 A.M. at the superintendent's office.

Bids will be received until 3:00 P.M., June 20, 2005, at which time they will be publicly opened and read aloud. Wumperton School District reserves the right to accept or reject any and/or all bids. Wumperton School District is an Equal Opportunity Employer.

S. Smith, Superintendent
Wumperton School District

NOTES

1. L. Bonner, "Myths, Misconceptions, and Realities About Public Procurement Automation," *School Business Affairs* 55 (1989): 25.

2. W. B. Thiel, "Facilities Planning: Developing the Specifications," *School Business Affairs* 71 (2005): 37–39.

3. J. Dobbin and M. Jenkins, "Supply Chain Management: Are You Maximizing Your Procurement Activity?" *School Business Affairs* 66 (2000): 45.

4. W. R. Gratton, "Let's Get Specific: Clear Specifications Save Time and Money," *School Business Affairs* 60 (1994): 31.

5. J. Beales, "By Request," *American School Board Journal* 182 (1995): 25.

6. K. E. Finkel, "Writing the Right Contract: Getting What You Want," *School Business Affairs* 64 (1998): 40.

4

Privatization of Elementary and Secondary Education

Frank Brown

Privatization in public education is as old as public education in America.[1] School officials have always purchased supplies and equipment. In fact, as schools grew from one-room schoolhouses to larger and more modern schools and school systems, the use of private vendors expanded. Officials now use private vendors for transportation, food services, computer systems, communication systems, janitorial services, and insurance and health services. The list of items can be expanded to include construction contracts, playgrounds, and financial services. If anything, it would be difficult to operate public schools today without the use of private vendors who provide these important services. Yet privatization took on a different dimension in the 1970s with contracting out with private vendors for classroom instruction and the management of programs and schools. Few will argue with the use of private contractors to build new schools or to provide food services, yet many question the use of private vendors to replace public school teachers with contracted instructors or administrators with private management teams.

This chapter refers to three different privatization situations. First, most public and private schools contract out for certain services, such as to supply students and faculty with food, transport children to and from school, and purchase school supplies. Second, some states allow local school boards to employ private companies to manage public schools for a fee. This is new in America. Typically, these privately managed schools are low-performance ones regarding student test scores, and most are charter schools. Charter schools are public schools with special exemptions from standard state regulations. The third example of privatization involves public educational vouchers that allow children from poor families to use public funds to attend private schools, including religious schools, that may be outside their attendance zones.[2] To date, three cities offer educational vouchers to children from economically disadvantaged families: Milwaukee, Wisconsin; Cleveland, Ohio; and Washington, D.C. In general, a state must convince a court that a state or the federal government has a compelling reason to allow public funds to be used to support education in religious elementary and secondary education. The state of Florida allows students from failing schools to receive state grants or vouchers to attend schools outside their school attendance zones or districts, while the other programs are limited to specific cities.

Privatization in public elementary and secondary schools is designed to improve education by injecting market incentives into the system.[3] There are several major market influences on education, such as political (and ideological), economic, and educational. Politics trumps other markets, as it defines other areas of interest.[4] Yet, in reality, educational reform is a metaphor for political, economic, and educational agendas. At first glance, these agendas should be obvious to the casual educational observer. However, due to the confluence of issues involved, the goals of privatization in education is muddled. Other metaphors for privatization of education are family choice, deregulation, and democratic values. Even so, the one thing that is clear about low academic productivity in America's public schools is that most poorly educated children are located in poorly funded schools. The majority of poorly performing schools are located in communities where most students come from racial and ethnic minority households. These residents possess less economic and political power than those who live outside these communities. Yet many educational reformers who propose radical solutions to the problems of poorly performing schools are traditionally the opponents of residents in these communities.

EXPERIMENTS WITH CHOICE

The movement promoting the use of educational vouchers, charter schools, and the private management of public schools is based on the principle of the free market.[5] This is based on the notion that more competition produces better academically performing public schools. Yet there are still scant positive results from market forces in education.[6] In this mix, students can use public vouchers to attend private schools in three cities in Florida. Private management of charter public schools also exists in many school systems where approved by their respective state governments. In more than 30 states, school boards can experiment with charter schools. Since Minnesota passed the first charter schools law in 1991, other sates and the District of Columbia have statutes authorizing charter schools, expanding from 252 schools with 58,620 students in 1995 to approximately 2,695 schools in 2003 with 684,000 students. Some charter schools are operated by non-profit community groups, and many employ outside private venders to manage these schools.

There is no evidence that charter schools educate children better than regular public schools, as shown by comparing schools in the District of Columbia with 17% of their students enrolled in charter schools.[7] Charter school students in the District of Columbia were no more difficult to educate than students in traditionally administered public schools, as some had claimed. Moreover, despite 15 years of experience, charter schools in Minnesota have yet to demonstrate positive results when compared to traditional public schools.[8]

EDUCATIONAL VOUCHERS

The voucher programs in Cleveland, Milwaukee, and the District of Columbia are designed for poor students, while the Florida program applies to students in all academically failing public schools. In Milwaukee and Cleveland, voucher systems were created for poor urban students. The National Center for the Study of Privatization in Education (www.ncspe.org) provides much of the data for this review.[9] Vouchers not only allow families to make decisions regarding how public money should be spent on their children but are also expected to create an educational market where schools must compete for students. Opponents of vouchers fear that education does not respond to market forces and that vouchers will create greater inequalities.

Cleveland Program

The Cleveland voucher program gained attention because it was the test case for vouchers in religious schools that the Supreme Court upheld.[10] The Cleveland program began in 1995 for low-income students who wished to attend private or suburban schools with the state paying $2,250 in tuition for each child. During the 2001–2002 school year, about 4,300 students received vouchers to attend private or religious schools. Insofar as suburban schools refused to participate, almost all of the students attended religious schools. In 2000, the Cleveland program enrolled approximately 3,000 students for a total cost of about $12 million, of which $7.5 million went directly for vouchers and the remainder for the cost of transportation. Most vouchers went to students who were already enrolled in religious schools; only about 200 students from the public schools received vouchers.

Of more than 75,000 children in the Cleveland City Schools, more than 80% are from low-income minority families. Families with incomes below 200% of poverty had priority and were eligible to receive 90% of private school tuition up to $2,250. For these lowest-income families, participating private schools may not charge a co-payment greater than $250 per child. Yet for all other families, the program pays 75% of tuition costs, up to $1,875, with no co-payment cap. Higher-income families receive vouchers only if the number of available vouchers exceeds the number of low-income children who participate. Voucher payments depend on where parents choose to enroll their children. If parents choose private schools, checks are made payable to the parents, who then endorse the checks over to the school. Parents who elect to keep their children in public schools while seeking tutorial assistance through grants must arrange for registered tutors to help their children and submit the bills to the state for payment. Students from low-income families receive 90% of the amount charged for such services up to $360; all other children receive 75% of $360.

The number of tutorial grants offered must equal the number of vouchers provided to students enrolled in participating private or adjacent public school districts. In the 1999–2000 school year, 46 of the 56 private schools (82%) participating in the voucher program were religiously affiliated. Approximately 3,700 students participated in the program, of whom 96% were enrolled in religious schools; 60% were from families with incomes below the poverty line; and about 1,400 students received tutorial assistance. In 2000, approximately 96% of the students receiving public vouchers in Cleveland attended religious schools.

Milwaukee Voucher Program

In 1997, the Milwaukee voucher program paid up to $5,100 per student in 2000, $38 million for 4,200 students enrolled in religious schools, and 2,300 enrolled in private non-religious schools.[11] Wisconsin State Democratic Representative Polly Williams of Milwaukee, herself an African American and early national spokesperson for vouchers, admitted that she "knew that once they [conservatives] figured they didn't need me as a Black cover, they would take control of vouchers and use them for their own selfish interest."[12] She thought that conservatives would remove the separation of church and state as well as remove the income cap set at the $23,000 per year level for a family of four, and that the city administration would use the voucher program to attract white people back into the city by promising "you don't have to go to Milwaukee schools with Black children because we have opened a way for you"[13] to send your children to school with other white children. Yet, as Representative Williams discovered, her goal of pursuing a better education for poor African American children was less important in the bigger scheme: a return to racially segregated schools.

Florida Voucher Program

In Florida, the state allowed the use of state funds to enable children in failing public schools to attend other public schools or private schools; the state allows corporations to support state-approved scholarships for low-income students and get their state taxes reduced dollar-for-dollar based on the total amount of their contributions to the program. To date, the future of the program is in doubt because an intermediate state appellate court in Florida affirmed that the program violated the no-aid provision of the state constitution by providing indirect benefits to "sectarian" schools due to their having received tax dollars through the voucher program.[14] The Florida program allows parents of students in low-performing schools to enroll their children in private schools with $4,500 per year vouchers. However, the state will cover only $4,500 and parents pay any additional costs.

FEDERAL PROGRAMS

The federal government is getting into the school choice movement with its financial support of charter schools, magnet schools, and ability of school districts to use federally funded Title I money to allow students to transfer out of low-performing schools to higher-performing ones.[15] The federal government requires local educational agencies (LEAs) to provide choice options for Title I students enrolled in low-performing schools for two consecutive years, unless forbidden by court-ordered desegregation plans or by state statutes.[16] This requirement seems like a self-fulfilling prophecy, because by definition, Title I programs are located in low-performing schools.

The Washington, D.C., legislation permits the secretary of education to launch a five-year pilot voucher program beginning in the fall of 2005. The voucher will provide annual, taxpayer-funded grants of up to $7,500 a year for 1,600 children to attend private and religious schools. These vouchers, or opportunity scholarships, are limited to children in families earning up to 185% of the poverty level, about $36,000 for a family of four, with priority going to children attending low-performing public schools.

RESULTS AND PROMISES

In order to understand the impact of vouchers on students and school systems, it is important to know about the size of vouchers in dollar terms, who qualifies for vouchers, the financing of vouchers, the rules governing private schools that accept vouchers, and how individuals and private schools react to specific voucher policies. Given a choice in selecting schools for their children, many parents place great weight on the demographics of a school's population, which generally results in greater segregation of students by race and social class.[17]

An interesting question relates to limits on the use of vouchers to educate poor children. Two states allow vouchers to be used in private schools or in another public school district. The costs of attending many private schools are beyond what public vouchers can purchase, but what about using vouchers to attend schools in other public school districts? Vouchers have strong support from wealthy individuals, but at the same time, wealthy school districts where many of these wealthy individuals live are opposed to children from poor districts attending schools with their children.[18] School boards outside of Milwaukee, Cleveland, and the District of Columbia are not required to participate in the voucher programs designed for mostly African American children from poor families by accepting them in their schools. Wealthy public school districts do not participate in voucher programs and typically place a "bounty" on non-residents who fraudulently enroll children in their schools. This situation poses a problem for voucher programs that try to enroll low-achieving students into high-achieving public schools. For example, a mother in Cleveland went to jail for enrolling her son in a wealthy suburban school.[19] Further, Illinois makes it illegal to register a child in another district; it is a misdemeanor punishable by up to 30 days in jail, a $500 fine, and tuition reimbursement.

Privatization implies that under free market conditions, maximum output and organizational efficiency can best be accomplished if parents have the opportunity to make a choice along with private management companies; this also implies that citizens should encourage private vendors to enter public education with the profit motive in mind to increase productivity. There is a belief by voucher advocates not only that the profit motive should be an advantage whether a school is operated with private or public funds via a state voucher or a performance contract with a local public school system because it increases competition, but also that competition is good for education. Yet the history of "markets" in education has not been positive.[20] As an illustration, to date, the Cleveland program, where approximately 90% of participating students are white and attend Catholic schools,[21] has done little to educate poor minority children. Further, there are not enough places in the private schools to accommodate all of the low-performing voucher students.

VOUCHER SUMMARY

Proponents of school choice give black parents the impression that simply having the option to choose the school their children will attend gives them control over the education of their children.[22] The history of such programs is that there are a limited number of options because of geographical distance to some schools and the attractiveness of these schools for middle-class families with more political influence. Also, once parents leave their children at private schools, there is little evidence they will have control over what happens. Chile has 25 years of experience with voucher programs and the results are similar to those in American schools with voucher programs.[23] With the Chilean experience, parents were positive in getting their choice of a school for their children, but the evidence revealed that middle and wealthy children were enrolled in higher-performing schools rather than with poor children in low-performing schools.

Poor parents may have less of a voice or influence with private schools than with public schools. Moreover, multiple private school options may not be available. It is true parents can exercise influence by withdrawing their children from a private school, but what are the options if they take this action, return to the public schools, or enroll their child in a private school of less quality (assuming that their first choice was of superior quality)? In the absence of more politically powerful consumers, vouchers may not purchase superior schooling for poor children, and an expansion of vouchers to all income groups may further segment schools by race, ethnicity, income, and ability.[24]

CHARTER SCHOOLS AND PRIVATE SCHOOL MANAGEMENT

More than 30 states have authorized semi-autonomous public schools known as charter schools. In these states, parents may organize charter schools with public funds on the same per pupil expenditure basis as other schools in the district if they can recruit enough students to enroll. The parents may operate the school themselves or contract with a private company to manage the school for a fee. Further, private companies, which generally try to make a profit by reducing administrative costs, may also contract directly with a local school board to manage their schools or contract to manage a charter school within the district controlled by parents.

In theory, charter schools foster competition, since they may accept students from within or outside a single district. To date, most charter schools are located in urban areas and operate in poor minority neighborhoods.

Getting parents in the "better" economic parts of a district to enroll their children in a charter school in a poor neighborhood has not proven successful. It will take years to systematically evaluate the academic success of charter schools. However, several state accountability systems that mandate annual testing of students in charter schools should provide better data on their effectiveness. In general, students in charter schools score below those in traditional public schools on standardized achievement tests, except for the few charter schools organized and operated by middle-class parents. Recently, a number of charter schools closed, while some failed to open because of a lack of enough students, staff, or adequate facilities.

Nationwide, charter schools account for about 2,695 of the nation's 85,000 public schools. Most are small and aimed at disadvantaged elementary and middle school students. Federal and state support is available to aid with planning and start-up costs of charter schools. Charter schools receive state and federal categorical funds to meet the need of high-cost students such as Title I students and special literacy programs. Federal planning and implementation grants provide funding for charter schools for up to three years. Many states provide transportation for children attending charter schools comparable to that for those in regular public schools or mandate that boards provide transportation at no cost. A few states provide funds for transportation for students attending charter schools.

In 2001, private vendors managed more than 200 public schools that enrolled approximately 100,000 students.[25] This is a small portion of the 53 million public school enrollment, and financial success for these private management companies is rare. The Tesseract Group, Inc., which evolved from Education Alternatives, Inc., failed to get its school management contracts renewed in Dade County, Florida; Baltimore, Maryland; and Hartford, Connecticut; it also recently sold two Arizona charter schools due to mounting financial losses. However, Nobel Learning Communities, Inc., of Media, Pennsylvania, bought the schools and now operates 151 small private and public charter schools in 16 states.[26]

Edison, the largest private managed vendor of public schools, is in a battle with a Detroit area school board that may force it out of the district. Edison's president and founder, H. Christopher Whittle, stated that Edison intends to reduce its growth figures and terminate contracts with several districts. With mixed results, Edison manages 134 for-profit schools, enrolling about 74,000 students in 22 states, including such locales as Las Vegas, Boston, and Detroit. They have lost schools in New York City and Wichita, Kansas. Edison has never made a profit, and in 2002 the company lost two-thirds of its value.[27] What can Philadelphia expect now that Edison is set to take over their public school system? Based on what Edison is accomplishing in Flint, Michigan, with at-risk students in poor neighborhoods, Philadelphia can expect 90 minutes of reading lessons each morning, in which teachers follow a set curriculum called *Success for All*; standardized tests taken on computers each week; quick disciplinary hearings for students who misbehave in class; and a computer in each home.[28]

In general, charter schools have not shown academic advantages over traditional public schools and are just advanced versions of the magnet schools that surfaced in the 1970s. A study of charter schools in Michigan suggests that charter schools there are not "public" in the sense of control over what and how students are taught and how schools are administered.[29] Charter schools in Michigan received more funds than public schools for the same number of students—producing less for more. And there appears to be less of an incentive on the part of state officials to provide meaningful oversight or to close failing charter schools.

CHOICE AND PRIVATE MANAGEMENT OF PUBLIC SCHOOLS

Contracting with a private vendor to manage a public school generally provides parents other choices. Parents ordinarily enroll their children in the same school they attended before the change in management, with the same teachers and schoolmates, regardless of who administers the school. Also, due to distance, money, peer pressure, and parental knowledge, school choice for the poor is more limited than for those who have the means to leave a district, enroll their children in private schools, or secure special treatment for their children in public schools. The inability of poor parents to choose quality schools for their children is central to a discussion of choice because it involves children from poor minority communities.[30]

OTHER STATE-SPONSORED PRIVATE INITIATIVES

Six states provide programs that allow parents or corporations tax incentives to fund private education.[31] Arizona, Florida, Illinois, Iowa, Minnesota, and Pennsylvania provide tuition tax credit to parents who enroll their children in private schools.[32] Arizona, Illinois, Iowa, and Minnesota apply tax credits to all citizens in their respective states, but Florida and Pennsylvania granted tax credits only to private corporations who assisted with payment of tuition to attend private or out-of-district schools. Further, at least two Florida corporations have given $5 million to the Florida scholarship program. The Florida program is capped at $50 million total and limited to $3,500 per student. In Pennsylvania, a business may provide up to $100,000 yearly to a scholarship fund or to projects that improve public schools, and take as much as a $90,000 tax credit. The state has capped the program at $30 million per year.

Arizona, Minnesota, Illinois, and Iowa offer similar programs designed for individuals to help fund public or private schools. Arizona taxpayers may take up to $650 credit of contributions to a "school-tuition organization" providing scholarships to children other than their own. Illinois parents get a credit for up to $500 in costs of tuition, books, and laboratory fees at private or public schools. Iowa parents get a credit of up to $250 for private school tuition, public school fees, or home schooling costs. In Minnesota, households with incomes of up to $33,500 can receive up to $2,000 credit against tuition, tutoring, and other school expenses. Higher-income households can reduce taxable income by expenses of up to $1,625 per child.

PRIVATIZATION AS POLITICAL SYMBOLISM

The genesis of privatization was the Supreme Court's decision in *Brown v. Board of Education, Topeka*,[33] which declared state-supported school segregation by race to be unconstitutional.[34] *Brown* motivated school systems, first in the South and later in the North, that were opposed to school desegregation to experiment with school choice in opposition to racial integration. The backlash against integration increased after the passage of the 1964 Civil Rights Law, which gave the Department of Justice the authority and resources to enforce *Brown*. School desegregation in the South and race riots in urban centers in the North combined to give the Republican Party a powerful weapon to attract conservative voters using the rhetoric of school "choice." In 1968, candidate Richard Nixon proposed his "southern strategy" to help him win the presidency.[35] The southern strategy worked North and South. Later, Ronald Reagan also applied this strategy. Reagan's action indicated symbolically to voters that he supported federal tax-exempt credits for tuition to help families offset the cost of enrolling their children in segregated academies. He also recommended federal vouchers and tuition tax credits against federal income taxes to support attendance at private academies. While Congress never enacted federal tax credits, the proposal started the movement to implement family choice measures such as the use of educational vouchers, charter schools, and tuition tax credits.

DISCUSSION

The privatization of public education involves the use of market incentives to improve education without additional financial resources as for-profit public schools in America are managed by private companies. This sounds confusing because the general public calls the private management of public schools "privatization" of public schools. It merely means that private companies are allowed to manage public schools for a profit.

The school choice movement in public schools is expected to decline within a decade because of several factors: federal budget deficits will slow plans to expand charter schools and voucher programs; there is a strong preference for neighborhood schools; public school vouchers cannot constitute a viable option to replace public education; the profits that can be made from managing schools are not enough to entice more private companies into the field; parents of children in failing schools will increase their opposition to the private management of the schools; elected public school officials will continue to oppose the private management of public schools; teachers' unions will continue to oppose this process; wealthy school districts have not found a need to use private companies to manage their schools or get involved with voucher programs; and since the major incentive behind the school choice movement, the opposition of white parents to court-ordered school desegregation, has ended, it is no longer a major factor in drafting school district boundaries.

Voucher supporters argue that vouchers promote innovation and diversity, competition among students and teachers, and a more flexible employment relationship. Financial access is not an issue with public education, they maintain, because public schooling is available to everyone. Opponents of vouchers argue that innovation and diversity are best served by the public schools; competition for students is not fair where all parents are not equally informed or interested; and vouchers will weaken the teaching profession, destroy the public schools, and return religion to the public schools.

In order to understand the impact of vouchers on students and school districts and to make informed decisions about their merits and demerits, the public needs all of the facts. People need to know the size of vouchers in dollar terms; who qualifies for vouchers; how vouchers are financed; the rules governing private schools that accept vouchers; and how individuals and private schools react to specific voucher policies.[36] Further, since there are not enough private schools to accommodate a large shift of public school students to private schools, people do not know what type of private schools will be established to meet such a demand. Neither is it clear whether these private schools are more effective in attracting high-quality teachers.

The desire for school choice, vouchers, or privatization should not be based solely on benefits to students. Using vouchers or the private management of public schools for poor urban children in any form is a risky enterprise, and it is often a metaphor for other goals. When the southern strategy is complete, a majority of Supreme Court justices will be individuals with racially and socially conservative views. The Court has ended court-ordered desegregated public education programs.[37] This action should decrease the demand for vouchers and privatization of public education.

A few minorities have bought into the use of vouchers to "fix the system" with parental choice where their children are educated. Yet the resources that poor parents have are simply no match with those available to the white conservatives who push their agenda.[38] The fact is that most poor parents will not have the money to have viable choices beyond the public school system. There is a rule in politics, that one should never play another man's game, because one can only lose. The use of vouchers to support education is the game of the wealthy and politically powerful.

There are not likely to be major changes in improving the education for poor minority children with voucher programs such as the one in Cleveland.[39] Further, there are not enough places in the private schools to accommodate all of the low-performing students, since suburban schools have shown no desire to participate in voucher programs, charter schools, or magnet schools to improve education for poor children and to increase integration. It should be remembered that *Brown v. Board of Education, Topeka* did little to desegregate the public schools because of such strong political opposition to it, and most poor black children continue to attend segregated, substandard schools.

Howard Fuller, a former superintendent in Milwaukee, site of the first voucher program, stated that his organization did not get into the voucher movement to give public money to educate middle-class white children. However, 90% of the children in the Cleveland voucher program are white and attend Catholic schools. Suburban schools refuse to participate in the voucher program for the same reason they opposed busing to integrate publics; they did not want to open their schools up to children from the inner cities.

If one assesses school choice from an educational perspective, the experiment is just beginning and needs more data over time before its success or failure can be judged. Even so, if one considers its impact on improving education for poor children, the experiment is a failure; most continue to be poorly educated. On the other hand, if one views it from a political perspective, it is enjoying temporary success, since candidates who use this symbolism as a political strategy always seem to be favored to win elections. These politicians look for support from big business and suburban voters who feel that since their taxes are paying for wasteful government programs for the poor, they favor vouchers and the privatization of urban schools but not for their schools.

Even if Americans were not divided along racial and social-class lines, politics would still play a significant role in the allocation of school resources for the simple reason that education is the largest component of local and state budgets. And educational resources are not evenly distributed. Inner-city schools are generally underfunded when compared to suburban schools. It is interesting to consider why there are so many conservative politicians from wealthy neighborhoods fighting to help inner-city children with state-funded vouchers. It is easier to get a program started for the poor and expand the program later to help the rich.

Again, the public will have to await the education success of the several choice options discussed for more long-term evaluations before conclusions may be drawn. A confluence of other social and economic issues may help determine the success or failure of privatization. On the political side, politicians who support these efforts won more votes than their opponents. Most choice programs are aimed at poor children. Wealthy communities have been content to watch the privatization movement with neutrality; with the rich on the sidelines, it is difficult to predict the long-term future of the movement. Polls reveal that most Americans oppose government tuition vouchers for parents to send their children to independent private or religious schools. Experiments will have to produce dramatic results for inner-city children before there is a change in public opinion about vouchers, charter schools, and the private management of public schools. School systems that contract out for instructional services must provide administrators with the training necessary to enter into agreements that will benefit children and meet the public's demand for fiscal accountability.[40] However, the Chilean experience[41] of having vouchers for more than 20 years suggests that poor parents believe they get the choice of good academic schools for their children, yet the results reveal that they do not get the best available schools for their children.[42]

School choice plans and privatization of public schools are likely to come to a halt within a decade as the educational leaders refocus on accountability measures which will lead to greater equality of funding for children in educationally disadvantaged schools. Choice and privatization plans separate schoolchildren by race and social class. However, in the near future, the minority population will become the majority and should bring changes in the education system. Given the winner-take-all format of national presidential elections in the United States, it will be difficult for a candidate to win with a southern strategy within a few years and continue to promote choice plans that separate children by race and social class.

In short, middle-class parents want their children in schools with other middle-class students, and poor parents want their children in schools with fewer poor students. Parents and their children are not the only constituents of public schools; teachers are also major players in the school choice movement.[43] Yet, in general, teachers oppose school choice options unless it is within the public school system.

Experience with school choice reveals that after the first year, most students get their first choice because they select the same school that they chose the first year. Thus, market conditions only operate in making the first choice; the mechanism of withdrawal and competition does not work as promoted by market advocates.[44] Educational suppliers are limited to the number of children living in a specific community due to the fact that public funds are finite and based on enrollments; once parents with more information and resources make their choices, it limits the choices of other households. This is not the market model that comes to mind when we shop for food and other household goods; these market conditions are not available to the urban poor where suppliers are few.

In America, many markets do not seek consumers from among the poor. Clearly, the education markets follow this trend. High-quality education suppliers have not fought to take advantage of public education vouchers that serve poor minority children. Public education does not respond to true market conditions. Education as a market owes its quality to state funding levels, not consumer demands (assuming all parents want the best for their children), by employing less-qualified teachers, having higher student/teacher ratios, and offering fewer support services. The motive for vouchers and privatizing public education in America is declining and will probably soon disappear, as is evident by minimum participation in the voucher program by poor African American children in Milwaukee and Cleveland. At the same time, public schools will continue to contract out with private vendors for such services as transportation, food, school supplies, and construction of facilities. If there is a hidden agenda by the rich to offer greater choices to poor parents, it may be tied to the larger economy and tax burden for their corporations. The rich will pay less for education if instructional services are contracted out to non-state employees. If contracted teachers taught most public school classes, states would not have to provide them with fringe benefits such as retirement plans and medical plans, and these teachers would lose the constitutional protections available to public employees. There is a theory in education, that educational reform is always a plan to redistribute power among individuals or groups.[45] As this is merely a speculation about motives, the nation will have to wait for more positive results from school choice plans in America and elsewhere in the world, such as in Belgium, Chile, Colombia, the Czech Republic, Holland, New Zealand, Scotland, and Sweden.[46] Finally, one must remember that all choice programs are different, depending on a state and country; this makes comparisons difficult based on the several components of such programs.

CONCLUSION

The use of private vendors to provide traditional services will continue, but the privatization of instruction in public schools should decline or disappear in the next two decades. This appears to be the case because the motivation to create privatization of public school instructional and management programs came from efforts to reduce the impact of school desegregation under *Brown v. Board of Education, Topeka*. Now that the Supreme Court has ruled that race may not be used to desegregate public schools, the reduced motivation to produce special schools after a return to neighborhoods should diminish a desire for privatization of instruction.

NOTES

1. F. Brown and R. C. Hunter, "Privatization of Public Education: The Past, Present and Future," in *Primer on Legal Affairs for School Business Officials*, ed. C. J. Russo, H. B. Polansky, and R. C. Wood (Reston, Va.: Association of School Business Officials, 2001), 41–62.

2. F. Brown, "The Voucher Movement After Brown: The End or the Beginning?" *School Business Affairs* 69 (January 2003): 4–8.

3. F. Brown, "Privatization of Public Elementary and Secondary Education in the United States of America," *Education and the Law* 14, nos. 1–2 (2002): 99–116.

4. B. Levin, "Race and School Choice," in *School Choice and Social Controversy: Politics, Policy, and Law*, ed. Stephen D. Sugarman and Frank R. Kemerer (Washington, D.C.: Brookings Institution Press, 1999), 266–299; H. M. Levin and C. R. Belfield, *Vouchers and Public Policy: When Ideology Trumps Evidence*, National Center for the Study of Privatization in Education, Teachers College, Columbia University, 2004, http://ncspe.org/kpublications-files/OP95.

5. H. M. Levin and C. R. Belfield, *The Marketplace in Education*, Occasional Paper No. 86, National Center for the Study of Privatization in Education, Teachers College, Columbia University, 2003, www.ncspe.org.

6. Levin, "Race and School Choice"; and Levin and Belfield, *Vouchers and Public Policy*.

7. J. Buckley, M. Schneider, and Y. Shang, *Are Charter School Students Harder to Educate? Evidence from Washington, DC*, National Center for the Study of Privatization in Education, Teachers College, Columbia University, 2004, http://ncspe.org/kpublications-files/OP96.

8. Levin, "Race and School Choice"; Levin and Belfield, *Vouchers and Public Policy*; Levin and Belfield, *The Marketplace in Education*.

9. H. M. Levin, *A Comprehensive Framework for Evaluating Educational Vouchers*, National Center for the Study of Privatization in Education, Teachers College, Columbia University, 2001, http://ncspe.org/kpublications-files/OP05.

10. *Zelman v. Simmons-Harris*, 536 U.S. 639 (2002).

11. F. Howard Nelson, Rachel Drown, Edward Muir, and Nancy Van Meter, "Public Money and Privatization in K–12 Education," in *Education Finance in the New Millennium*, ed. Stephen Chaikind and William J. Fowler Jr. (Larchmont, N.Y.: Eye on Education, 2001), 173–192.

12. Bob Peterson and Barbara Miner, "Vouchers, the Right and the Race Card," in *Civil Rights Since 1787: A Reader on the Black Struggle*, ed. Jonathan Birnbaum and Clarence Taylor (New York: New York University Press, 2000), 819–822.

13. Peterson and Miner, "Vouchers, the Right and the Race Card."

14. J. Kronholz, "High Court's Ruling Will Fuel Fight Over School Vouchers," *Wall Street Journal*, February 19, 2002, A28; *Bush v. Holmes*, 886 So.2d 340 (Fla. Dist. Ct. App., 2004).

15. Brown, "The Voucher Movement After Brown." See also F. Brown, "Nixon's 'Southern Strategy' and Forces Against Brown," *Journal of Negro Education* 73, no. 3 (2004): 191–208.

16. R. Paige, "Dear Colleague, Letter to Education Officials Regarding Implementation of No Child Left Behind and Guidance on Public School Choice," U.S. Secretary of Education, Department of Education, Washington, D.C., June 14, 2002.

17. D. Goldhaber, "The Interface Between Public and Private Schooling: Market Pressure and the Impact on Performance," in *Improving Educational Productivity*, ed. David H. Monk, Herbert J. Walberg, and Margaret C. Wang (Greenwich, Conn.: Information Age Publishing, 2001), 47–76.

18. C. E. Finn Jr., "Cheating the Child to Save the 'System,'" *New York Times*, May 17, 1997, 17.

19. T. Lewin, "Schools Get Tough on Illegal Students From Other Places," *New York Times*, April 20, 1997, 1.

20. C. E. Richards, S. Rima, and M. B. Sawicky, *Risky Business: Private Management of Public Schools* (Washington, D.C.: Economic Policy Institute, 1996). See also Levin, "Race and School Choice"; and Buckley, Schneider, and Shang, *Are Charter School Students Harder to Educate?*

21. K. Zernike, "Vouchers: A Shift, but Just How Big?" *New York Times*, June 30, 2002, 3.

22. Levin and Belfield, *Vouchers and Public Policy*.

23. P. Gonzalez, A. Mizala, and P. Romaguera, *Vouchers, Inequalities and the Chilean Experience*, National Center for the Study of Privatization in Education, Teachers College, Columbia University, 2004, http://ncspe.org/publications-files/op94.pdf. See also G. Elacqua and E. de Gobierno, *School Choice in Chile: An Analysis of Parental Preferences and Search Behavior*, National Center for the

Study of Privatization in Education, Teachers College, Columbia University, 2004, http://ncspe.org/publications-files/op97.pdf.

24. I. V. Sawhill and S. L. Smith, "Vouchers for Elementary and Secondary Education," in C. Eugene Steuerle, Van Doorn Ooms, George Peterson, and Robert D. Reishauer, *Vouchers and the Provision of Public Services* (Washington, D.C.: Brookings Institution, 2000), 251–290.

25. M. F. Addonizio, "New Revenues for Public Schools: Blurring the Line Between Public and Private Finance," in *Education Finance in the New Millennium*, ed. Stephen Chaikind and William J. Fowler Jr. (Larchmont, N.Y.: Eye on Education, 2001), 159–171.

26. Addonizio, "New Revenues for Public Schools," 166.

27. Addonizio, "New Revenues for Public Schools."

28. J. Steinberg and D. Henriques, "Edison Schools Gets Reprieve: $40 Million in Financing," *Wall Street Journal*, June 5, 2002, C1, C7.

29. G. Miron and C. Nelson, *What's Public About Charter Schools? Lessons Learned About Choice and Accountability* (Thousand Oaks, Calif.: Corwin Press, 2002).

30. J. Wilgoren, "Chicago Uses Preschool to Lure Middle Class," *New York Times*, June 15, 2001, A1, A20; A. Molnar, *Giving Kids the Business: The Commercialization of America's Schools* (Boulder, Colo.: Westview Press, 1996); T. Henry, "Are School Vouchers Worthwhile?" *USA Today*, April 11, 1996, 1D.

31. J. Kronholz, "High Court's Ruling Will Fuel Fight Over School Vouchers," *Wall Street Journal*, February 19, 2002, A28.

32. H. M. Levin, *Where Can I Find Out More About Charter Schools*, 2005, www.ncspe.org/inforead.php?mysub=2.

33. *Brown v. Board of Education, Topeka*, 347 U.S. 483 (1954).

34. B. Levin, "Race and School Choice."

35. Brown, "Nixon's 'Southern Strategy' and Forces Against Brown."

36. Goldhaber, "The Interface Between Public and Private Schooling."

37. *Belk v. Charlotte-Mecklenburg Bd. of Educ.*, 233 F.3d 232 (4th Cir., 2000), rehearing en banc, 269 F.3d 305 (4th Cir., 2001), reconsideration denied sub nom.; *Belk v. Capacchione*, 274 F.3d 814 (4th Cir., 2001), cert. denied sub nom.; *Capacchione v. Charlotte-Mecklenburg Bd. of Educ.*, 535 U.S. 986 (2002).

38. Wilgoren, "Chicago Uses Preschool to Lure Middle Cass."

39. Zernike, "Vouchers: A Shift, but Just How Big?"

40. Richards, Rima, and Sawicky, *Risky Business*.

41. Gonzalez, Mizala, and Romaguera, *Vouchers, Inequalities and the Chilean Experience*; Elacqua and de Gobierno, *School Choice in Chile*.

42. Gonzalez, Mizala, and Romaguera, *Vouchers, Inequalities and the Chilean Experience*; Elacqua and de Gobierno, *School Choice in Chile*.

43. W. G. Buss, "Teachers, Teachers Unions, and School Choice," in *School Choice and Social Controversy*, ed. Sugarman and Kemerer, 300–331.

44. E. R. House, *Schools for Sale: Why Free Market Policies Won't Improve America's Schools, and What Will* (New York: Teachers College Press, 1998).

45. R. King, A. Swanson, and S. R. Sweetland, *School Finance: Achieving High Standards with Equality and Efficiency*, 3rd ed. (Boston: Allyn and Bacon, 2003).

46. Gonzalez, Mizala, and Romaguera, *Vouchers, Inequalities and the Chilean Experience*; Elacqua and de Gobierno, *School Choice in Chile*.

5

Transportation

Ralph D. Mawdsley

Every year, approximately 440,000 public school buses travel about 4.3 billion miles to transport 23.5 million children to and from school and school-related activities. The school bus occupant fatality rate of 0.2 fatalities per 100 million vehicle miles traveled (VMT) is much lower than the rates for passenger cars (1.5 per 100 million VMT) or light trucks and vans (1.3 per 100 million VMT). School bus transportation is thus one of the safest forms of transportation in the United States.[1]

In fact, between 1991 and 2001, only 0.33% of the more than 406,000 fatal traffic crashes were classified as school transportation related. More specifically, only 9% of the 1,479 school bus related fatalities were occupants of the buses, even though almost half of the crashes with other vehicles and 46% of all fatalities involving school bus passengers were front-end collisions. Of the 100 crashes that occurred between 1991 and 2001 involving at least one fatality of a school bus occupant, 55 involved another vehicle. In the remaining 45 single vehicle crashes, the first harmful events were striking a fixed object (23), a person falling from the bus (9), overturning (8), the bus colliding with a train (3), the bus colliding with an object not fixed (2), and other (5).[2]

The statistics underscore that despite the safety record of school buses when compared with other motor vehicles, the operation of school buses still represents a potential risk to boards, passengers, and those who encounter the buses as pedestrians or motorists. The purpose of this chapter is to explore some of the common areas where boards can be exposed to legal risks in operating school buses so that school business officials and other educational leaders can be better informed about these issues. While the limited amount of space does not permit an exhaustive discussion of legal problems in these areas, an identification of some of the more frequently litigated topics may be useful to those responsible for providing transportation for school systems.

SCHOOL BUS SAFETY REQUIREMENTS

While school buses represent a comparatively safe means of transportation, they must be operated by competent and skilled personnel. The buses also need regular maintenance inspections to make certain they comply with appropriate safety standards. Comprehensive safety requirements for school buses have most assuredly played a major role in their safety record. Moreover, although bus safety requirements are not necessarily uniform among states, there is consistency for such items as regular inspections,[3] passenger seating capacities,[4] use of stop signal arms and lights,[5] location of fire extinguisher,[6] and mandatory special licenses[7] and seat belts for drivers.[8]

Variances among the states regarding safety features have prompted the Department of Transportation (DOT) to adopt guidelines and standards pertaining to the manufacture, equipping, and operation of school buses. Among these guidelines are the use of a rod in front of a bus to keep children within the direct view of the driver; use of signal arms and lights by local transit buses when transporting schoolchildren; semi-annual bus inspections; twice-a-year emergency evacuation drills for students riding buses; and passenger seat belts for buses with less than 10,000 pounds gross weight rating.[9] Further, the DOT has enacted highly detailed and technical performance requirements for school bus design and manufacture to protect passengers in the event of crashes.[10]

Singularly missing are state or federal seat belt requirements on buses in excess of 10,000 pounds gross weight that carry many of the nation's children to and from schools. The National Transportation Safety Board, following up on a 1987 study, recommended that lap belts not be required on large buses, in part because such restraints would not have made a difference in saving passenger lives. However, the study indicated that states could require lap belts if they wanted to.[11] The two leading reported state cases addressing liability for buses that lack seat belts for children, albeit with different results, are discussed below.

The supreme court of Alabama refused to find that school buses without seat belts violated the state's Extended Manufacturer's Liability Doctrine.[12] The court determined that even though the state legislature required drivers to wear seat belts, it had not intended children to do the same. In addition, the court was of the opinion that since a school bus without pupil seat belts was not inherently defective or dangerous for purposes of products liability, it would not impose liability over their non-use.

Conversely, an appellate court in Oklahoma decided that a litigable question was presented under a products liability theory where a school bus did not have passenger seat belts.[13] The defendants in both Alabama and Oklahoma were bus manufacturers, but if they were to be found liable, the question remains as to whether boards could be held accountable should school buses be considered dangerously defective because they lack pupil seat belts or, if buses have seat belts, whether failure to properly instruct on their use constitutes negligence.

Insofar as the Oklahoma case indicated that liability under state law existed even where bus standards met federal guidelines, the responsibility is on state legislatures to consider whether compliance with federal standards should eliminate state causes of action. In other words, if a state legislature explicitly adopts the federal standards, as at least one state has done, such an action presumably could limit potential liability only to violations of federal requirements.[14] Absent such legislative action, school bus safety and design standards may be influenced more by litigation than legislation.

Regardless of the ongoing debate over seat belts for students,[15] the owners, and operators, of school buses clearly have a responsibility to check vehicles regularly for defects. Whether owners meet their standard of care for students transported by waiting to correct defects after they have become known is problematic. This difficulty is illustrated by an appellate decision from Georgia[16] wherein the court suggested that the standard of care is not whether the bus owner inspected vehicles for defects after they became known, but whether a company established an ongoing maintenance program to replace parts that had deteriorated. Similarly, an appellate court in North Carolina held that a private school was liable for a student's death when a bus stalled along a busy highway.[17] The court concluded that the school was responsible because even though it knew about the bus's mechanical malfunctions, its only solution was to provide the driver with a set of jumper cables.

Another troublesome area is whether boards can avoid liability by contracting with private bus companies to transport students. Generally, if state law considers bus companies to be independent contractors, then boards are not likely to be liable for negligence of company employees either in driving or maintaining vehicles, as long as transporting children is not determined to be inherently dangerous work.[18] If a board chooses to contract out for bus services, it may be advisable to include an indemnification provision in the contract with the transportation company. The contractual language should indemnify the board for damages it may sustain due to an injury involving a school bus.[19]

Regardless of whatever strategies school boards may engage in to reduce or limit liability, the presence of unsafe buses on public streets is an invitation for a suit. If boards use their own buses, they need regular preventative maintenance plans. On the other hand, if boards contract out for bus transportation, they need to include a company's maintenance record as part of the bidding process for the lowest responsible bidder. Hopefully, lowest responsible bidder statutes in states permit boards to reject low bidders with inadequate safety records.[20]

BUS STOP LOCATIONS

The selection of bus stops presents a litigious issue, since students are instructed to wait at locations not of their choosing that may be in unsafe or heavily traveled areas. At the same time, school boards are normally not liable for injuries that students suffer as they cross streets or walk along roads on their way to bus stops.[21] Moreover, boards are not likely to be responsible for injuries to students caused by other pupils at bus stops, but may be accountable for injuries caused by non-students.[22]

In many states, the location of bus stops may be considered a planning function and therefore immune from liability under governmental immunity.[23] Even so, liability may be predicated on negligent design of bus routes.[24] Although this distinction regarding liability is neither easy to understand nor consistently followed, liability may attach where a court considers that the issue is not one of the location of a bus stop but rather a design problem with variables such as the locations of the homes of students or dangerous conditions of which the district is knowledgeable. For example, an appellate court in Illinois decided that a student who was injured while crossing a railroad track after disembarking from a bus was entitled to a jury trial because school board officials did not have the vehicle stop at an alternative location which would not have required children to cross the tracks.[25] Similarly, an appellate court in Florida ruled that a school system was liable for $175,000 in damages over the death of a 12-year-old student despite problems that were associated with a bus stop that it maintained.[26]Among the difficulties with the location were near misses of students by cars and the absence of any traffic signals, signs, markers, or barriers designating the area as a bus stop.

An even more troublesome situation exists where the actions of school bus drivers who drop off children is related to liability insurance coverage and governmental immunity. In such a case, the supreme court of Georgia upheld a $1,000,000 judgment against a school board after a bus driver dropped off a kindergarten student in a hazardous location at an unapproved stop, requiring the child to walk along a dangerous road where he was struck and killed by a car.[27] The court reasoned that since the accident occurred after the child was dropped off, it did not come within a comprehensive insurance policy exclusion for injuries resulting from bus use. Insofar as insurance coverage applied in this case, the board lost its governmental immunity argument.

The supreme court of Connecticut addressed a case involving a comprehensive insurance policy that covered bus usage such that the state's immunity statute could have been invoked only if an injury occurred outside such use. In this case, a special education student was sexually assaulted by another special education student after both departed their school bus and entered the school. In finding that this was the result of bus use, the court noted that just as a board has a duty to deliver students safely to a bus stop, so also do officials have a duty to deliver students safely to school personnel.[28]

To a large extent, school boards rely on information from parents in designing bus routes and stops. Even so, boards may be liable due to the unilateral acts of students who select alternate bus stops. In one case, the supreme court of Kansas affirmed that a school board was not liable for a student's injury when his parents selected a bus stop on the side of the road nearest their home but the driver had no knowledge that they had chosen one across the street from their residence.[29] However, knowledge by a driver that a parent has made a mistake affects immediately the responsibility to see that a child safely crosses the street, rather than wait for a school board to change the location of a bus stop to the other side of a street.

When students miss a bus at their designated stops, the legal issues are twofold whether a board is liable for students hurrying to another designated bus stop and whether it is responsible for picking up pupils at undesignated locations. A board can be liable in the former situation only if it has communicated its endorsement of the practice so that parents have come to rely on an alternate bus stop route.[30] Liability can occur in the latter anytime officials know that an undesignated stop is being used.[31] However, self-help efforts by parents to compensate if their child misses a bus can impact on other obligations. For example, an appellate court in New York[32] pointed out that a bus driver who ordinarily did not transport the injured child in question did not have a duty to activate the vehicle's flashers after a parent flagged him down.

RESPONSIBILITY EN ROUTE TO AND FROM SCHOOL

School boards must satisfy a minimum standard of care in transporting students. If a board operates its own buses, then the standard is usually ordinary care, proportionate to the age and ability of children to care for themselves.[33] Yet in some states, buses operated by private companies under leases to boards may be held to the higher standard of care for common carriers.[34]

Even though bus rides to school are relatively brief, students can become disruptive or ill. As illustrated by a case from Ohio, the standard of care that applies to a bus driver or school board can affect liability.[35] The Sixth Circuit affirmed that a board was not liable under a federal civil rights claim where a child who was a passenger on a school bus died of heart failure. The court maintained that since the driver reasonably thought that the student was only experiencing an epileptic seizure and took her home without medical intervention, this incident did not demonstrate a practice or custom of deliberate indifference, the standard required for recovery under section 1983 of the Civil Rights Act of 1964. A central issue before the court was how much knowledge school officials must have about a student's special conditions before they become responsible to train bus drivers to address those needs. Insofar as cases are always fact specific, the court was not satisfied that the board had sufficient notice about seizures on buses to require a training program. However, denial of recovery under federal law does not mean that a party might not be successful under state law.

Litigations filed pursuant to section 1983 concern violations of liberty and/or property interests under the Fourteenth Amendment and are frequently referred to as constitutional torts. While such constitutional torts may involve different substantive proof requirements from negligence claims under state law, the results may be the same as in the Sixth Circuit's decision in states that require proof of gross negligence or reckless disregard, which is very similar in definition to deliberate indifference, before recovery is possible under a negligence theory. On the other hand, the result in the Sixth Circuit might well be different in states that permit liability under the lower common-law ordinary standard of care for negligence. Under either approach, liability depends on what board officials and a bus driver knew about an individual student's needs and how much they were disregarded in the past.

The Sixth Circuit's opinion raises larger questions over training bus drivers to address emergencies. This complex issue has two broad aspects whether every board must have a plan to address the medical needs of students and whether bus drivers are expected to perform medical interventions or to exercise medical judgment concerning options for a child who is ill. To date, the law provides no guidance.

School boards need to consider at least three additional questions. The first inquiry is whether all students who are ill should be taken to medical facilities, regardless of the kind of illness, or whether such a practice should be reserved only for specific children with special medical needs. The second query is whether all bus drivers need to be trained in emergency medical practices such as CPR or be prepared to administer other kinds of emergency care. The third question asks whether bus drivers who perform emergency care practices would be held to the ordinary standard of care associated with the mythical reasonable person, or to the higher standard associated with the medical professional possessing specialized knowledge and training.

The existence of a school board plan for addressing medical emergencies does not mean that bus drivers will have any direct intervention responsibilities. However, if a board has faced past medical emergencies, failure to have a plan may well demonstrate deliberate indifference or gross negligence at one end of the liability spectrum and very likely ordinary negligence at the other.

Increasing emphasis on mainstreaming or inclusion of special needs children in classrooms invariably means that these students must be transported to and from home or to and from other instructional sites during the school day. Contrary to an unanticipated medical emergency for which board officials had no advanced notice, these children have individual education plans (IEPs) which not only describe their needs but also, in most cases, prescribe treatment. In fact, the IEPs of some students are likely to require assistants to travel with them on school buses, while many of the children who are less challenged will have no one but the driver to help them in the event of a medical emergency. What is clear is that a board may not be able arbitrarily to segregate all special needs children on special buses, even if the purpose is to concentrate them so that a driver with medical training is available, since doing so could, at the least, be discrimination under section 504 of the Rehabilitation Act of 1973.

The importance of a plan for dealing with medical emergencies is based on the notice school officials have regarding the emergency situations that have arisen on school buses. Much the same reasoning can apply to addressing problems of disruptive student conduct on buses.

Bus drivers are regularly called on to deal with disruptive students. Fortunately, most of the disruption does not pose a threat of physical harm to students. Yet compressing students into the confined space of school buses presents a double source of problems. Problems can arise on the one hand from students who are in close proximity to each other and cannot readily escape their tormentors, and on the other hand from parents who cannot understand why order cannot be maintained in a confined space. Other than the obvious reaction, in the form of suits by parents and by students who have been the victims of disruptive students, an interesting potpourri of proposed solutions is present. Alternatives for restraining disruptive students include lap belts, although one study suggests that they are more harmful to students in the event of a crash than if no belts were used;[36] video cameras, which produced improvement in conduct but at the expense of approximately $1,000 per bus;[37] and volunteers on buses, so that drivers can concentrate on driving.[38]

When students create disruptions on school buses, drivers are expected to respond appropriately. For example, in a case from Texas, the Fifth Circuit, fortunately for bus drivers, reversed itself in determining that even though a parent had been permitted in an earlier case to sue a bus driver but not the school board after their son was beaten unconscious on a school bus during a fight, the standard for the board and the driver should have been the same under a federal constitutional tort theory.[39] Neither the board nor the driver can be liable where the school district lacked a special relationship with the injured child. Thus, although the conduct of the driver in the earlier case was considered culpable since he continued to drive his bus to a convenience store to call his supervisor after being apprised of an injured student rather than drive the student to a hospital, that reasoning was no longer valid. Special relationship requires that a student be placed involuntarily in a custodial relationship, which generally will not apply to bus transportation. Worth noting is that this Fifth Circuit case represented a constitutional tort approach to a transportation-related injury, not a common-law negligence claim. Federal courts will not translate negligence claims into constitutional tort claims.

To demonstrate the difference between constitutional tort and negligence, an appellate court in New York decided that a school board was liable for a $100,000 judgment under a state common-law negligence theory for a student who suffered a permanent eye injury after being struck by an object that was thrown by a fellow passenger.[40] The court relied on the fact that the bus driver had been advised of the disruptive behavior 15 minutes prior to the injury but failed to take appropriate steps to stop the misconduct.

Responsibility for student-safe buses extends to occurrences involving circumstances other than medical emergencies and disruptive behavior by students. The importance of repeated warnings to students was illustrated in a case involving students who frequently stuck their hands, arms, or heads out of bus windows. In this case, an administrator assigned a teacher to serve as a monitor in assisting buses to pull safely out of the school parking area by giving the driver directions as he backed the bus up. The teacher was also expected to warn students to keep their hands and arms in the bus. After giving several warnings to a number of students to keep their heads and arms in the bus, the monitor signaled for the bus to back up; suddenly, a 12-year-old student stuck his head out of a window and was fatally injured when his head struck a guide wire that was in close proximity to the bus. The supreme court of Tennessee agreed that the board was not liable for ordinary negligence based on the teacher's repeated warnings coupled with the student's age.[41] This case highlights the issue that reasonableness of a board's conduct depends on a variety of factors, among which are the age and maturity of students. The possibility might exist that with younger children, even repeated warnings may not be enough to prevent liability. Thus, a bus driver of young children may have to take such measures as requiring all of a vehicle's windows to be closed until the vehicle moves forward.

A persistent problem, but one that has not generated litigation, is student clothing becoming stuck in the door of a school bus. Not unlike other situations involving lack of a driver's attention to care, this problem has two dimensions that probably affect the dearth of case law. First, since most states exempt school bus operations under governmental immunity, disembarking students would be considered to be school bus operation. The one exception, of course, would be if a state's immunity statute waives a board's immunity up to the amount of liability insurance coverage. The legal issues dealing with the interaction of negligence, insurance, and governmental immunity are so complex and confusing that any judgment on behalf of an injured child can be assured of a long and expensive appeals process, extending any possible recovery far into the future. Second, while school bus drivers are not covered by governmental immunity, they normally are not considered good sources of recovery for large judgments. Drivers who have been inattentive enough to fail to see that students have caught their clothing in a bus door probably have been fired, which in turn, without a source of income, makes them even more judgment proof. Accordingly, mandatory liability insurance for bus drivers, apart from that for school districts, would seem to be a good investment.

FAILURE TO USE SAFETY EQUIPMENT

State laws uniformly require school buses to have certain safety equipment such as signal arms and flashers that must be used when students enter or disembark from the vehicles. The responsibility of bus drivers to use flashers and signal arms to assure that students safely cross a street is virtually absolute. Deactivation of lights prematurely or failure to activate them at all can generate liability for the bus driver, even if not for the school system.[42] For example, a board in Washington was liable for the death of a 13-year-old student where there was undisputed evidence that the bus driver discharged her along a road without using flashers or a stop sign and without keeping her in sight until after she had crossed the street. The court's observation regarding use of safety equipment is worth noting: "The laws . . . governing school bus operators establish uniform guidelines that do not vary according to the age of the student, his or her familiarity with the surroundings, or other individual factors."[43]

The purpose of safety equipment is to assure that other motorists are aware of the presence of students. Although bus drivers are ordinarily aware of which side of the road a student lives on, children may occasionally cross a road after exiting a bus. A school board may be liable where a bus driver is aware of the student's intentions. For example, the supreme court of appeals of West Virginia[44] ruled that a board was liable where a driver discharged a student on the side of the street on which she lived but failed to keep the flashers on when she crossed the road behind the bus to her mailbox on the other side of the street. Similarly, responsibility can extend to a student who lives on the side of the street on which she is discharged, but school officials are aware that children frequently cross the street to meet members of their family on the other side.[45]

The responsibility to use flashers can lead to unanticipated results. The supreme court of Louisiana decided that a board was responsible not only for the death of a four-year-old boy who was struck by a car after the flashers had been discontinued before he reached the other side of the street, but also for emotional damages to the driver of the car that struck the child.[46]

However, as exemplified by a case from New York, the obligation to use flashers and stop signs has a limit. In this case the court maintained that the board was not liable as a matter of law where a child safely crossed a first street but was then struck by a car while he was attempting to cross a second street.[47]

ALTERNATIVE MEANS OF STUDENT TRANSPORTATION

Few areas seem as volatile as the matter of students who select alternate means of transportation to or from school or to and from school sites or field trips during the academic day. The problem can be further complicated when parents consent to such alternative arrangements while others do not.

The law is clear that, except as mandated by state statutes, boards are not required to provide bus transportation. The only notable exception to this general rule is when students with disabilities have provisions for transportation in their IEPs. A board would face liability to a student with an IEP, since failure to provide transportation could be construed as denying the child the right to a free appropriate public education under the Individuals with Disabilities in Education Act.

Generally, boards are not liable for injuries sustained by students who selected alternate forms of transportation to or from schools. This rule is based not only on the rationale that educators' responsibility does not begin until children are on buses in the morning but also that boards cannot compel students to ride buses home at night. Exceptions arise where boards or their employees assumed responsibility that a child will ride the bus or have contributed to the student's failure to ride the bus. For example, an appellate court in New York was of the opinion that the father of a 15-year-old student who was injured in a car while riding home from school did not state a triable cause of action for negligence where a school counselor's response to his demand that his child ride a school bus home was too vague to create an affirmative duty for the board.[48] However, an inference from this case is that clear unequivocal promises that educators place a student on a school bus and not permit the child to take alternative transportation might be enforceable. In a different kind of alternative transportation case, an appellate court in Wisconsin posited that a bus driver, but not the board, was liable for injuries sustained by a child who was struck by a car while riding his bike to school as a result of being suspended from the bus by the driver.[49] The court thought that the board was not liable because a school rule clearly stated that only an administrator could suspend a student from riding on a school bus. Especially damaging here was the driver's failure to notify the child's parents that he was suspended from the bus.

The most troublesome area continues to be use of private cars. Ordinarily, the mere fact that students use their own cars for a school-sponsored activity does not in itself generate liability.[50] However, a board can be responsible if it provides bus transportation but grants an exception for a student who uses a car[51] or whose unauthorized use of a car is known by school officials.[52] This rule was reflected in a case from Ohio where an appellate court asserted that an injured student was able to satisfy the bulk of his $314,650 judgment against the school's insurer because a private car in which he was injured was considered a "hired vehicle" within the terms of the district's liability insurance.[53] The court also noted that the person in charge of the field trip that the student was on asked for volunteers to drive their family cars.

Courts have usually been reluctant to find boards liable where students are injured in cars while traveling from one school site to another.[54] Along these lines, some boards enacted "driving/riding policies" requiring parental permission before students can ride in private cars from one school site to another. Even a board's failure to provide adequate supervision of such a policy may not create liability in a state that requires gross negligence to generate liability.[55] While courts have not always clearly articulated their reasons for not imposing liability (other than in situations involving governmental immunity), they may simply be responding to the reality that, unless school officials have made specific promises to parents regarding private vehicles or requested their use by parents or students, requiring educators to supervise their parking lots is more than can reasonably be expected.

CONCLUSION

Legal issues involving transportation for students present a collage of interacting liability issues. Selecting bus stops and providing safe bus rides are standard expectations. Moreover, safety has been undergirded by a host of state and federal statutory and regulatory requirements pertaining to safety equipment. Courts have little latitude for tolerance by bus drivers who fail to use safety equipment, especially flashers and stop signs. Courts are more understanding of the difficulties confronting school officials who monitor district policies over the use of private cars. Yet this reluctance to find liability should not prevent schools from having policies affecting use of private cars, at the very least to alert students to the risks involved in riding with other students who may or may not have appropriate private liability coverage.

Clearly, providing school bus transportation is a considerable responsibility. To this end, school boards are expected to have adequate training programs in place for drivers and safety inspection programs for the buses.

NOTES

1. School Bus Research Plan, 63 Fed. Reg. 57089-57091 (October 26, 1998) (to be codified at 49 CFR Part 571).

2. See *Traffic Safety Related Facts 2001: School Transportation-Related Crashes*, DOT HS 809 479 (U.S. Department of Transportation, National Highway Traffic Safety Administration, 2001).

3. See, for example, Minnesota Statutes Annotated § 169.451 (West, 2001).

4. See, for example, Delaware Code Annotated, tit. 14, § 2911 (West, 2004).

5. Iowa Code Annotated 321.372 (West, 2004).

6. See, for example, California Education Code § 39838 (West, 2004).

7. See, for example, Alabama Code § 16-27-4 (West, 2004).

8. See, for example, 625 Illinois Compiled Statutes Annotated 5/12-807 (West, 2004).

9. U.S. Department of Transportation, Highway Safety Program Guideline No. 17 (23 C.F.R. § 1204.4), Washington, D.C., 1991. See also *National Transportation Safety Board Study: Crashworthiness of Small Poststandard School Buses* 14 (Report No. NTSB/SS-89/02).

10. 49 Code of Federal Regulations § 571.220 (Standard No. 220; School bus rollover protection), § 571.221 (Standard No. 221; School body joint strength), and § 571.222 (Standard No. 222; School bus passenger seating and crash protection), 1990.

11. See *National Safety Board Safety Study: Crashworthiness of Large Poststandard Schoolbuses* 73-96 (Report No. NTSB/SS-87/01).

12. *Dentson v. Eddins & Lee Bus Sales*, 491 So.2d 942 (Ala., 1986). This decision was reaffirmed in dismissal of a lawsuit challenging the lack of air bags in cars, *Schwartz v. Volvo North America Corp.*, 554 So.2d 927 (Ala., 1989).

13. *Attocknie v. Carpenter Mfg.*, 901 P.2d 221 (Okla. Ct. App., 1995).

14. See *O'Connor v. Mahopac Cent. Sch. Dist.*, 692 N.Y.S.2d 76 (N.Y. App. Div., 1999).

15. See, for example, Fla. Statutes Annotated § 316.6145 (West, 2005).

16. *Kirby v. Spate*, 448 S.E.2d 7 (Ga. Ct. App., 1994). See, generally, Ralph Mawdsley, "Should Seat Belts Be Required on All School Buses," *Education Law Report* 105 (1996).

17. *Sharpe v. Quality Educ., Inc.*, 296 S.E.2d 661 (N.C. Ct. App., 1982). See also, *NSBA Legal Clips*, February 24, 2005: school districts are beginning to install Global Positioning System (GPS) units on their buses in order to track their location, which allows districts to locate buses with mechanical troubles and to monitor the speed of buses.

18. See *Dixon v. Whitfield*, 654 So.2d 1230 (Fla. Dist. Ct. App., 1995); *Settles v. Incorporated Village of Freeport*, 503 N.Y.S.2d 945 (N.Y. Sup. Ct., 1986).

19. See *Merrimack Sch. Dist. v. National Sch. Bus Serv.*, 661 A.2d 1197 (N.H., 1995).

20. See *Dineen v. Town of Kittery*, 639 A.2d 101 (Me., 1994) (court approved bid $30,000 higher than low bid).

21. See *Young v. Salt Lake City Sch. Dist.*, 52 P.3d 1230 (Utah, 2002); *Cavalier v. Ward*, 723 So.2d 480 (La. Ct. App., 1998); *Norton v. Canandaigua City Sch. Dist.*, 624 N.Y.S.2d 695 (N.Y. App. Div., 1995); *Powell v. Dist. of Columbia*, 634 A.2d 403 (D. D.C., 1993).

22. Compare *Fornaro v. Kerry*, 527 N.Y.S.2d 61 (N.Y. App. Div., 1988), and *Harker v. Rochester City School Dist.*, 661 N.Y.S.2d 332 (N.Y. App. Div., 1997) with *Moore v. Wood County Bd. of Educ.*, 489 S.E.2d 1 (W. Va., 1997).

23. See *Hewett v. Miller*, 898 S.W.2d 213 (Tenn. Ct. App., 1994).

24. See *Houle v. Galloway Sch. Lines*, 643 A.2d 822 (R.I., 1994).

25. *Garrett v. Grant Sch. Dist. No. 124*, 487 N.E.2d 699 (Ill. App. Ct., 1985).

26. *Duval County Sch. Bd. v. Dutko*, 483 So.2d 492 (Fla. Dist. Ct. App., 1986).

27. *Burke County Sch. Dist. v. Roberts*, 482 S.E.2d 283 (Ga., 1997).

28. *Board of Educ. of Bridgeport v. St. Paul Fire and Marine Insur. Co.*, 801 A.2d 752 (Conn., 2002).

29. *Hackler v. School Dist. No. 500 of Kansas City*, 777 P.2d 839 (Kan., 1989).

30. See *Stokes v. Tulsa*, 875 P.2d 445 (Okla. Ct. App., 1994).

31. See *DiCabo v. Raab*, 516 N.Y.S.2d 995 (N.Y. App. Div., 1987).

32. See *Keiser v. Elmer*, 639 N.Y.S.2d 118 (N.Y. App. Div., 1996).

33. See *Bruce v. Hasbrouk*, 620 N.Y.S.2d 562 (N.Y. App. Div., 1994).

34. See *Sharpe v. Quality Educ.*, 296 S.E.2d 661 (N.C. Ct. App., 1982).

35. *Sargi v. Kent City Bd. of Educ.*, 70 F.3d 907 (6th Cir., 1995).

36. See *National Safety Board Safety Study: Crashworthiness of Large Poststandard Schoolbuses*, 73, 78, 95, 97.

37. "Watching More Than the Road: Head Start Bus Will Have Video Monitor," *Times Picayune*, February 25, 2003, WL 3994598; "Say Cheese!" *Education Week*, September 21, 1994, 4. See also Kyle Zambarano, "Rhode Island's Right to a Safe School: A Means to an End or an End Without Means," *Roger Williams University Law Review* 8 (2003): 417 n. 196; Andrew McClurg, "Bringing Privacy Law out of the Closet: A Tort Theory of Liability for Intrusion in Public Places," *North Carolina Law Review* 723 (1995): 1020 n. 172 (reporting hundreds of school districts using video cameras to curb unruly students).

38. See, for example, Ohio Revised Code § 3327.16 (Baldwin, 1994) (includes volunteer adults and responsible older students, but they are expressly not employees and are not compensated).

39. *Lopez v. Houston Indep. Sch. Dist.*, 817 F.2d 351 (5th Cir., 1987), overruled in *Walton v. Alexander*, 44 F.3d 1297 (5th Cir., 1995). The reason for the change was the U.S. Supreme Court's decision in *DeShaney v. Winnebago County*

Department of Social Servs., 489 U.S. 189 (1989), reversing liability imposed on social services because it lacked special relationship with child severely injured by parent. But see, *Goga v. Binghamton City Sch. Dist.*, 754 N.Y.S.2d 739 (N.Y. App. Div., 2003), no special relationship between school district and driver where driver injured in stopping students fighting on bus.

40. *Blair v. Board of Educ. of Servurne-Earlville Cent. Sch.*, 448 N.Y.S.2d 566 (N.Y. App. Div., 1982).

41. *Arnold v. Hayslett*, 655 S.W.2d 941 (Tenn., 1983).

42. See, for example, *Chainini v. Board of Educ. of New York City*, 639 N.Y.S.2d 971 (N.Y., 1995).

43. *Yurkovich v. Rose*, 847 P.2d 925 (Wash. Ct. App., 1993).

44. *Yeager v. Morgan*, 429 S.E.2d 61 (W. Va., 1993).

45. See *Farley v. El Tejon Unified Sch. Dist.*, 274 Cal. Rptr. 780 (Cal. Ct. App., 1990).

46. *Clomon v. Monroe City Sch. Bd.*, 572 So.2d 571 (La., 1990).

47. *Womack v. Duvernay*, 645 N.Y.S.2d 831 (N.Y. App. Div., 1996).

48. *Wenger v. Goodell*, 733 N.Y.S.2d 523 (N.Y. App. Div., 2001).

49. *Toeller v. Mutual Serv. Cas. Ins. Co.*, 340 N.W.2d 923 (Wis. Ct. App., 1983). See also *Hollins v. Richland County Sch. Dist. One*, 427 S.E.2d 654 (S.C., 1993).

50. See *Bradshaw v. Rawlings*, 612 F.2d 135 (3d Cir., 1979).

51. See *Williamson v. Board of Educ. of Berne-Knox*, 375 N.Y.S.2d 221 (N.Y. App. Div., 1975).

52. See *Sumter County v. Pritchett*, 186 S.E.2d 798 (S.C., 1971).

53. *Caston v. Buckeye Union Ins. Co.*, 456 N.E.2d 1270 (Ohio Ct. App., 1982). See also *Andresen v. Employers Mut. Cas. Co.*, 461 N.W.2d 181 (Iowa, 1990).

54. See *Wickey v. Sparks*, 642 N.E.2d 262 (Ind. Ct. App. 1994); *Capuzzi v. Heller*, 558 A.2d 596 (Pa. Commw. Ct., 1989).

55. See *Steele v. Auburn Vocational Sch. Dist.*, 661 N.E.2d 767 (Ohio Ct. App., 1994); *Richardson v. Hambright*, 374 S.E.2d 296 (S.C., 1988).

6

Technology in Education

Timothy E. Morse

School business officials are cognizant of the noteworthy technology-related expenditures they authorize annually. On average, Americans spend $7 billion per year on school computing technologies.[1] Given the size of this investment, school business officials and other interested constituencies such as parents and elected officials are interested in knowing what return, in terms of gains in students' academic achievement, they are receiving on their investment. Yet to date, researchers have not clearly established how technology can be used effectively and efficiently to positively impact each student's academic progress.

In lieu of such data, school business officials must unilaterally develop a solid rationale to support the decisions they make with respect to technology expenditures. That is, in the absence of an existing diagnostic-prescriptive approach to school-based technology applications—an approach in which a student need is identified and a technology-based remedy is prescribed—school business officials must consider a host of variables as they decide how to budget for technology expenditures. As was alluded to by former Secretary of Education Richard Riley, the question that must be addressed is not whether technology will impact our nation's schools, but how and to what extent students will use the technology that is available. He stated: "This debate has never been about technology. It has been about what our children have the opportunity to do. . . . It's about connecting students to a whole new world of learning resources and offering the mind the opportunity to expand and take on a new and challenging future."[2]

As for now, the potential for school technology to impact our nation's students is limited. That is, while $7 billion per year is being spent on school computing technologies, a typical student's access to this technology is still measured in minutes per week. Yet as is discussed below, emerging computer technologies, such as the handheld computer, are setting the stage for the day when every student will have access to a computer throughout an entire school day and beyond. Hence, as computer technology becomes a staple within American schools, much the way that textbooks, papers, and pencils currently are, school personnel will simultaneously have to plan for its equitable use among students.

Given these circumstances, this chapter presents information to assist school business officials to plan for technology expenditures that will enable them to address extensive, yet equitable, student use of computer technology. The chapter begins with a discussion of basic legal issues. Specifically, it reviews the idea that school business officials must establish acceptable use policies to govern who can use school technology as well as how it can be used. The chapter then considers information pertaining to the emerging era of pervasive computing, since this model for computer use will enable every student to have full-time access to this technology. Finally, the chapter highlights topics that are directly related to the equitable use of technology. After discussing issues related to the digital divide, the chapter explores two topics that are dedicated to the premise that appropriate technology use can ensure every student's full participation at school: universal design for learning and assistive technology.

ACCEPTABLE USE POLICY

The rapid pace of technological change presents a tremendous challenge to school business officials who are working to address the extensive and equitable use of technology by the students in their schools. As new devices and uses for these devices evolve, governing laws are created. Thus, unless someone is a lawyer or a similarly trained professional whose area of expertise is school technology, it is virtually impossible to remain abreast of the legal issues that pertain to the appropriate use of technology. To this end, readers of this chapter are encouraged to consult other sources to obtain an in-depth examination of this topic.[3]

For the purposes of this chapter, it is necessary to speak to the foundational legal issues that school business officials must address with respect to extensive and equitable technology use by students. An acceptable use policy (AUP) is the natural starting point whereby a school board can explain how technology should be used to enhance student achievement and the conditions under which technology can be used.[4] Moreover, most school boards essentially do not have a choice about creating an AUP, since the Children's Internet Protection Act (CIPA), which became law in December 2000, requires systems receiving E-rate funds to have board-approved AUPs.

Wenkart and Darden listed the following features of sound AUPs: such policies put parents and students on notice about the rules for acceptable use of school technology; diminish parents' and students' expectations that electronic communications are private; establish parameters for acceptable student behavior while using school technology; allow school officials to discipline those who violate the terms of the policy; specify that school personnel will, to the extent possible, supervise technology access.[5] The authors also noted that AUPs should be reviewed annually, given the rapid pace of technological change. Further, they stressed that this approach becomes a contract between the school, student, and parent or guardian, informing everyone about what is "acceptable use" and, therefore, protecting the school against later claims. One final issue that they considered and which needs to be resolved with respect to AUPs is whether school boards prefer to have a single policy that covers both students and employees or separate policies for these groups. Either way, once created, a well-crafted AUP will provide a solid foundation upon which school personnel can build other technology-related policies and procedures.

THE ERA OF PERVASIVE COMPUTING

As school officials work to establish an AUP for their relevant constituencies, they also must continue to address the limited student use, currently measured in minutes per student per week, of their existing computing technology. The inevitable, pending emergence of the era of pervasive computing apparently will enable school personnel to ensure extensive technology use by virtually every student.

Citing cost and capability data pertaining to emerging mobile computing technology, as well as highlighting historical references to the widespread adoption of other technological innovations such as fax machines, microwaves, and cell phones, predictions are that portable wireless computer use will be widespread in our nation's schools by the end of this decade. Portable wireless devices (PWDs) refers to the class of portable, Internet-capable computers that include both handheld and tablet computers; it also appears that in the future every student will be able to access their own PWDs 24 hours per day, seven days per week. Bull referred to this inevitable state of affairs as the era of pervasive computing.[6] It is worth noting that since handheld computers that possess the same power as three-year-old desktops are readily more affordable than existing tablet computers ($250 vs. $1,700) and will be more affordable for schools, this discussion of PWDs refers only to handheld computers.

The establishment of the era of pervasive computing will ensure extensive computing technology use by every student. The challenge for school business officials will be to plan and budget appropriately for the relevant issues that will emerge. Accordingly, the following items will need to be addressed.

1. Professional development. School business officials must anticipate the costs that will be associated with training teachers how to use PWDs. In particular, this requires at least three expenditures. First, teachers will have to be taught how to operate this new computing technology. Second, teachers will need to be taught how to present instruction using PWDs and then be allowed the time needed to modify their existing lesson plans and related elements such as the physical arrangement of their classrooms. Third, at least some teachers will have to be provided with opportunities to participate in developing appropriate applications such as software programs for use with PWDs. Teachers may develop these applications independently or in concert with commercial firms.

2. Creation of appropriate infrastructures. School systems will have spent considerable funds wiring their facilities to ensure access to the Internet. Naturally, a question that readily comes to mind when one begins to consider the extensive use of devices that allow for wireless Internet access is how, or even if, an existing infrastructure

will still be useful. Put another way, were the monies that were used to build this infrastructure wasted? The answer is that since an existing infrastructure can still be useful even though it may be used in a different way,[7] the funds that have been spent to create one will not have been wasted. In particular, access points should be established within existing wired infrastructures that can serve as the gateways through which wireless PWDs obtain Internet connections. Further, while PWDs already possess tremendous computing power and hold great promise with respect to what students can do with them, they will not completely eliminate the need for the existing desktop and laptop machines that are connected to a school's existing infrastructure. As the computing powers and capabilities of these machines continue to increase, they can be used to complete tasks such as creating multimedia instructional materials that simply cannot be completed with PWDs.

3. Acquisition and replacement costs. While individual PWDs are relatively inexpensive, the costs of acquiring devices for each student, as well as desktop and laptop computers that will still be needed, will have to be considered. Similarly, there will be expenses for applications and various PWD accessories. As is the case with laptops and desktops, school boards will have to purchase software that can run exclusively on PWDs. Regarding accessories, some unique items will have to be budgeted for, such as expansion cards (the PWD equivalent of floppy disks), carrying cases to protect PWDs should they be dropped accidentally, screen protectors to extend the usefulness of PWD touch-sensitive display screens, and replacement styli for the pencil-like instrument that come with PWDs and are used to input data via the touch-sensitive screen but can be easily misplaced or lost.

A related issue that school business officials will have to address is replacement costs for PWDs. Given their size and portability, these devices will be more prone to theft and damage from everyday use than existing school computing technologies. As a result, a number of relevant issues, for which there are no ready answers, will have to be addressed in a policy and procedures document. For instance, one issue is who will pay the replacement costs of devices if they are damaged through willful neglect? While it is easy to say that students (and their parents) are responsible for replacement costs, many families that live in poverty may not be able to afford these costs. If, as predicted, these devices are used throughout a school day to complete school-based tasks, will it be practical for school officials to enforce such a policy when students cannot afford to purchase the primary "tool" that is needed to complete their work? A related consideration pertains to the fact that it is more cost-effective to replace an entire PWD than it is to repair it. Hence, school business officials may need to consider dedicating funds to an appropriate insurance policy that covers wholesale replacement costs rather than an on-site technology support staff that traditionally has been paid to repair broken technology.

4. Small-scale appropriate use studies. A variety of researchers strongly advocate spending time and resources conducting small-scale studies investigating appropriate uses for PWDs before adopting them for use on a wider scale. School business officials can heed this advice by funding exploratory investigations, from existing budgets, at the classroom or building level and then use the data obtained from these studies to plan how to budget for district-wide adoption of PWDs.

ELIMINATING THE TANGIBLE DIGITAL DIVIDE

When the era of pervasive computing comes to pass, school business officials will be able to obliterate the existing limited student use of school computing technology. It therefore seems logical to conclude that, simultaneously, all vestiges of inequitable computer use will be readily addressed. Equitable computer use is an important issue for several reasons. First, in order to be able to determine how technology use impacts each student's academic achievement, it is necessary that each child's use of technology be included in measures of this phenomenon. Second, by ensuring equitable student use of technology, school business officials will reduce or eliminate their legal exposure. For example, federal law mandates that students with disabilities, a group that historically has suffered from discriminatory practices by public school personnel, be given full access to the general education curriculum, which in most, if not all, instances will eventually include the use of computing technology. Third, a close examination of equity of technology use issues reveals cost savings that cannot be realized otherwise.

Regrettably, all vestiges of inequitable computer use will not be readily addressed with the onset of the era of pervasive computing. Yet there is reason to hope that these inequities can eventually be eliminated if the relevant key issues are addressed thoughtfully head-on.

Presently the inequitable use of computer technology has been referred to as the digital divide. According to Gorski, this term "has traditionally described inequalities in access to computers and the Internet between groups of people based on one or more social or cultural identifiers"[8] such as socioeconomic status or gender. Recent data reported by the Department of Commerce indicated that in American society certain social groups, such as whites and those with higher income and education levels, have above-average levels of computer ownership and access.[9] Further, available data reveal that these inequities extend into our nation's schools, as schools attended by students from families living in poverty as well as students from diverse ethnic backgrounds are likely to offer less access to technology.[10] While this divide is narrowing, meaning that computer technology use among subgroups is evening out, it is probably fair to say that the gap will not be eliminated until computer technology is as affordable as other widespread technologies such as cellular phones. The emergence of low-cost PWDs affords school business officials the opportunity to eliminate this divide within our nation's schools. Ironically, the widespread use of PWDs will redefine the meaning for the term digital divide.

THE INTANGIBLE DIGITAL DIVIDE

While the term digital divide is now used to refer to access to computer technology, once this technology is equally accessible to members of all subgroups in society, the term will be used to refer to how computer technology is used by various subgroups. Simply stated, a more multidimensional definition for the term digital divide acknowledges that existing computer technology is used differently by different subgroups in society, and these different uses will continue with the widespread implementation of PWDs unless this aspect of the digital divide is directly addressed.[11]

Examples of the ways computer technology is used differently by different subgroups in society include the following. First, in far too many situations, low-achieving students come to view technology as a high-priced reinforcer to which they are allowed access only after behaving in a certain way, while their higher-achieving peers come to view it as a tool to assist them in the completion of work that requires the use of higher-order thinking and problem-solving skills. Second, some students, through completing skill and drill exercises on the computer, come to view computers as devices that control their behavior by presenting activities to which they must respond. On the other hand, students who are allowed to use computers to manipulate data to solve complex problems learn that they control this device to meet their needs, and not vice versa. Third, members of some subgroups, such as students living in poverty and females, simply need to see more role models using computer technology in the performance of daily tasks. Hence, educators will be well served to identify instances where the intangible digital divide exists in their schools and plan to eliminate it during the era of pervasive computing.

UNIVERSAL DESIGN FOR LEARNING

The extensive use of computer technology will also be realized as another concept that pertains to how students interact with computing technology is more fully developed: universal design for learning (UDL). UDL refers to the design of instructional materials such that they are able to be used by the widest possible range of learners.[12] In schools, where much of the information students are expected to acquire is presented through instructional materials that utilize one format, print, many students are denied access to this information for a number of reasons. For instance, some have visual impairments and cannot see the printed word, while others are dyslexic and are unable to decode the text even though they can readily acquire the knowledge presented through it; still others have physical disabilities that simply prevent them from turning the pages containing the print. To this end, using the principle of UDL and today's digital, computer-based technology, print-based materials are designed from the outset to accommodate the range of learners previously described. One digital textbook could contain the capability to be printed in Braille for a student with a visual impairment, read aloud for a student with dyslexia, and navigated, through its virtual pages, with the click of a mouse by a student with a physical impairment.[13]

UDL is based on the concept of universal design as it emerged in the field of architecture. This movement, named by Ron Mace, was based on the idea of designing buildings and various structures from the outset to be accessible by everyone.[14] For instance, instead of retrofitting buildings with ramps and elevators to allow individuals mobile in wheelchairs to access them, architects incorporated these features into the design of the building from the outset. In so doing, they learned that this was a more cost-efficient approach that proved to be more useful to the population as a whole than was originally anticipated. For example, while curb cuts were initially designed and installed to accommodate people with disabilities, it soon became apparent that this design feature allowed a much wider segment of the population—people with strollers, luggage, bicycles, or shopping carts—to access sidewalks when they otherwise would not have readily been able to do so.

As students are able to spend more time using computer technology, school business officials should seek to acquire compatible instructional materials such as software and textbooks on CD-ROM that incorporate the principles of UDL. Currently, these types of materials are in short supply. One major reason for this state of affairs is that publishers have not settled on a standard format in which to create these materials. When these materials are more readily available, they will enable school business officials to realize cost savings by purchasing one set of instructional materials that can be used by every student in a school, rather than having to purchase multiple versions of the same set of instructional materials so that students with various needs can have access to the same knowledge.

ASSISTIVE TECHNOLOGY

Until the principle of UDL becomes more commonplace, one segment of a school's population, students with disabilities, will need to continue to use what are referred to as assistive technologies to meet the demands that are placed on them in school settings. Assistive technologies refer to devices or solutions that improve an individual's functional capacity by enabling an individual with a disability to perform a task he or she otherwise could not perform because a disability prevents him or her from doing so.[15] For example, assistive technologies, such as an adapted keyboard or speech recognition software, might enable an individual with a fine motor impairment to produce legible text, a task that the individual could not perform in a typical fashion using a pen or pencil.

The use of assistive technology by students with disabilities is governed by federal special education law, the Individuals with Disabilities Education Act (IDEA).[16] The IDEA defines both assistive technology devices and assistive technology services. An assistive technology device is "any item, piece of equipment, or product system, whether acquired commercially off-the-shelf, modified, or customized, that is used to increase, maintain, or improve functional capabilities of children with disabilities."[17] Assistive technology services are defined as "any service that directly assists a child with a disability in the selection, acquisition, or use of an assistive technology device."[18] In accordance with these definitions, the IDEA requires school personnel to perform a number of activities whenever they believe a student with a disability needs to be provided an assistive technology in order to receive a free appropriate public education.[19] These activities include, but are not limited to, the following:

1. A comprehensive evaluation must be conducted to determine a student's assistive technology needs. Given that the application of assistive technologies to the field of special education is relatively new,[20] conducting an appropriate assistive technology evaluation presents a noteworthy challenge to school personnel. Presently, educators cannot earn a state-sponsored certification which acknowledges their ability to conduct such an evaluation. Similarly, there are no commercially produced valid and reliable instruments that can be used to identify the assistive technology device that is appropriate for an individual.[21] Yet even if such an instrument were available, it is questionable if it could keep track of the tens of thousands of assistive technologies that presently exist, as well as those that are developed daily.

   Given these circumstances, school officials must opt to contract with individuals they believe are sufficiently qualified to conduct assistive technology assessments or build capacity within their districts to conduct these assessments by having professionals or groups of professionals acquire available training for the purpose of being able to conduct these assessments. While there is merit in opting for the latter approach, as it enables school systems to become self-sufficient at this endeavor, educators need to be cognizant of the fact that assistive technology evaluations are time- and labor-intensive, since they require observations of children in one or more school settings, interviews with students and significant others, and trials with potential devices. Further, educators should recall that assessments are ongoing: once a device is selected, changes in a child's environment or personal capabilities will trigger the need to conduct another evaluation.

2. School boards are responsible for acquiring and maintaining needed devices. While school business officials must budget for the acquisition of assistive technology devices, this does not mean they will have to purchase every device a student needs. The law allows officials to ask parents to use their private insurance to acquire devices, provided this does not result in hardship to them in the form of increased premiums. Likewise, to meet their legal mandate to acquire needed assistive technologies, educators can rely on the goodwill of non-profit organizations. In many instances certain organizations, such as a Lion's Club, will purchase a device for a student with a particular disability, in this instance, visual impairments. Finally, devices do not necessarily have to be purchased outright. Many companies allow devices to be leased with an option to apply some of the fees paid for the lease to be credited toward its purchase. This option can be particularly attractive where an assistive technology evaluation identified several devices that a student needs. Leasing with an option to buy may also enable the assistive technology decision-making process to move forward in these situations, since school personnel would not be locked into a device about which they have some reservations.

Once they have acquired such devices, school board officials are responsible, under the law, for maintaining, repairing, and replacing them. In some situations, a district's technology department will possess the resources that are needed to maintain and repair devices. However, in other instances, school business officials will need to make arrangements, via warranties and service agreements, with the manufacturer to cover maintenance and repair costs. In some cases, schools will not have the option of repairing a device, since the manufacturer has determined that it is more cost-efficient to replace, rather than repair, an item. School business officials should investigate the use of insurance policies for these contingencies. Also, officials should explore writing policies and procedures to govern instances where a student's willful negligence creates a need to replace a device.

3. Schools must train the student and significant others how to use devices. This aspect of the IDEA refers to the fact that not only students, but also individuals who interact with them as part of their special education program, must be trained in how to use the device. This group could include the student's parents/legal guardians, peers, related service personnel, and employer. Some boards opt to use their assistive technology evaluation team to conduct this training and, in doing so, plan for the manpower and related costs that are associated with this undertaking.

Many school business officials are aware of the excess costs associated with the operation of special education programs. Regrettably, some of these costs result from the fact that more litigation revolves around special education issues than any other area of education. Yet other costs result from the unique needs of students with disabilities, such as the need to use an assistive technology. Thus, in an effort to meet all students' needs and keep technology expenditures to a minimum, school business officials must be well versed about assistive technology issues.

CONCLUSION

As the discussion above indicates, school business officials must address a number of existing and emerging issues as they plan for the extensive and equitable use of technology by their district's students. Ironically the rapid pace of technological change both hinders and assists school business officials in their efforts. On the one hand, this rapid pace of change makes it difficult to remain abreast of relevant legal issues that, in many instances, are being developed simultaneously with new technologies. Yet school business officials must make an effort to remain abreast of these issues in order to limit their legal exposure. As was noted near the outset of this chapter, school boards should lay a solid legal foundation by creating an acceptable use policy that governs who can use school computing technology as well as the purposes that are to be served by its use.

On the other hand, this rapid pace of technological change is enabling school districts to eliminate the existing tangible digital divide by ensuring that every student is provided access to computing technology. As important is the fact that, with the emergence of portable wireless devices in the era of pervasive computing, this access will be much more extensive than anything realized to date, measured in hours of student use per day rather than just minutes. Additionally, when the concept of universal design for learning is applied to the applications that are used with these technologies, this access will be broader than ever, as the wide range of learner variance that exists within our nation's schools will be accommodated. For the small number of students who need additional supports to access the curriculum, a large number of assistive technologies are also available.

School officials who work in public schools are ever mindful of their duty to educate each student. While computing technology is not yet affordable and accessible for every student, it is becoming so. Hence, the issue that school officials must now prepare to address is not whether computing technology will be used extensively by every student, but how each student will do so.

NOTES

1. G. Bull, G. Bull, J. Garofalo, and J. Harris, "Grand Challenges: Preparing for the Technological Tipping Point," *Learning and Leading with Technology* 29 (2002): 6–12.

2. U.S. Department of Education, *e-Learning: Putting a World Class Education at the Fingertips of All Children* (Washington, D.C.: Author, 2000).

3. E. C. Darden, ed., *Legal Issues and Education Technology: A School Leader's Guide*, 2nd ed. (Alexandria, Va.: National School Boards Association, 2001).

4. R. D. Wenkart and E. C. Darden, "Student Learning and the Law of School Technology," in *Legal Issues and Education Technology: A School Leader's Guide*, 2nd ed. Darden (Alexandria, Va.: National School Boards Association, 2001), 1–30.

5. Wenkart and Darden, "Student Learning and the Law of School Technology."

6. Bull, Bull, Garofalo, and Harris, "Grand Challenges."

7. L. Goldberg, "Lose the Wires? Network Design for a Wireless World," *Learning and Leading with Technology* 29 (2002): 28–31.

8. P. C. Gorski, "Dismantling the Digital Divide: A Multicultural Education Framework," *Multicultural Education* 10, no. 1 (2002): 28.

9. U.S. Department of Commerce, *Falling Through the Net: Toward Digital Inclusion* (Washington, D.C.: Author, 2000). Retrieved June 4, 2003, from www .ntia.oc.gov/ntiahome/digitaldivide/.

10. M. R. Brown, K. Higgins, and K. Hartley, "Teachers and Technology Equity," *Teaching Exceptional Children* 33, no. 4 (2001): 32–39; C. Clark and P. Gorski, "Multicultural Education and the Digital Divide: Focus on Race, Language, Socioeconomic Class, Sex, and Disability," *Multicultural Perspectives* 3, no. 3 (2001): 39–44.

11. T. E. Morse, "Ensuring Equality of Opportunity in the Digital Age," *Education and Urban Society* 36, no. 3 (2004): 1–14.

12. B. Pisha and P. Coyne, "Smart From the Start: The Promise of Universal Design for Learning," *Remedial and Special Education* 22 (2001): 197–203; D. Rose, "Universal Design for Learning," associate editor column, *JSET E-journal* 15, no. 1 (2000). Retrieved December 5, 2004, from http://jset.unlv.edu/15.1/ asseds/rose.html.

13. S. Stahl, "The NFF: A National File Format for Accessible Instructional Materials," *JSET E-journal* 18, no. 2 (2003). Retrieved December 5, 2004, from http://jset.unlv.edu/18.2T/tasseds/stahl.html.

14. A. Meyer and D. H. Rose, "Universal Design for Individual Differences," *Educational Leadership* 58, no. 3 (2000): 39–43.

15. J. F. Melichar and A. E. Blackhurst, *Introduction to a Functional Approach to Assistive Technology* [Training Module]. Department of Special Education and Rehabilitation Counseling, University of Kentucky, Lexington, 1993.

16. 20 U.S.C. § 1400 et seq. (1997).

17. 20 U.S.C. § 1401 (a)(1) (1997).

18. 20 U.S.C. § 1401 (a)(2) (1997).

19. S. J. Smith and E. D. Jones, "The Obligation to Provide Assistive Technology: Enhancing General Curriculum Access," *Journal of Law and Education* 28 (1999): 247–265.

20. A. E. Blackhurst, "Perspectives on Technology in Special Education," *Teaching Exceptional Children* 29, no. 5 (1997): 41–48.

21. E. H. Watts, M. O'Brian, and B. W. Wojcik, "Four Models of Assistive Technology Consideration: How Do They Compare to Recommended Educational Assessment Practices?" *Journal of Special Education Technology* 19, no. 1 (2004): 43–56.

7

Negligence

Charles Russo

A major challenge facing educators is how to maintain a safe, risk-free learning environment for students. Whether students are in class, playing in school yards, or participating in extracurricular activities, educators run the risk of liability for injuries that children suffer if they breach their duty to protect the youngsters from unreasonable risks of harm. The nearly impossible task of insulating educators and their school systems from all liability aside, awareness of the principles constituting the legal duty to supervise students properly and the defenses to the tort of negligence can go a long way toward protecting a school and its personnel. Insofar as negligence can result in unwelcomed litigation, school business officials and other educational leaders can help protect themselves and their districts by familiarizing themselves with the basic elements of this important topic.

Negligence is a common-law tort involving fault when one's unintentional conduct breaches a duty of care and injures another person or persons. In school settings, boards and their employees have a duty to protect students from reasonably foreseeable risks of harm. Even so, educators are not insurers of student safety, since most injuries in schools derive from what the law calls unavoidable, or pure, accidents, meaning those for which no legal fault lies, and they cannot reasonably be expected to supervise and control students continuously.[1]

In order for school officials to be liable for negligence, injured parties must prove that educators failed to meet the elements of negligence: duty and the related concept of foreseeability; breach; injury; and causation. Further, school officials must not have been able to assert a defense such as immunity, assumption of risk, or contributory/comparative negligence that can help reduce or even eliminate liability. In reviewing the elements of negligence, it is important to realize that since they are not mutually exclusive, any number of the cases discussed herein can be used to demonstrate multiple points of law. Moreover, since the facts are essential in deciding whether a party was negligent, the following discussion and use of exemplary cases help to illustrate some of the wide array of issues that arise in school settings.

ELEMENTS OF NEGLIGENCE

Duty

In the law of negligence, absent a legal relationship, a person has no duty to act. It is thus important to recognize that educators who act within the scope of their duties, whether in classrooms, at other schools in a system, or as part of co-curricular or extra-curricular activities on campus or off, have a duty to assist all students in a group even if they do not know an individual or children personally. This duty arises based on educators' legal relationship with their school boards and is not limited to children (or others) from the building where they work. Given the significance of the element of duty, it is safe to say that most negligence cases can be viewed in the broad context of adequacy of supervision. Insofar as adequate student supervision should prevent injuries from reasonably foreseeable dangers, all activities must be supervised depending on such factors as their nature and the ages of the children involved.

Once the law recognizes the existence of a legal relationship, educators have the duty to anticipate reasonably foreseeable injuries or risks to students and take reasonable steps to try to protect them from harm. In recognizing that foreseeability is a highly flexible concept that varies based on a student's age and physical condition as well as the degree of danger inherent in a situation, the law does not expect educators to foresee all harm that might befall children. Rather, educators are responsible for only those mishaps that can reasonably be anticipated or of which they are actually aware.

If school officials take reasonable precautions but an intervening act that could not have been foreseen occurs, they are not likely to be liable.

For example, where teachers could not have anticipated that students were going to pull chairs out from under peers as they attempted to sit down, courts have refused to impose liability.[2] Other courts refused to impose liability for such unanticipated events as where a student slipped and was injured during a classroom skit[3] or due to spontaneous fighting[4] unless one child was clearly the aggressor and school officials failed to intervene.[5] On the other hand, depending on the circumstances, not all courts agree on whether boards should be liable if children are injured while using playground equipment.[6]

While the requisite level of supervision may decrease before the opening of a school day and after students are dismissed, once officials know, or should know, that children are present, they must take precautions to ensure their safety. For example, where a principal was aware that students were playing football before classes began because he directed them to play in the specific location where a child was injured, the supreme court of Idaho held that a trial was necessary to consider whether his duty to supervise the students had been breached.[7]

Conversely, where a student was struck by a car after being chased off school grounds by a peer before class, he and his mother unsuccessfully sued the board for negligence.[8] The supreme court of Kansas affirmed that the student could not recover for negligence absent evidence that officials affirmatively assumed a duty to render services to protect or supervise him before classes began, since he was not in their custody or control.

Litigation often arises when students throw, or propel, various objects around schools and school grounds. For example, in an older case, where a child was struck in the eye by a paper clip that a classmate shot from a rubber band, the supreme court of New Jersey found the principal liable for his injuries.[9] The court noted that since the principal was present at school but had not set rules for children as they gathered before entering classes, had not assigned teachers or others to assist him in supervising children at that time, and was engaged in activities other than overseeing the students when the accident took place, he was liable.

On the other hand, the supreme court of Wyoming decided that neither a school board nor teacher's aid were liable where a seven-year-old was partially blinded by a small rock which was thrown by a fellow student and bounced off a larger rock while they were at recess.[10] The court observed that since the teacher's aid who was supervising the playground where the accident occurred walked by the students approximately 30 seconds before the accident took place but did not see anything out of the ordinary, and the injury was not foreseeable, neither she nor the board was responsible. In like fashion, an appellate court in Ohio affirmed that a board was not liable for a first-grader's injuries after he was struck in the eye by a dirt-ball thrown by a fourth-grader, since the older child's action was not foreseeable.[11]

In a case that overlaps with sports and dangerous activities, where a 16-year-old female high school football player suffered serious internal injuries as a result of being tackled cleanly by a player from the other team, she and her mother sued their school board for negligent supervision.[12] Even though it voiced its concern over the seriousness of the student's injuries, an appellate court in Maryland affirmed that the board did not have a duty to warn the student or her mother of the obvious risks posed by her voluntary participation in interscholastic football because the foreseeable risk of injury was normal and obvious.

As violence continues in and around school activities, parties are increasingly filing suit in attempts to render school officials liable for student deaths and injuries. For example, the tragic shootings at Columbine High School in April 1999 that left 15 people dead, including a teacher and the two students who undertook the rampage, and injured others, gave rise to a series of unsuccessful lawsuits against the board and other public officials.[13]

Two other cases illustrate the types of issues that educators face with regard to violence in and around schools. In Louisiana, the mother of a student who was shot and killed in a parking lot after a school-sponsored fund-raising dance sued the board and the club where the event occurred over an alleged lack of security. An appellate court ruled that the board had not breached its duty of care, since officials lacked the requisite degree of foreseeability that would have imposed a duty on them to provide additional security in the parking lot.[14] The court also decided that the club owner was not liable for the student's death, since there was only slight foreseeability and gravity of harm from the criminal acts of a third party in the parking lot.

In a similar vein, where a student was shot by an unknown assailant while leaving a dance at his high school cafeteria, an appellate court in New York affirmed a grant of summary judgment in favor of a board in his suit that sought to recover for his injuries.[15] The court agreed that the student's claim of inadequate supervision lacked merit, since officials could not reasonably have foreseen that the shooting would take place.

Breach

Two important elements must be taken into account when considering whether educators have breached their duty of care. The first relates to the fact that educators can breach their duties in one of two ways. First, educators can breach their duty by not acting when there is a duty to act; this is referred to as nonfeasance. Second, educators can breach their duty by failing to act properly when there is a duty to act; this is known as misfeasance. In addition, where educators act improperly, or with evil intent, they commit malfeasance, more properly an intentional tort, as in cases involving sexual misconduct with students. Further, if school officials are aware that employees are failing to meet their responsibilities, whether due to nonfeasance, misfeasance, or malfeasance, then they, and their boards, may be liable for the tortious conduct of staff members.

The second major consideration under breach is the standard of care that educators must follow. In evaluating whether individuals have met the requisite level of care, courts have adopted a common-law standard of reasonableness. Courts typically instruct juries to consider educators' behavior in light of the legal fiction known as the reasonable person, also known as the reasonably prudent person. Although stopping short of establishing a clear hierarchy, based on education and years of experience working with children, a reasonable teacher is likely to be expected to provide a higher standard of care than a reasonable person but not to the same level as a reasonable parent. That is, courts have tried to create an objective standard that requires teachers to provide the same level of care as reasonably prudent professionals of similar education and background. This degree of care is ordinarily based on equivalent age, training, education, experience, maturity, and other relevant characteristics.

A sports case illustrates the significance of applying the proper standard in negligence cases. When a high school football player who was being considered for an athletic scholarship to college broke his neck while correctly executing a block, the New York Court of Appeals declared that the coach should not have been judged under the same standard of care as a reasonably prudent parent.[16] Instead, the court followed the general rule, declaring that since the student voluntarily participated in the game, the coach satisfied the less demanding standard of ordinary reasonable care. Similarly, where a high school football player sued his school board after his coaches, both of whom had teaching certificates and coaching endorsements, allowed him to return to a game in which he had suffered a head injury, the supreme court of Nebraska held that the proper standard of care for the coaches was that of a reasonably prudent person with a teaching certificate and coaching endorsement, rather than the lower standard of the reasonable person who did not possess such credentials.[17] The court explained that since coaches with coaching endorsements received specialized training in athletic injuries, including head injuries, they should have met the heightened standard of care. The court remanded for a determination of whether they acted in accord with this higher standard.

Injury

In order for an aggrieved party to prevail, an injury must be one for which compensation can be awarded. For example, if a student who was running through a school hallway slipped and fell on water that had leaked from a drinking fountain and had been accumulating on the floor for at least an hour, three factors would need to be examined. The first question is whether school officials had a duty to keep the floor safe and clean. Assuming the obvious, that officials had such a duty, the related question of foreseeability comes into play. To the extent that officials should have foreseen that such an incident could have occurred, they should have had the water cleaned up reasonably quickly. Second, the issue of the school's duty and possible breach, in terms of supervising the area, must be answered. The third concern is the nature of the child's injuries. If the child's only injury was a wet pair of pants, then it is highly unlikely that his claim will proceed. However, if the child broke his leg on falling, then there is a greater likelihood that this may be deemed an injury for which compensation can be awarded.

To the extent that the existence of a physical harm is present in most of the cases discussed in this section, one additional unusual case, from Louisiana, exemplifies causation by illustrating the nature of an injury. An appellate affirmed that a school board was liable for the emotional injuries that a kindergarten-aged child suffered when a physical education teacher told him that he hanged his friends with a jump rope.[18] The court found that since evidence revealed that the child was a well-adjusted five-year-old before the teacher pretended that his friends were dead, he and his parents were entitled to remuneration for his injuries.

Causation

The final element in establishing liability for negligence is that school personnel must be the legal or proximate cause of injuries brought about by their breaches. Put another way, as situations evolve, the last person or persons in a temporal chain of events who could have taken steps to prevent an injury from occurring is typically considered as at least contributing to the legal cause.

Two cases from New York illustrate judicial reasoning in this regard. As two middle school students engaged in roughhousing during recess, shortly after they stopped fighting, one child threw a stick and injured the eye of the other. When parents filed a negligence claim, an appellate court ruled that since there was insufficient actual or constructive notice of dangerous conduct that such an injury would have occurred, educators did not breach their duty of adequate supervision.[19] The court added that any negligence on the part of educators did not proximately cause the student's injury because the time span between the fight and the stick-throwing incident was so short that greater supervision could not have prevented the injury. The court also noted that the student's supervisory negligence claim was without merit, since he was a willing participant in the incident.

A board challenged the denial of its motion for summary judgment in a case filed by a high school student who was assaulted in school after school hours by a former student. An appellate court in New York reversed in favor of the board on the ground that it was not liable absent a showing that the attack was foreseeable.[20] The court acknowledged not only that although there were previous trespassing incidents by former students after school hours, none involved physical violence against students, but also that any negligence by the school officials was not the proximate cause of the student's injuries.

OFF SCHOOL GROUNDS

The duty to supervise students on school grounds is clear. Amid efforts to
extend the scope of duty beyond school grounds, it is important to em-
phasize that common law sets the duty of school officials as coextensive
with their physical custody and control over children.

When boards provide transportation for children, they extend their
boundaries via the bus to the bus stop where students board and leave
buses.[21] As can be expected, the use of school buses to transport students
has generated a fair amount of litigation. As noted in chapter 5, on transportation, as long as bus stops are not located in unreasonably dangerous
places, boards are unlikely to be liable for injuries to children that occur
there.[22] Further, boards have no duty to ensure that students reach designated bus stops safely prior to the arrival of school buses[23] and, as long as
the distance from home is reasonable, children can be required to walk to
bus stops.

On the homeward trip, the duty of bus drivers is to see that children
have crossed a road to the opposite side of the street if necessary.[24] In such
a case, an appellate court in Georgia rejected a board's motion for summary judgment in the wrongful death action a mother brought against it,
the school bus driver, and another driver after the other driver struck and
killed her daughter.[25] After the mother and other driver reached a settlement agreement, the court affirmed that material issues of fact existed as
to whether the bus driver initiated the boarding procedure for children.

In a case from New York, parents of a student who was injured when
struck by a car as he exited a bus sued the bus company, driver, and school
board. An appellate court affirmed that the bus company's failure to equip the
vehicle as a school bus did not violate a law regulating school buses, since it
was inapplicable to a bus that was not used solely to transport students.[26]

Where a second-grader who was dropped off early by his school bus
driver died as a result of injuries that he sustained while attempting to
climb into his house through a window, his parents sued the board for negligence. The supreme court of Ohio held that while the board waived its
right to statutory immunity, a genuine issue of material fact existed as to
whether the driver violated the statute prohibiting school bus drivers from
starting their vehicles until after the children leaving them have reached
places of safety.[27]

In a case that overlaps with field trips, the parents of first-graders and chaperones who were injured when a school bus driver lost control of his vehicle challenged a jury verdict in favor of the school and driver. Reversing in favor of the plaintiffs, an appellate panel in Indiana was of the opinion that the trial court committed a reversible error in not instructing the jury that it reasonably could have inferred that the driver should not have lost control of her bus as much as she did on a clear, dry spring day.[28]

School-sponsored field trips require special supervisory precautions because children are taken to unfamiliar places. While there are no specific rules, the younger students are, the greater the amount, and degree, of supervision that educators must provide. When a sixth-grader was raped by acquaintances after she left the park where a class field trip was taking place, the supervising teacher had left the park without her, stopped by her house, and returned to school. Although the teacher contacted the child's mother, she did not disclose the incident to officials at the school. The New York Court of Appeals decided that the board was liable, since evidence supported a jury's verdict that the rape was a foreseeable result of the danger created by the failure of educators to supervise the outing adequately.[29]

On a field trip to a zoo, a parent whose son was assaulted by children from another school sued their board for negligent supervision. The federal trial court in the District of Columbia rejected the board's motion to dismiss the claim on the basis that its staff owed a duty to supervise its students in order to prevent foreseeable harm such as the type that befell the child.[30]

Difficulties can often arise when students are permitted, as part of open-campus policies, to leave school. In Louisiana, after a junior high school student checked herself out in violation of a school policy that authorized only the principal or vice principal to allow a child to leave during regular class hours, she was sexually molested by a stranger while walking home through a bad neighborhood. An appellate court affirmed that the board and officials breached their duty, since the scope of their supervisory responsibilities encompassed the foreseeable risk that a female student walking through a bad neighborhood might fall victim to a criminal who frequented the area.[31]

On the other hand, another appellate court in Louisiana reviewed whether a school board owed a duty to insure the safety of a child who ordinarily walked home alone from school after an extra-curricular activity. The board stationed crossing guards at the highway where the student was injured at the end of the school day but not at the completion of after-school activities. The court affirmed that since the one-hour time period that the guard was on duty was appropriate, it would have been unreasonable to impose a duty on school officials to require them to have students walk home in groups.[32]

As a final concern involving out of school activities, it is understandable that educators seek to limit liability for student participation in activities such as sports which can cause injuries. As long as officials carefully craft release forms, courts are unwilling to impose liability.[33] Yet courts are likely to invalidate releases that are too broad or vague. For example, the supreme court of Washington vitiated release forms which officials in different districts required students to sign before engaging in school-related activities such as interscholastic athletics. The court decided that the releases, which sought to protect the board from all future negligence, violated public policy.[34] Similarly, an appellate court in New York vitiated a release form that was executed by parents of a child who participated in youth wrestling activity which stated only that they absolved the president of the tournament and head coach of all risks beyond those inherent in wrestling.[35] The court affirmed that the release was void ab initio and did not bar their negligence action, because it failed to limit liability plainly and precisely.

DEFENSES

Even if an injured party has established that the elements of negligence are present, boards and their employees have three primary defenses available to limit or eliminate liability. The defenses recognize that even though boards and officials have the duty to look after students, they cannot be accountable for every possible harm that occurs during school hours.

Immunity

Immunity is the defense most frequently used by school systems. Immunity is based on the common-law principle, now supplemented widely by various statutes dealing with such aspects as recreational[36] and discretionary function[37] immunity laws, that the government, in and through its various branches and departments such as school boards, cannot be liable for the tortious acts of its officers or employees.

Contributory/Comparative Negligence

Both contributory and comparative negligence are premised on parties' having played a part in causing their injuries. Yet the difference between these similar-sounding defenses, which now apply in an almost equal number of jurisdictions, can be profound. Contributory negligence completely bars individuals from recovering for their injuries if they contributed in any way to the harm that they suffered.[38]

As courts and legislatures realized that the contributory negligence defense often led to inequitable results, an increasing number of jurisdictions adopted comparative negligence as a defense. Comparative negligence permits juries to apportion liability based on a percentage of relative fault between the parties, as most states that rely on comparative negligence allow plaintiffs to recover for the harm that they suffered if they are not more than 50% liable.[39] Some states may apply pure comparative negligence, which permits plaintiffs to recover even if they contributed more than 50% to their injuries.[40]

In a related concern involving liability, issues arise as to the appropriate standard to apply when children contribute to their injuries. Rather than expecting children to meet the same standard as adults, courts take their age and physical condition into account when the defense of comparative negligence is raised. As a general rule, courts agree that children under the age of seven are incapable of negligence for their own behavior, while those over the age of 14 may be accountable on a case by case basis. An appellate court in Louisiana ruled that a six-year-old child did not negligently cause his own injury even though he ran out into the street and into the side of a car while returning to school to wait for his mother.[41] The court observed that the six-year-old did not share in the fault for his injury because he acted in the manner that could have been expected of a child his age.

Assumption of Risk

Assumption of risk, which is also based on comparative fault, can reduce an injured party's recovery in proportion to the degree to which his or her culpable conduct contributed to an accident if the individual voluntarily exposed himself or herself to a known and appreciated risk of harm. As noted elsewhere in this chapter, this defense frequently applies in cases where students are hurt while participating in sports.

In New York, for example, an appellate court affirmed that a cheerleader who was injured during practice could not recover from her school board, since she assumed the risks of her sport and was practicing voluntarily under the supervision of her coach.[42] Another appellate court in New York agreed that a board could not be liable for injuries that an experienced high school varsity softball player sustained when she collided with chain-link fencing while chasing a fly ball.[43] The court acknowledged that since the player fully assumed and appreciated the risks inherent in playing softball, and that the condition of the fence was open and obvious, there was no triable issue as to whether the fence unreasonably increased her risk of injury. Other courts reached similar results involving baseball,[44] basketball,[45] field hockey,[46] gymnastics,[47] ice hockey,[48] swimming,[49] and wrestling.[50]

Courts are unwilling to apply assumption of risk as a defense in school settings where coaches had students warm up for games in hazardous locations prior to the start of a volleyball game,[51] for conducting a track practice in a high school hallway that unreasonably increased a student's risk of injury,[52] nor for providing adequate safety equipment for physical education classes dealing with such activities as in-line skating[53] and softball[54] or interscholastic sports such as football[55] and softball.[56]

CONCLUSION

Compliance with the rules of negligence and adequate supervision does not guarantee a perfectly safe school or complete immunity from litigation. However, the more carefully that school business officials and other educational leaders impress the need to follow these directions on board employees, the more likely they will have safe schools that are not subject to costly litigation that could have been avoided.

NOTES

1. *Mirand v. City of New York*, 614 N.Y.S.2d 372 (N.Y., 1994).
2. *Tomlinson v. Board of Educ. of Elmira*, 583 N.Y.S.2d 664 (N.Y. App. Div., 1992).
3. *Jones v. Jackson Public Schs.*, 760 So.2d 730 (Miss., 2000).

4. *Johnsen v. Carmel Cent. Sch. Dist.*, 716 N.Y.S.2d 403 (N.Y. App. Div., 2000); *Dadich v. Syosset High Sch.*, 717 N.Y.S.2d 634 (N.Y. App. Div., 2000).

5. *Shoemaker v. Whitney Point Cent. Sch. Dist.*, 750 N.Y.S.2d 355 (N.Y. App. Div., 2002).

6. For cases rejecting board liability see, for example, *Navarra v. Lynbrook Pub. Schs.*, 733 N.Y.S.2d 730 (N.Y. App. Div., 2001); *Sinto v. City of Long Beach*, 736 N.Y.S.2d 700 (N.Y. App. Div., 2002).

7. *Bauer v. Minidoka Sch. Dist. No. 331*, 778 P.2d 336 (Idaho, 1989).

8. *Glaser ex rel. Glaser v. Emporia Unified Sch. Dist. No. 253*, 21 P.3d 573 (Kan., 2001).

9. *Titus v. Lindberg*, 228 A.2d 65 (N.J., 1967).

10. *Fagan v. Summers*, 498 P.2d 1227 (Wyo., 1972).

11. *Allison v. Field Local Sch. Dist.*, 553 N.E.2d 1383 (Ohio Ct. App., 1990).

12. *Hammond v. Board of Educ. of Carroll County*, 639 A.2d 223 (Md. Ct. Spec. App., 1994).

13. See, for example, *Ruegsegger v. Jefferson County Sch. Dist. R–1*, 187 F.Supp.2d 1284 (D. Colo., 2001); *Rohrbough v. Stone*, 189 F.Supp.2d 1088 (D. Colo., 2002), reconsideration denied, 189 F.Supp.2d 1144 (D. Colo., 2002); *Schnurr v. Board of County Comm'rs*, 189 F.Supp.2d 1105 (D. Colo., 2001).

14. *Lee v. B & B Ventures*, 793 So.2d 215 (La. Ct. App., 2001).

15. *Jimenez v. City of New York*, 738 N.Y.S.2d 380 (N.Y. App. Div., 2002).

16. *Benitez v. New York City Bd. of Educ.*, 543 N.Y.S.2d 29 (N.Y., 1989).

17. *Cerny v. Cedar Bluffs Junior/Senior Pub. Sch.*, 679 N.W.2d 198 (Neb., 2004).

18. *Spears on Behalf of Spears v. Jefferson Parish Sch. Bd.*, 646 So.2d 1104 (La. Ct. App., 1994).

19. *Janukajtis v. Fallon*, 726 N.Y.S.2d 451 (N.Y. App. Div., 2001).

20. *Nossoughi v. Ramapo Cent. Sch. Dist.*, 731 N.Y.S.2d 78 (N.Y. App. Div., 2001).

21. *Pratt v. Robinson*, 384 N.Y.S.2d 749 (N.Y., 1976).

22. See, for example, *Moshier v. Phoenix Cent. Sch. Dist.*, 605 N.Y.S.2d 581 (N.Y. App. Div., 1993).

23. *Cavalier v. Ward*, 723 So.2d 480 (La. Ct. App., 1998).

24. *Johnson v. Svoboda*, 260 N.W.2d 530 (Iowa, 1977).

25. *DeKalb County Sch. Dist. v. Allen*, 561 S.E.2d 202 (Ga. Ct. App., 2002).

26. *Sigmond v. Liberty Lines Transit*, 689 N.Y.S.2d 239 (N.Y. App. Div., 1999).

27. *Turner v. Central Local Sch. Dist.*, 706 N.E.2d 1261 (Ohio, 1999).

28. *Aldana v. School City of East Chicago*, 769 N.E.2d 1201 (Ind. Ct. App., 2002).

29. *Bell v. Board of Educ. of the City of New York*, 665 N.Y.S.2d 42 (N.Y., 1997).

30. *Thomas v. City Lights Sch.*, 124 F.Supp.2d 707 (D.D.C., 2000).

31. *D.C. v. St. Landry Parish Sch. Bd.*, 802 So.2d 19 (La. Ct. App., 2001).

32. *Jackson v. Colvin*, 732 So.2d 530 (La. Ct. App., 1998).

33. *Aaris v. Las Virgenes Unified Sch. Dist.*, 75 Cal.Rptr.2d 801 (Cal. Ct. App., 1998); *Sharon v. City of Newton*, 769 N.E.2d 738 (Mass., 2002).

34. *Wagenblast v. Odessa Sch. Dist. No. 105-157-166J*, 758 P.2d 968 (Wash., 1988).

35. *Alexander v. Kendall Cent. Sch. Dist.*, 634 N.Y.S.2d 318 (N.Y. App. Div., 1995).

36. See, for example, *Auman v. School Dist. of Stanley–Boyd*, 635 N.W.2d 762 (Wis., 2001).

37. See, for example, *Arteman v. Clinton Community Unit Sch. Dist.*, 763 N.E.2d 756 (Ill., 2002).

38. See, for example, *Daniel v. City of Morganton*, 479 S.E.2d 263 (N.C. Ct. App., 1997).

39. See, for example, *Millus v. Milford*, 735 N.Y.S.2d 202 (N.Y. App. Div., 2002); *Johnson ex rel. Johnson v. Dumas*, 811 So.2d 1085 (La. Ct. App., 2002).

40. *Church v. Massey*, 697 So.2d 407, 412 (Miss., 1997) (criticizing improper jury instructions on pure comparative negligence); *Jennings v. Southwood*, 521 N.W.2d 230 (Mich. Ct. App., 1994).

41. *Sutton v. Duplessis*, 584 So.2d 362 (La. Ct. App., 1991).

42. *Fisher v. Syosset Cent. Sch. Dist.*, 694 N.Y.S.2d 691 (N.Y. App. Div., 1999).

43. *Schoppman v. Plainedge Union Free Sch. Dist.*, 746 N.Y.S.2d 325 (N.Y. App. Div., 2002).

44. *Yanero v. Davis*, 65 S.W.3d 510 (Ky., 2001).

45. *Milea v. Our Lady of Miracles*, 736 N.Y.S.2d 84 (N.Y. App. Div., 2002).

46. *Sandler ex rel. Sandler v. Half Hollow Hills West High Sch.*, 672 N.Y.S.2d 120 (N.Y. App. Div., 1998).

47. *Weber v. William Floyd Sch. Dist.*, 707 N.Y.S.2d 231 (N.Y. App. Div., 2000).

48. *Greenberg by Greenberg v. North Shore Cent. Sch. Dist. No. 1*, 619 N.Y.S.2d 151 (N.Y. App. Div., 1994).

49. *Aronson v. Horace Mann-Barnard Sch.*, 637 N.Y.S.2d 410 (N.Y. App. Div., 1996) leave to appeal denied, 651 N.Y.S.2d 15 (N.Y.,1996); *Kahn v. East Side Union High Sch. Dist.*, 117 Cal.Rptr.2d 356 (Cal. Ct. App., 2002).

50. *Lilley v. Elk Grove Unified Sch. Dist.*, 80 Cal.Rptr.2d 638 (Cal. Ct. App., 1998).

51. *Gilbert ex rel. Gilbert v. Lyndonville Cent. Sch. Dist.*, 730 N.Y.S.2d 638 (N.Y. App. Div., 2001).

52. *Kane ex rel. Kane v. North Colonie Cent. Sch. Dist.*, 708 N.Y.S.2d 203 (N.Y. App. Div., 2000).

53. *Jackson v. Lawrence Public Sch. Dist.*, 735 N.Y.S.2d 570 (N.Y. App. Div., 2001). But see *Arteman v. Clinton Community Unit Sch. Dist.*, 763 N.E.2d 756 (Ill., 2002) (refusing to impose liability for a rollerblading accident in a physical education class based on discretionary function immunity).

54. *Muniz v. Warwick Sch. Dist.*, 743 N.Y.S.2d 113 (N.Y. App. Div., 2002).

55. *Harvey v. Ouachita Parish Sch. Bd.*, 674 So.2d 372 (La. Ct. App., 1996).

56. *Zmitrowitz ex rel. Zmitrowitz v. Roman Catholic Diocese of Syracuse*, 710 N.Y.S.2d 453 (N.Y. App. Div., 2000).

8

Supervision and Evaluation of School Employees

C. Daniel Raisch

Beginning with the inception of compulsory attendance laws in public education in the United States in the mid-1800s, school personnel have been employed, supervised, and evaluated in some way by board members and/or administrators.[1] As schooling has become more institutionalized, the hiring, supervision, and evaluation process has become more prescriptive. Moreover, the formalization of the evaluation process has been accompanied by an increased awareness of the potential losses school personnel could incur in light of negative evaluations.[2] As a form of protection against perceived improper supervision, transfers, or recalls, and/or negative evaluations that often resulted in dismissals, school employees began to seek legal redress. Consequently, most public school employees are now covered by an array of statutory procedures that administration must adhere to when hiring, supervising, and evaluating their personnel.[3]

Beyond conducting and overseeing evaluations, the non-renewals of contracts, and the dismissals of employees, administrators encounter the difficult task of deciding their staffing needs for the coming year. As part of this process, administrators must consider a wide range of issues, including a staff member's competence, classroom management abilities, instructional performance, rights, and privilege in relation to evaluation documents, when deciding the future of their employees. Insofar as the supervision and evaluation process may impact upon the size of a staff,[4] it is important to have specific policies in place to help ensure a school's efficient operation.

Litigation has proliferated around issues relating to the processes and procedures used by administrators as they screen, employ, supervise, and evaluate their staffs. In addition, establishing criteria for hiring, supervising, and evaluating personnel has created additional disputes between school boards, administrators, and employees. In light of these concerns, this chapter describes the major issues confronting school employees and administrators concerning the management, supervision, and evaluation of educational personnel. Understanding how the legal system has resolved some of these complex issues should be of assistance in administrative decision-making.

This chapter begins by reviewing some of the basic assumptions related to hiring, supervision, and evaluation. Among these assumptions is the concept that the management, supervision, and evaluation of employees is not confined to personnel performance and behavior in specifically defined jobs but can extend to such other areas as cooperation with administration, relationships with parents and other staff, outside employment, or personal conduct. The chapter next considers the various types of supervision and evaluation. In particular, the chapter explores formative and summative observations and evaluations, statutes, and regulations. Such a discussion is warranted, as these issues often prove confusing and open to possible litigation.

HIRING, SUPERVISION, AND EVALUATION

The screening, hiring, supervision, and evaluation of faculty and staff generally involve the process of establishing standards and written procedures along with the development of performance criteria. Key elements in this process are gathering information relating to the specific need (a position description of the opening) and the performance expectations, and establishing minimum expectations in order to determine an employee's effectiveness. On the basis of supervision and evaluation, at least as it relates to non-tenured staff members, these efforts are ordinarily directed at improving performance or lead to a determination whether to non-renew or terminate their contracts. The areas of supervision and evaluation have become major components in the field of education law.[5]

POLICY DEVELOPMENT

It is imperative that each school system have policies on recruiting, hiring, supervision, and evaluation that have been approved by their boards, since districts leave themselves subject to legal action in the absence of such written directives. For example, in a case from Ohio, a local board's failure to follow state law requiring it to adopt evaluation procedures warranted the reinstatement of an ineffective non-tenured teacher.[6] Consequently the policy and procedures should be crafted so as to determine and specify the competencies, skills, and conduct required of personnel being employed, supervised, and evaluated.[7]

In many states, evaluation policies are required by statute, while in others collective bargaining policies dictate the human resources procedures. Regardless, policies and procedures must be written in understandable language and reviewed by all stakeholders before they are approved and implemented. Failure to establish employee management policies and procedures with clearly defined standards of performance leaves administrators open to the charge of arbitrary and capricious conduct. In fact, such a charge of arbitrary conduct may even raise the inference that the administration has kept its evaluation policies and procedures hidden in order to discriminate against employees.[8]

As important as it is to have policies and procedures which are relevant to employment decisions, difficulties surface when they are not uniformly administered. As an example, a board or administrator, in most cases, may not hire a new employee or transfer an existing employee without first following state and/or local policies.[9] When hirings or evaluations are necessary but not conducted uniformly, an adversely affected employee may contend that an employment decision is invalid and unsupported by the evidence. Such a claim may be based on the argument that the terms of employment include the right to be supervised and the right to have a reasonable time and perhaps support to improve unacceptable performance. The failure to have such essential conditions may invalidate any form of discipline or dismissal if based on reasons that would be appropriate to evaluation.[10]

The preceding text primarily referred to the academic interest of the school. However, in public schools, extra-curricular activities personnel are covered by contracts. In most states, the extra-curricular employees do not have the same protection as a classroom teacher, for instance.[11]

HUMAN RESOURCE PROCESSES: RECRUITMENT AND SELECTION

In order for school districts to become and remain effective organizations, they must identify, attract, hire, and retain competent personnel. However, attracting, employing, and retaining effective personnel have become more difficult in recent years. This is especially true in poor and/or urban areas of our nation.[12] Certain teacher shortages affect some schools across our country to varying degrees; in particular, urban districts face unique challenges due to changing enrollment patterns, charter schools, vouchers, and challenging working conditions. Effective recruitment and selection will hopefully produce a pool of viable applicants that exceeds the vacant position to be filled. Many states now require passing an assessment test in pedagogy and content before a standard teaching license is issued.[13]

METHODS OF SUPERVISION AND EVALUATION

The most commonly used methods for supervising and evaluating school personnel are those conducted by administrators or supervisors, peers, one-self, students, and parents.[14] Administrative evaluations involve the observation of faculty and staff by using a set of criteria usually agreed upon by the supervisor and the employee. The standards are usually established through an ongoing negotiation and collaboration process conducted between an employee's association and the administration. The observations are conducted in the employee's place of work, usually the classroom, or in the case of a non-teaching employee, the normal work setting.

Peer review, although resisted by many teachers' unions, refers to the observation of employees by a colleague. This method is based on the assumption that peers are in the best position to evaluate another employee's strengths and weaknesses because they are subject to some of the same evaluative criteria for effectiveness, have greater opportunity for day to day observations, and possess the special expertise to make judgments regarding performance.[15]

Self-evaluation has met with mixed results. However, Glickman recommends the use of self-assessment as a means of ensuring that how the employees perceive themselves is consistent with how others perceive them.[16] This is also a very useful yet non-threatening method to use. The results of the self-evaluation should be shared with another professional in an effort to produce positive changes.

The process of allowing elementary or secondary students to evaluate their teachers, although common in higher education, is at best controversial at the K–12 level. One assumption for using student feedback is that students see teachers and other employees every day and therefore are daily consumers and are entitled to some input into the evaluation process. Involving students in teacher evaluations, through student reports, surveys, systematic interviews, and focus groups, can make positive changes in teacher-student relationships. Although evidence indicates some chance for disparaging opinions, there is a greater likelihood of an expression of appreciation for a teacher's performance.[17]

Teacher's connections with parents cover a wide range of activities. Some teachers desire considerable distance from parents because they view their primary work and responsibility as being with students. Other teachers resent intrusions in their work schedules when parents break into their days and disrupt instruction. Involving parents in teacher evaluation, through parent reports, surveys, interviews, and focus groups, changes these relationships. In general, greater involvement of parents in teacher evaluation can help make teacher-parent relationships more positive.[18] Such an approach can make parents even more involved in the education of their children.

The methods utilized to observe and evaluate staff should include standards which are understood and approved by both the employee and the administration. Standards may include knowledge of subject, pedagogy, organization, management, evaluation of students, professional responsibilities, student/parent/administration relationships, and personal qualities. Further, evaluations may focus on particular areas of performance but should support strengths while addressing areas in which an employee may be deficient or is having difficulties.[19]

PURPOSES OF SUPERVISION AND EVALUATION

The purpose of supervision and evaluation varies depending on who initiates the process and the audience to whom it is addressed. On a general level, the stated purposes of supervision and evaluation are usually to improve performance, such as classroom instruction by a teacher or greater management of students by a bus driver.[20]

There are two basic forms of supervision and evaluation: formative and summative. Each serves a distinct purpose. Although the courts have not articulated this formative/summative distinction clearly, this consideration is implied by the underlying purposes of supervision and evaluation as reflected by statute, policy, or contract.[21]

Formative observations are important from the educational organization's point of view, even if they are less significant from a legal standpoint.[22] This form of observation should be used to guide teachers or other employees in improving their skills. Summative evaluations, on the other hand, are usually conducted as a basis for employment status decisions, such as whether performance warrants retention, non-renewal, dismissal, promotion, or the awarding of tenure.

If formative observations are used primarily to improve employee performance and only incidentally for use in determining whether to retain or dismiss individuals, administrative failure to follow procedures is less likely to weaken personnel decisions.[23] Formative observations should not be considered evaluations, but a subset of the evaluation process. Generally, observations are undertaken with the expressed purpose of judging overall effectiveness and performance of the individual faculty or staff member, as compared with deciding whether an employee has met the minimum competencies expected. Using the terms supervision and evaluation interchangeably is a major reason there is so much confusion and why unclear policies and procedures lead to litigations. In fact, in a case where a policy stated that evaluations should be made, this fact did not give a non-tenured employee a constitutionally protected property right in the renewal of her contract where evaluation/observations were not conducted.[24]

Summative evaluation refers to the procedure that uses the observation data to make conclusive personnel decisions. Evaluation procedures specifically designed to apply to employment determinations must be vigilantly followed, as they confer important rights on the individual which must be strictly adhered to.[25] Tenured employees usually have distinctive rights in the summative process, although some notable exceptions involving non-tenured employees do exist. Where evaluation is mandatory under statute, state rule, local policy, or contract, it may be a jurisdictional prerequisite to an employment action. Formal evaluation of this sort affords school employees some measure of job protection by requiring that they are evaluated properly and informed with regard to job performance so that deficient performance may be corrected. To a great extent, observations and evaluations serve a function similar to a warning or remediation notice before faculty or staff are disciplined or dismissed.[26]

SUPERVISION AND EVALUATION PROCEDURES

Supervision and evaluation are often simultaneously made up of what is considered both a formal and informal process. In the formal case, it is a process that follows prescribed policies and procedures that should include approved forms, agreed-upon time lines, acceptable taping (audio or video), and approved supervising personnel. Informal procedures, such as "management by walking around" informal observations and effective listening techniques, can be used to confirm formal observations.[27]

In general, the courts have no expected validation of evaluation instruments. Instead, the courts have recognized that an evaluation of teacher competence is necessarily a highly subjective determination that does not easily lend itself to precise qualifications for judicial review.[28] It should be observed, though, that past rulings from the courts do not necessarily mean that future decisions will be as permissive. Therefore, it would be unwise not to validate all evaluation instruments. A number of objective evaluation instruments are available, regardless of the evaluation methods used.[29]

Standardized testing and especially competency tests are among the most controversial methods of evaluation. Only a few states require educators to pass a competency test to retain a teaching license. Even so, many use competency tests as a prerequisite to the issuance of the initial teaching license.[30] A number of questions permeate the case law on competency testing. First is the central importance of the validity of the test. Second is the concern held by courts with respect to the disproportionate effect such tests have on a particular class of persons. A final noteworthy concern is the pervasive attitude of judicial consideration and deference to the decisions of educational policy-makers.[31] If used judiciously, and with a clearly identified purpose, testing is a tool that can serve to help both an educator and the supervising administrator make decisions that could positively guide the educator's future.

CONTENT AND CONSTITUTIONAL REQUIREMENTS

Courts are hesitant to find procedures mandatory or even applicable to employment decisions unless they are clearly defined. Historically, the evaluation process has not been considered a necessary condition for an employee among other employment actions.[32] At the same time, substantial compliance is considered adequate where evaluation is required, because courts will not allow a slight technical procedural oversight to thwart decision-making, provided an employee is given adequate notice that his or her performance needed improvement.[33]

The basic components of a legally defensible supervision and evaluation system should include predetermined, job-related standards for assessing performance, notice of the deficiencies, opportunity and support to improve performance, and time to remediate the deficiencies. One court used a two-prong test for determining remediability. The judicial test asked whether damage had been done to the students, faculty, or school, and whether the conduct resulting in that damage could have been corrected had the administrators warned the teacher.[34] In general, employees who are more senior in teaching experience and who possess tenure are typically extended more time in which to address a remedial deficiency.[35]

Evaluations are especially significant in the dismissal of employees based on incompetence.[36] Often, problems with tenured employees arise yet are never mentioned in the observation or evaluation data. It is important to list areas of concern in writing, for failure to do so may suggest satisfactory performance.[37] Lack of proper evaluations does not deter personnel actions for reasons unrelated to those being evaluated.[38]

Regardless of the circumstances, when administrators are involved in the evaluation of educators, they must follow procedural due process. Procedural due process includes the use of an evaluation instrument that is objective, and that provides adequate notice to the educator of the standards that will be used, and an opportunity to understand the standards. In addition, an educator must be given an opportunity (time and assistance) to remediate deficiencies cited in the evaluation.

Finally, tenured teachers have a reasonable expectancy that their positions will be continuous. Such expectation of a continuing contract is the meaning of tenure. Courts have held that this is a sufficient property right to warrant the protection of the due process.[39] To the extent that probationary or limited contract teachers have no claim to a property right, they have minimal, if any, rights to procedural due process other than those that may be found in collective bargaining agreements.

PLANS AND TIME FOR IMPROVEMENT

Once an employee has been identified as needing remediation, it is critical to have plans and procedures in place to make sure he or she has both the time and assistance to improve. Some states allow both procedural and substantive challenges, often providing for review or appeals panels.[40] Generally, the time to improve is considered in terms of months, not weeks or days.[41] For example, an employee who has been repeatedly notified of late reports to the principal's office might be given until the end of the following term before progressive discipline measures are fully implemented. This does not mean that more serious offenses should not be dealt with in a much shorter time period. Some deficiencies related to competency may be regarded as irremediable. Consequently, for example, a teacher with poor classroom management skills that could cause injury to students may not be given as much time to improve as a teacher who files late reports.

In considering the nature of the deficiency, courts typically weigh the property interest of an employee, giving consideration to the length of time that may be necessary to correct the deficiency in relationship to the possible harm for schoolchildren should the employee be permitted a period of remediation.[42] It should be noted that other rights, such as privilege, can come into play in the process of supervising and evaluating employees.

Comments made by administrators during the evaluation process, even if not correct, are usually given some degree of privilege or immunity. The defense of privilege is predicated on the public policy that where there is a great enough public interest in encouraging uninhibited freedom of expression to require the sacrifice of the right of the individual to protect his or her reputation by civil suit, the law recognizes that false, defamatory matter may be published without civil liability.[43] Privilege can be distinguished from immunity in that, rather than providing a defense for an admitted defamation, statements are deemed never to have been defamatory in the first instance. Moreover, the defense is more closely linked to the occasion on which the statement was made than to the identity of the person making the statement.

It is important for school officials to have a clear understanding of state law related to privilege/immunity. Whether a privilege or immunity applies generally depends on the applicable defamation statutes or case law in a given state. Consequently it is critical for administrators to understand state school law statutes. In one case, the supreme court of Missouri held that the superintendent had absolute protection because his remarks, which led to the non-renewal of a teacher's contract, were made public at the request and with the consent of the plaintiff, who requested reasons for such action at a public meeting.[44] The court was satisfied that the superintendent stated very specific reasons for the dismissal action.

An additional issue to consider is whether a speaker has made a statement of fact or opinion. Courts have usually held that personal opinions, as well as true statements, are protected. Usually, only statements of fact may serve as a basis for liability in a defamation suit. It is important for administrators to be accurate with the statements made about employees in public. Any comments that may harm an employee's reputation must be substantially true if the administrator is to be protected in a defamation case. Educational administrators should always exercise both caution and discretion with regard to dispensing personnel information.

EMPLOYEE DISCIPLINE

Just as school boards have the right to hire employees, they also have the right and responsibility to discipline staff members.[45] A progressive discipline decision could cover a wide range of actions, including reprimands that are verbal or written, suspensions with or without pay, demotion, or dismissal. Unless an employee's conduct is so extreme that a single instance would justify cause for dismissal, the range of discipline usually follows the standard progressive pattern. Under this system, an employee could be given notice of the unacceptable conduct. If the conduct continues, the discipline can escalate through suspension to dismissal.[46]

Statutes and case law vary on grounds for dismissal. Most statutes include immorality, insubordination, neglect of duty, incompetence, and other good and just causes as reasons for dismissal. Dismissal for cause may be undertaken against either tenured or non-tenured employees. A board may wait for the expiration of a non-tenured employee's contract and give notice of intent to non-renew. In effect, this allows the employee the opportunity to complete the school year, and it provides the board with the opportunity to replace the person when the contract expires, rather than face a potential challenge for violating due process.

Insofar as an employee's contract may be a property right, dismissal requires a board to provide an individual with due process that includes notice and a hearing at which it must determine whether there is good and just cause for a dismissal. Public employees with property rights in continued employment are entitled to notice of charges against them, an explanation of the evidence, and an opportunity to present reasons why they should not have their contracts terminated. The Supreme Court ruled in *Cleveland Board of Education v. Loudermill* that minimal due process under the provisions of the Fourteenth Amendment guarantees a tenured school employee the right to a pretermination hearing to evaluate whether there are reasonable grounds to believe that the charges against the individual are true and supported by evidence.[47]

CONCLUSION

The process of recruiting, hiring, observing, supervising, and evaluating school employees can be a very complex, often confusing undertaking, with expectations that all educators must learn to work with. School administrators must be cautious to follow minimum fairness guidelines in making sure that all employees have proper notice, assistance, and time to make necessary improvements for their continued employment. The employees have an expectation of following reasonable procedures, guidelines, and time commitments, as well as a right to expect reasonable assistance to improve performance. Additionally, they have the responsibility to exhibit reasonable improvement in their performance. If administrators and staff work together to improve supervision, then the most important people in the process, students, will benefit.

NOTES

1. L. Rossow and J. Parkinson, *The Law of Teacher Evaluation* (Dayton, Ohio: Education Law Association, 2003).

2. J. Beckman, *Meeting Legal Challenges* (Lancaster, Pa.: Technomic Publishing, 1996).

3. K. D. Peterson, *Teacher Evaluation: A Comprehensive Guide to New Directions and Practices* (Thousand Oaks, Calif.: Corwin Press, 1995).

4. See Rossow and Parkinson, *The Law of Teacher Evaluation*.

5. K. Frels and J. L. Horton, *A Documentation System for Teacher Improvement or Termination*, 4th ed. (Topeka, Kans.: National Organization on Legal Problems of Education, 1994).

6. *Farmer v. Kelleys Island Bd. of Educ.*, 594 N.E.2nd 204 (Ohio Com. Pleas, 1992).

7. *Teboro v. Cold Spring Harbor Cent. Sch. Dist.*, 510 N.Y.S.2d 655 (N.Y. App. Div., 1987).

8. Rossow and Parkinson, *The Law of Teacher Evaluation*.

9. *AFL-CIO v. Board of Educ.*, 767 N.E.2d 549, 436 (Mass., 2002); *Juniel v. Park Forest-Chicago Heights School Dist. 163*, 176 F.Supp.2d 842 (N.D. Ill., 2001).

10. *Roberts v. Lincoln County School Dist. No. One*, 676 P.2d 577 (Wyo., 1984).

11. See Alabama Code 1975 §16-24-1; *Kingsford v. Salt Lake City Sch. Dist.*, 247 F.3d 1123 (Utah, 2001).

12. P. Young and W. Castetter, *The Human Resource Function in Educational Administration*, 8th ed. (Upper Saddle River, N.J.: Pearson, 2004).

13. For example, the Ohio Department of Education's rule 3301-24-05 describes various types of school licensure offered in Ohio and one of the requirements is the successful completion of an examination prescribed by the State Board of Education. Also, see *Massachusetts Fed'n of Teachers v. Board of Educ.*, 767 N.E.2nd 549 (Mass., 2002).

14. C. D. Glickman, S. P. Gordon, and J. M. Ross-Gordon, *Supervision of Instruction*, 3rd ed. (Boston: Allyn and Bacon, 1995).

15. J. A. Rapp, *Education Law*, vol. 1 (New York: Matthew Bender, 1995).

16. Glickman, Gordon, and Ross-Gordon, *Supervision of Instruction*.

17. Peterson, *Teacher Evaluation*.

18. Peterson, *Teacher Evaluation*.

19. *Eshom v. Board of Educ.*, 364 N.W.2d 7 (Neb., 1985).

20. Glickman, Gordon, and Ross-Gordon, *Supervision of Instruction*.

21. Rapp, *Education Law*.

22. *Board of Educ. v. Ballard*, 507 A.2d 192, 196 (Md. Ct. Spec. App., 1986).

23. *Willis v. Winefield Sch. Dist. No. 3*, 603 P.2nd 962 (Colo. Ct. App., 1979).

24. *Roberts v. Lincoln County Sch. Dist. No. One*, 676 P.2nd 577 (Wyo., 1984).

25. *Wilt v. Flanigan*, 294 S.E.2d 189, 194 (W. Va., 1982).

26. *Board of Educ. v. Ballard.*

27. *Eshom v. Board of Educ.*

28. *Beauchamp v. Davis*, 550 F.2d 959, 961 (4th Cir., 1977).

29. J. S. Cangelosi, *Evaluating Classroom Instruction* (New York: Longman, 1991).

30. For example, see Ohio Administrative Code (OAC) 3301-24.

31. L. F. Rossow and J. Parkinson, *The Law of Teacher Evaluation* (Topeka, Kans.: National Organization on Legal Problems of Education, 1992).

32. *Anaclerio v. Skinner*, 134 Cal.Rptr. 303 (Cal. Ct. App., 1976).

33. *Governing Bd. of El Dorado Union High Sch. Dist. v. Commission on Professional Competence*, 217 Cal.Rptr. 457 (Cal. Ct. App., 1985).

34. *Gilliland v. Board of Educ. of Pleasant View Consol. Sch. Dist. No. 622*, 365 N.E.2d 322 (Ill., 1977).

35. *Ganyo v. Independent Sch. Dist. No. 832*, 311 N.W.2d 497 (Minn., 1981).

36. *Eshom v. Board of Educ.*

37. Rapp, *Education Law.*

38. *Illinois Educ. Ass'n. Local Community High Sch. Dist. 218 v. Board of Educ.*, 340 N.E.2nd 7 (Ill., 1975).

39. *Board of Regents v. Roth*, 408 U.S. 564 (1972).

40. *Thompson v. Board of Educ.*, 838 S.W.2d 390 (Ky., 1992).

41. *deOliveira v. State Board of Educ.*, 511 N.E.2d 178 (Ill. App. Ct., 1987).

42. *Knapp v. Whitaker*, 577 F.Supp. 1265 (C.D. Ill., 1984).

43. *Bigelow v. Brumley*, 37 N.E.2d 584, 588 (Oh., 1941).

44. *Williams v. School Dist. of Springfield R-12*, 447 S.W.2d 256 (Mo., 1969).

45. Beckman, *Meeting Legal Challenges.*

46. Beckman, *Meeting Legal Challenges.*

47. *Cleveland Board of Education v. Loudermill*, 470 U.S. 532 (1985).

9

Employee Rights

Ralph D. Mawdsley

Each year only about 200 school employment cases, excluding those dealing with collective bargaining and tort liability issues, are reported in the
United States. About one-half of these cases involve federal issues under
federal anti-discrimination statutes and under the Constitution's substantive
and procedural rights. The balance of the reported cases concern state issues
pertaining to contract language, employee discipline and dismissal under
state laws, employee benefits, and certification/licensure requirements.

This chapter surveys legal issues pertaining to federal statutory and constitutional rights. Although a wide range of issues also arise under state law,
a consideration of the unique features of each state's laws and court decisions is beyond the scope of the limited amount of space for this chapter.

DISCRIMINATION IN EMPLOYMENT

Discrimination claims can arise under state or federal statutes. Even so,
most suits identifying state law as a claim also invoke federal law, if for
no other reason than states tend to follow federal law in interpreting their
own anti-discrimination laws. However, states may also act under their
own laws to protect categories that may be the same or different from
those under federal law. Thus, for example, some states explicitly provide
protection for marital status and sexual orientation, categories that are not
explicitly mentioned in federal law.

Federal non-discrimination statutes are divided into two broad groups: those prohibiting discrimination in employment and those forbidding discrimination in educational institutions receiving federal assistance. The employment statutes include Title VII of the Civil Rights Act of 1964,[1] which prohibits discrimination on the basis of race, color, religion, sex, and/or national origin; the Age Discrimination in Employment Act of 1967 (ADEA),[2] which outlaws discrimination against persons 40 years of age or older; the Americans With Disabilities Act of 1990 (ADA),[3] which forbids discrimination on the basis of disabilities in employment by state and local governments and in public accommodations; and the Family and Medical Leave Act (FMLA),[4] which affords employees the right to extended leave for personal and family medical needs and illnesses. A less litigated federal statute, the Uniform Services Employment and Reemployment Act (USERRA), prohibits discrimination based on membership, application for membership, performance of service, application for service, or obligation of a person in the uniformed services.[5]

Statutes requiring the reception of federal assistance include the Rehabilitation Act of 1973 (section 504),[6] which prohibits discrimination based on disabilities; Title IX of the Educational Amendments of 1972,[7] which forbids gender discrimination; the Equal Pay Act of 1963,[8] which prohibits gender-based wage discrimination; and Title VI of the Civil Rights Act of 1964,[9] which forbids discrimination based on race, color, or national origin.

Remedies for discrimination can also be pursued under two other federal statutes that can apply to both employment and non-employment situations. Section 1981 of the Civil Rights Act of 1866[10] prohibits discrimination on the basis of national origin and race in the making of contracts. Section 1983 of the Civil Rights Act of 1871,[11] which contains no discriminatory categories of its own, is a vehicle for seeking damages for violations of federal constitutional and statutory rights.

STATING A DISCRIMINATION CLAIM

Persons alleging discrimination have a specified number of days referred to as a statute of limitations in which to bring their claims, a limitation that courts normally follow precisely unless equity requires a waiver.[12] Where a plaintiff alleges a continuing pattern of behavior, courts generally permit acts prior to the statutory limit to be included in a complaint.[13]

In order to survive dismissal of a complaint, a plaintiff must make a prima facie statement of the facts. Ordinarily, a prima facie statement in a discrimination case involves the following elements: the plaintiff fits within the protected definition of the statute; the plaintiff was qualified for the benefit; the plaintiff was denied a benefit under the applicable statute on the basis of membership in the particular category; someone outside of the plaintiff's category received the benefit.[14] Once a plaintiff presents a prima facie claim, a defendant can produce evidence of a legitimate and non-discriminatory reason for an employment action, which may be sufficient to defeat the discrimination claim if the plaintiff does not demonstrate that it is pretextual.[15] Generally, boards prevail when their reasons for employment decisions are not pretextual, such as correcting a district's worsening financial conditions,[16] selecting employees who fit advertised needs,[17] or removing employees who are disruptive.[18]

School employees have no discrimination claim if they have not experienced an adverse employment decision. Generally, reassignment of teachers to other teaching positions is not considered an adverse action as long as a teacher's pay, benefits, and working conditions remain unchanged.[19]

SPECIFIC CATEGORIES PROTECTED UNDER FEDERAL LAW

Laws prohibiting discrimination address a person's alleged differences in treatment based on membership in specific categories. A court must determine whether a difference in treatment has occurred and whether that difference was related to a person's membership in a protected category.

Sexual Orientation

Sexual orientation is not expressly protected under federal statutes.[20] However, the courts have recognized some protection regarding same-sex conduct under Title VII and the Equal Protection Clause. The Supreme Court has held that a male employee, under Title VII, could sue his employer for alleged same-sex, sex-related, humiliating actions and physical assaults from other employees.[21] The Court held that the prohibition against "sex" discrimination under Title VII included same-sex actions. The implications of this case are somewhat unclear but would seem to extend to employer harassment or retaliation in employment decisions based on an employee's sexual preference. Yet other courts have more clearly found a measure of protection for gay/lesbian teachers under the Equal Protection Clause, where one teacher alleged that his contract had been non-renewed due to his sexual orientation[22] and a second teacher alleged that school officials had not taken effective action in response to her being harassed by students.[23]

Race

One of the most prolific areas of litigation under Title VII involves claims that persons were discriminated against in employment based on race. Although many plaintiffs are African American, an increasing number of plaintiffs are Caucasian employees who allege what is sometimes referred to as reverse discrimination.[24] In fact, Caucasian employees alleging discrimination in schools where the overwhelming majority of teachers are black are entitled to sue, not only under Title VII, but also under section 1981.[25]

Claims involving race can involve either disparate treatment or disparate impact. Disparate treatment cases require plaintiffs to prove intent to discriminate,[26] while disparate impact can involve evidence, such as statistics, from which a trier of fact can reasonably infer discrimination.[27]

Race discrimination, as with national origin and sex, very much depends in stating a prima facie case in terms of comparison with other categories of employees. Employees who allege that they have been treated differently must be able to draw accurate comparisons. In evaluating whether two employees are similarly situated, a court can consider past as well as current conduct in assessing whether the quality or quantity of differences among the facts differentiates the comparison between employees on some factor other than race.[28]

While harassment or hostile environment are terms most frequently identified with discrimination based on gender, the claim can be raised in cases involving race. In evaluating such claims, courts apply the same criteria used in gender harassment and hostile environment cases. Accordingly, a federal trial court in Maryland found that two comments allegedly made by a supervisor to a black employee, "the kind of people you are supposed to spit on" and the school staff was a bunch of "African fools," did not rise to the level of racially hostile environment because they were not sufficiently pervasive so as to render the work environment objectively abusive.[29]

National Origin

National origin applies to ethnicity and countries of origin, not to other kinds of geographic differences.[30] Issues involving national origin very closely parallel those involving race, and suits alleging violations of both categories are fairly common.[31]

One unique aspect of national origin can be alleged differences in treatment based on language accents. The federal trial court in Kansas held that a teacher whose heavily accented English could not be understood by students failed to state a national origin claim where it agreed with school officials that she refused to address language concerns that affected her teaching effectiveness.[32] However, a federal trial court in New York determined that a directive to a custodian not to speak to teachers while cleaning rooms after school because his accent made understanding him difficult without concentrated listening stated a claim for discrimination.[33]

Disparate impact can apply in national origin cases as well as in those involving race. In such a case, a federal trial court in New York was satisfied Latino and African American teachers presented a Title VII claim where a school board required them to pass one of two tests to keep their teaching licenses.[34] The court reasoned that the tests, which were designed to assess the teaching program of applicants, had a severe and disparate impact on both minority groups.

Sex (Gender)

Both Title VII and Title IX forbid discrimination based on sex, but most courts agree that employees can bring gender claims only under Title VII, leaving Title IX for students.[35] Gender discrimination claims can arise where employment decisions are made based on gender or where employees were subjected to harassing conduct.

School boards generally have discretion in choosing whom to hire but must have a non-discriminatory reason for their selections. A federal trial court in Michigan thought that a female applicant for a boys' varsity basketball head coach position stated a prima facie claim where a male with less experience was selected.[36] The applicant was currently the girls' varsity basketball coach. In denying summary judgment for the board, the court observed that the trier of fact would have to consider whether its proffered reason for acting, that it did not hire the woman due to overlapping schedules between boys' and girls' basketball, represented existing policy or a contrived pretext for not hiring her.

Comments reflective of sexual stereotyping can be the grist of a sex discrimination suit. The Second Circuit ruled that both a principal and director of pupil personnel in New York engaged in sexual stereotyping when a school counselor was denied tenure following her return from maternity leave. Some of the comments that the court found dispositive as to the discrimination claim related to the spacing of the counselor's children and her not waiting to have a second child until the first was in school. In addition, the director questioned whether the counselor could perform her administrative tasks with a small child at home.[37]

Comments alone will not always state a gender discrimination claim. In affirming a school board in Florida's motion for summary judgment, the Eleventh Circuit agreed that a male applicant who was not hired for a teaching position did not present a prima facie case based on two statues with derogatory statements regarding men that were located on the female principal's desk.[38] The court asserted that the presence of the statues and words simply did not manifest an intention to discriminate under Title VII.

Sexual harassment claims dominate Title VII suits concerning gender. The Supreme Court, in *Clark County School District v. Breeden (Clark County)*, cast doubt on whether a single act is sufficient to present a harassment claim. In *Clark County*, a female employee in Nevada alleged punishment following a comment by a supervisor in the presence of the plaintiff that "I hear that making love to her is like making love to the Grand Canyon." In reversing the Ninth Circuit's decision for the employee, the Court was of the opinion that "no reasonable person could have believed that the single incident recounted above violated Title VII's standard."[39]

Particularly troublesome issues surround hostile environment claims involving employees who were involved in past sexual relationships. Courts have been very clear that sexual harassment must be based on gender. Thus, the Eleventh Circuit held that a male teacher in Florida failed to state a Title VII claim where abusive treatment by a female teacher toward him, after the two were involved in a past sexual relationship, was not based on his gender but on personal animosity resulting from the dissolution of their intimate relationship.[40] The supreme court of Michigan reached the same conclusion under state law in a similar set of facts.[41]

A victim of harassment can recover both compensatory and punitive damages.[42] However, the Supreme Court decided in *Faragher v. City of Boca Raton*[43] that an employer is liable for damages for sexual harassment only for "tangible employment action." In interpreting this requirement, the Fourth Circuit determined that a supervisor's assignment of extra work as part of an alleged hostile environment did not constitute tangible employment action.[44] Other federal circuits have accepted this work assignment standard as long as the extra assignment is not excessive.[45]

Age

Reflecting the graying of America, age discrimination claims are the fastest growing area of discrimination. The ADEA protects employees who are 40 years of age or older from discrimination. A prima facie case can be established even though persons given favorable treatment are over 40 as long as they are younger than the plaintiff.[46]

The statute exempts treatment "based on reasonable factors other than age"[47] and discharge or discipline "for good cause."[48] The statute also permits employers to raise affirmative defenses where treatment is based on "a bona fide occupational qualification reasonably necessary to the normal operation of the particular business"[49] or where they are acting pursuant to the terms of a bona fide seniority or employee benefit plans.[50]

Numerous discrimination claims are filed each year alleging discrimination by job applicants over 40 who were unsuccessful in being hired or promoted. As in the other areas, employers prevail if they can provide a legitimate, non-discriminatory reason for acting. Thus, school boards have prevailed where the younger persons selected had better academic qualifications[51] or a better interview.[52]

As with other discrimination areas, changes of assignments for workers over 40 do not state ADEA claims as long as the changes do not significantly disadvantage the employee.[53] A federal trial court in New York upheld the transfer of a 69-year-old custodian from an elementary to a high school and the change of his hours from 11:00 a.m.–8:00 p.m. to 2:00 p.m.–11:00 p.m.[54] The court reflected that a lateral transfer with no reduction in wages or of job responsibilities did not rise to the level of a materially adverse job action under the ADEA.

The Equal Employment Opportunity Commission (EEOC), which is responsible for enforcing the ADEA, took issue with a board's tying the hiring of new teachers to the steps on a salary scale. However, the Seventh Circuit upheld an Illinois school board's decision not to hire a 63-year-old applicant whose 30 years of experience would have exceeded the limit the board had placed on the amount it would spend on a new teacher.[55] The court rejected the EEOC's disparate impact theory that connecting years of experience to hiring decisions disparately affected age. The court reasoned that an economic reason for a hiring decision represented a nondiscriminatory reason.

The most controversial areas involving ADEA concern providing benefits and early retirement incentive plans where age is a factor. The Supreme Court has upheld a private-sector, collective-bargaining-agreement benefits plan that eliminated health care benefits for retired employees except as to current employees age 50 or older.[56] In rejecting an ADEA claim by employees ages 40 to 50, the Court reasoned that the ADEA did not stop an employer from favoring older employees over younger ones. Regarding early retirement plans, courts have upheld plans that provide payment upon completion of a specified number of years of service, but have invalidated plans that tied the amount of benefits to years of age.[57]

Religion

Title VII prohibits discrimination on the basis of religion. Religious discrimination claims arise in two different situations, one involving secular employers and the other involving religious employers. Secular employers such as public school boards may be required to address the religious beliefs of current or prospective employees that might impact employment requirements. On the other hand, religious employers frequently have beliefs incorporated into their employment practices and, thus, they make employment decisions reflecting those beliefs.

Secular employers are required to make reasonable accommodations to the religious beliefs and practices of employees unless doing so would represent an undue hardship. The Supreme Court, in *Ansonia Board of Education v. Philbrook*,[58] provided some guidance to an understanding of undue hardship. In *Ansonia*, the Court held that a school board in Connecticut, by having a policy that allowed three days of paid leave for personal business that could include religious days per year, made a reasonable accommodation to an employee whose religion required that he miss school for six days per year. The Court added that once the board made this reasonable accommodation, it was not required to demonstrate that alternatives to its accommodation proposed by the teacher constituted a hardship. Lower federal courts have interpreted undue hardship in such a way that boards are not required to incur even de minimis additional costs, which means that not only do they not have to hire extra or substitute workers,[59] but they also are not required to reassign employees so others can participate in religious observances.[60]

School boards have faced a variety of challenges to policies or practices that allegedly violated the practice of the religion of staff members. Courts have upheld board employment decisions that are adverse to the alleged religious beliefs of employees, such as removal of a teacher's name from the substitute list where he persisted in injecting his personal religious beliefs into the classroom,[61] reprimanding a biology teacher for refusing to teach the theory of evolution that contradicted his belief in creationism,[62] and discharging a sign-language teacher who refused, on religious grounds, to interpret literally words of profanity.[63]

Public school boards can be pressured by religious views of their constituents to take action against employees, but as the Eighth Circuit indicated in *Cowan v. Strafford R-VI School District*,[64] that action can be expensive. The case involved a Missouri school board's decision not to renew the contract of a second-grade teacher, a decision that was linked to her presenting a "magic rock" to each of her students and to parental religious concerns about the teaching of New Ageism. The evidence was found sufficient for a jury trial concerning Title VII religious discrimination. Although the court did not reinstate the teacher, it did uphold a two-year award of front pay.

Religious employers that have religious-based employment requirements are not expected to meet the reasonable accommodation requirements of secular employers. Title VII has a set of three exemptions for religious employers that allow these employers to discriminate on the basis of religion.

The first exempts hiring, discharge, or classification where religion is "a bona fide occupational qualification reasonably necessary to the operation of a particular business or enterprise."[65] A second exemption permits an institution controlled in whole or part by a religious entity (e.g., a church) to impose religious requirements for the purpose of "the propagation of a particular religion."[66] The third exemption permits a religious entity to impose its religious requirements on employees performing work connected with the carrying out of the entity's "activities."[67]

Disability

Prior to passage of the Americans With Disabilities Act (ADA)[68] in 1990, the vehicle to remedy disability discrimination in employment was the Rehabilitation Act of 1973 (section 504).[69] Both acts define those protected from discrimination virtually identically. Section 504 protects an "otherwise qualified individual," while ADA protects a "qualified individual with a disability."

Section 504 was limited in its application to organizations that received federal assistance.[70] The ADA overlapped the coverage of section 504 and extended protection to private employers. Title I of ADA prohibits discrimination by private employers with 15 or more employees involving "job application procedures, hiring, firing, advancement, compensation of training, and other terms, conditions, and privileges of employment."[71] Title II of ADA prohibits the same kind of discrimination by state and local entities, including public school boards.

Although the ADA is far more systematic and comprehensive in its construction and coverage than section 504, the virtual identity in both statutes as to the definition of prohibited discrimination has meant that section 504, with its longer history of interpretation, has become the template for analyzing alleged discriminatory conduct. The definition of a disability is the same under both statutes:[72] a physical or mental impairment that substantially limits one or more of the major life activities; a record of impairment; and a party's being regarded as having an impairment. Worth noting is that employees must have more than impairments to prevail under the ADA. Plaintiffs must also produce evidence that alleged impairments limit a major life function. Thus, merely because an employee has cancer[73] or any other affliction[74] is not enough to establish a prima facie case if the person is still able to perform the essential functions of the job.

Both statutes require employers to make reasonable accommodations to individuals with disabilities unless doing so would represent an undue hardship. Undue hardship is usually tied to an employer's financial resources and requires evaluation of a number of factors, such as the nature and cost of an accommodation, size of the employer's budget, size of the program, number of employees, and type of facilities and operation.[75]

Reasonable accommodations may include making existing facilities used by employees readily accessible to and useable by individuals with disabilities, such as use of ramps or adjusting the height of work areas,[76] and job restructuring, part-time or modified work schedules, reassignment to a vacant position, acquisition or modification of equipment or devices, appropriate adjustment or modifications of examinations, training materials or interpreters, and other similar accommodations for individuals with disabilities.[77] However, even with reasonable accommodations, employees must be able to perform essential job functions. Of course, determining which functions are essential is critical. For example, if a school counselor's attendance at school at 8:15 a.m. is an essential job function, then a counselor's request that she be permitted to report to work at a later time each morning would not represent a reasonable accommodation, since this would change the nature of the job.[78]

The ADA protects employees with communicable diseases, except that if employers have employees with communicable diseases handling food and cannot make reasonable accommodations, they may refuse to continue to assign such employees to jobs that involve food handling.[79] The ADA does not protect "any employee or applicant who is currently engaging in the illegal use of drugs," but does protect individuals who have completed supervised drug rehabilitation and are no longer engaging in the illegal use of drugs.[80]

The ADA permits employers to make business decisions that are "job-related and consistent with business necessity."[81] Such decisions can include requiring an employee to submit to a psychiatric examination where the individual's behavior causes school officials to be concerned about the physical safety of those who come into contact with the employee. If an examination is considered "job-related," that is, related to a concern for safety, the issue as to whether the employee is disabled is never reached.[82]

CONSTITUTIONAL RIGHTS

Employees are invested with substantive and procedural rights under the U.S. Constitution. The most frequently litigated substantive rights concern free expression, association, and privacy, while the procedural rights concern rights to a notice and a hearing.

SUBSTANTIVE RIGHTS

Substantive rights are those that restrict state and federal governments in the adoption and enforcement of rules and regulations that address how persons conduct their lives and interact with others.

Free Expression

The distinction between oral and written speech has become blurred in our technological age. As a result, free speech is generally merged with a free press under the First Amendment to protect what is referred to as free expression. Efforts by school boards to limit or prohibit employee expression are scrutinized carefully and are balanced against broad interests regarding curriculum content and protection of student and employee safety.

The extent to which employees have free expression rights depends on two concepts: forum and public concern. Forum analysis defines the kind of venue for free expression that has been created on school property, while public concern addresses the content of expression and the extent to which "it involves an issue of social, political, or other interest to the community."[83]

Generally, the expressive rights of employees outside a school are the same as for any other citizen. As such, the Supreme Court decided that a teacher has a protected right to expression of views in a letter to a newspaper, even where the letter opposed an upcoming levy.[84] However, conduct off school property can become the subject of school discipline where not protected by free expression or other constitutional rights or where it is disruptive to the school.[85]

Of the three kinds of forums that the Supreme Court identified in *Perry Education Association v. Perry Local Education Association*[86]—public, limited public, and non-public—the only two that apply to schools are limited public and non-public. Generally, public schools are non-public forums unless, by designation or practice, they have been opened up as a limited public forum.

A non-public forum requires only a rational basis for restriction of employee expression. While a non-public forum can include an entire school building, classrooms are the best examples. School boards have a rational claim in presenting and interpreting their own curriculum without having to allow for in-class presentations by persons with different viewpoints.[87] In addition, classroom speech can be regulated as long as a board's restriction has a reasonable pedagogical purpose.[88] In such a case, a principal can require a teacher to remove a pamphlet from his classroom that listed banned books, because insofar as it was not part of the curriculum, it was not protected by free speech.[89]

On the other hand, in a case of first impression, the Sixth Circuit, in *Cockrel v. Shelby County School District*,[90] determined that free speech protection can extend to persons invited by a teacher to speak in a classroom. In reversing summary judgment for a school board as to dismissal of an elementary teacher for inviting a person to speak in her class on industrial hemp, a substance prohibited in Kentucky, the court reasoned that the invitation represented a matter of public concern. The court observed that the teacher was entitled to have her interests balanced against those of the school board. Even though many parents wrote letters to the superintendent expressing concern about the teacher's conduct, the court discerned that her speech was not outweighed by the board's interest in efficient operation of the school and a harmonious workplace. At trial, the court explained that the board would have the burden of proving that the teacher was dismissed for a reason other than for exercising her free speech rights.

Cockrel stretches the limit of public concern for free speech by applying the concept not only to classrooms but also to a subject that one normally would expect school officials to be able to regulate. While the subject matter does not fit squarely in the areas that courts have identified as personal in nature[91] and outside public concern protection, neither does the area fit within the areas traditionally recognized as protected by public concern.[92] In any case, a school board can justify adverse employment actions for an employee's alleged exercise of free speech if doing so is necessary to prevent disruption,[93] loss of efficiency,[94] or loss of confidence and trust.[95]

Generally, officials in public schools can prohibit employee religious expression in schools, especially regarding the presentation of their religious views in class or distribution of religious materials in school. However, in an important case of first impression, the Eighth Circuit held that a school board in South Dakota violated the free speech rights of an elementary teacher by refusing her permission to meet with a Good News Club that met on school premises after school.[96] The court reversed an earlier order that would have limited the teacher to meeting with the club at schools other than where she taught. Reasoning that the teacher's after-school participation amounted to private speech, the court concluded that the after-school participation did not put the board at risk of violating the establishment clause.

Association

The constitutional right of association applies to two situations: participation in an organization that presents a particular viewpoint, and intimate social contacts such as with members of a family.[97] Efforts by school officials to punish or prohibit association in these two areas require more than a rational basis. In terms of organizations, courts have protected an employee's right of association as applied to membership in unions and political parties.[98] Regarding the second category of family intimacy, a federal trial court in Massachusetts maintained that a school committee's discharging an elementary teacher for living with the man she later married violated her right of association.[99]

The right of association can be imbued with free speech protection where the right of a teacher to live her lesbian lifestyle also includes the right to express her views regarding sexual orientation outside the classroom. In *Weaver v. Nebo School District*,[100] a public school teacher in Utah prevailed in her claims that a school board violated her expressive rights regarding her sexual orientation in prohibiting her from expressing her views outside of school and by removing her as coach of the volleyball team. All parties agreed, and the court did not express otherwise, that the school could prohibit the teacher from expressing her views regarding sexual orientation in the classroom.[101] Worth noting in this case is that, while the teacher's lifestyle generated comments from parents in the community, the school board produced no evidence that the teacher's lifestyle had caused disruption in the classroom or among members of the volley-ball team.

Privacy

Employee privacy interests arise in searches of classrooms and employee vehicles and in drug-testing policies. Privacy interests are grounded in the Fourteenth Amendment's liberty clause protection of bodily integrity and the Fourth Amendment's protection against unreasonable searches and seizures.

The Supreme Court has not addressed a school employee search and seizure case. In its leading non-education employee search and seizure case, *O'Connor v. Ortega (Ortega)*,[102] the Court looked for support to an earlier student search case, *New Jersey v. T.L.O.*[103] In *Ortega*, which involved a search of a hospital employee's locked office purportedly to conduct an inventory and to search for evidence of alleged sexual harassment charges, the Supreme Court appeared to adopt the reasonableness standard of *T.L.O.*

Whether a search is constitutional depends on an employee's expectation of privacy. In *Ortega*, which involved a locked office, the Court observed that an employer could enter a locked office at any time for business-related purposes—to conduct inventory, look for files or records, or investigate alleged acts of wrongdoing. However, the Court suggested that extending a search to an employee's personal items located in an office—briefcase, attaché case, purse—would require reasonable suspicion, presumably a reasonable belief that the object of the search may be located inside them.

Generally, school searches should not involve *Ortega*'s expectation of privacy, since teachers would have no such expectation in classrooms which are frequented by teachers, students, administrators, and custodians. In any case, school officials could address the expectation of privacy in classrooms in quite another way, simply by creating a policy stating that classrooms and the variety of storage places therein—desks, cabinets, file cabinets—are the property of the school and can be searched at any time.[104]

Insofar as searches of employee cars in school parking lots invoke no special constitutional issues, the Eleventh Circuit, in *Hearn v. Board of Public Education*,[105] upheld law enforcement officers' use of a drug-sniffing dog in the parking lot in Georgia. After the dog alerted the officers to a teacher's car, they entered the unlocked car and found a marijuana cigarette. The school board had a policy that employee failure to take urine tests if reasonable suspicion existed of drug use or possession would result in dismissal. In upholding the dismissal when the teacher refused to submit to a drug test within the policy's time limit of two hours, the court found that the vehicle search exceeded the reasonable suspicion standard because the positive alert of the dog satisfied the higher probable cause standard of the Fourth Amendment.

Drug testing can be suspicion based or suspicionless. Many school boards require all prospective employees to take suspicionless drug tests as part of the hiring process, but drug testing after that is generally, as was the case in *Hearn*, limited to reasonable suspicion that an employee is using, possessing, or selling drugs. Certainly, in school systems with collective bargaining agreements, the *Hearn* standard is likely to be the one included in contracts.

To date among federal appellate courts, only the Sixth Circuit, in *Knox County Education Association v. Knox County Board of Education*,[106] upheld a school board's suspicionless random drug-testing policy. The court reasoned that public school teachers, in their relationships with minor students, had enough in common with customs and law enforcement officers, who are subject to suspicionless searches, to justify the same kind of search.

PROCEDURAL RIGHTS

Employee constitutional rights regarding notice of termination and a hearing generally have been supplanted by state statutes or collective bargaining agreements. A constitutional right to notice of charges and a hearing date normally is associated only with employees who have a property interest or employees claiming damage to reputation that requires a name-clearing hearing. However, if collective bargaining agreements or state statutory remedies are adequate to address employees' alleged damages to their reputations, courts may deny them constitutional remedies.[107]

The extent to which employees have constitutional rights to hearings depends on whether they have property interests. Employees have property interests in contracts, an entitlement, if they have continuing contracts or a term contract and action is being taken to discharge them during the life of the term. In *Cleveland Board of Education v. Loudermill*,[108] the Supreme Court determined that an employee with a property interest in a position is entitled to a pretermination opportunity to respond to charges, in addition to post-termination statutory or collective bargaining hearing rights. The purpose of a pretermination hearing is to protect an employee's reputation that might result from improvident school board action. However, courts have taken the position that suspending employees with pay and benefits while investigating charges against them does not entitle employees to presuspension hearings.[109] Absent statutory due process protection of a contract property right, employees are entitled to notice of the charges and pretermination opportunities to respond.[110]

CONCLUSION

Employees have a panoply of federal statutory and constitutional rights. These substantive and procedural rights assure that school employees will not be subjected to unfair rules or unfair treatment. However, educational leaders, including school business officials, also have legitimate interests in managing school districts. Employee costs constitute the single largest expense for school districts, and school boards can expect that the business of the district will be carried out in an efficient and orderly manner. Thus, the rights that school employees might enjoy as citizens outside the schools must be tempered by school boards' responsibilities for presenting curriculum and instructing students. As conflict between employee and school board expectations will occur, school officials are advised to seek legal counsel in drafting appropriate policies that meet statutory and constitutional requirements.

NOTES

1. 42 U.S.C. § 2000 et seq.
2. 29 U.S.C. § 621 et seq.
3. 42 U.S.C. § 12101 et seq.
4. 29 U.S.C. § 2611 et seq.

130 Ralph D. Mawdsley

5. 38 U.S.C. § 4311.

6. 29 U.S.C. § 794.

7. 20 U.S.C. § 1681 et seq.

8. 29 U.S.C. § 206(d)(1).

9. 42 U.S.C. § 2000d.

10. 42 U.S.C. § 1981.

11. 42 U.S.C. § 1983.

12. See *Black v. Columbus Pub. Schs.*, 211 F.Supp.2d 975 (S.D. Ohio, 2002), affirmed, 79 Fed.Appx. 735 (6th Cir., 2003) (under Title VII, complaint must be filed within 300 days of discriminatory act).

13. See *Freeman v. Oakland Unified Sch. Dist.*, 291 F.3d 632 (9th Cir., 2002).

14. See *Stove v. Philadelphia Sch. Dist.*, 58 F.Supp.2d 598 (E.D. Pa., 1999), affirmed, 216 F.3d 1977 (3d Cir., 2000).

15. See *Cherry v. Ritnour Sch. Dist.*, 361 F.3d 474 (8th Cir., 2004).

16. See *Vance v. North Panola Sch. Dist.*, 31 F.Supp.2d 545 (N.D. Miss., 1998), affirmed, 189 F.3d 470 (5th Cir., 1999).

17. See *Walton v. Dougherty County Sch. Sys.*, 59 F.Supp.2d 1297 (M.D. Ga., 1999).

18. See *Tilghman v. Waterbury Bd. of Educ.*, 312 F.Supp.2d 185 (D. Conn., 2004).

19. See *Bell v. South Delta Sch. Dist.*, 325 F.Supp.2d 728 (S.D. Miss., 2004).

20. See *Byars v. Jamestown Teachers Ass'n.*, 195 F.Supp.2d 401 (W.D. N.Y., 2002).

21. *Oncale v. Sundowner Offshore Servs.*, 523 U.S. 75 (1998).

22. *Glover v. Williamsburg Sch. Dist.*, 20 F.Supp.2d 1160 (S.D. Ohio, 1998).

23. See *Lovell v. Hamilton Sch. Dist.*, 214 F.Supp.2d 319 (E.D. N.Y., 2002).

24. See *Lyons v. Memphis Bd. of Educ.*, 6 F.Supp.2d 734 (W.D. Tenn., 1997).

25. See *Mohr v. Chicago Sch. Reform Bd. of Trustees*, 155 F.Supp.2d 923 (N.D. Ill., 2001).

26. See *Williams v. Cleveland Pub. Schs.*, 733 A.2d 571 (N.J. Super. Ct., 1999); *Brewer v. Cleveland Pub. Schs.*, 701 N.E.2d 1023 (Ohio Ct. App., 1997).

27. Compare *Burks v. Amite County Sch. Dist.*, 708 So.2d 1366 (Miss., 1998) (disparate impact not established involving teacher renewals) with *Allen v. Alabama State Bd. of Educ.*, 216 F.3d 1263 (11th Cir., 1999) (upholding successful challenge to state test for teacher certificates where more black teachers than white teachers passed and were certificated).

28. See *Silvera v. Orange County Sch. Bd.*, 244 F.3d 1253 (11th Cir., 2001) (number and nature of arrests supported different treatment).

29. *Nicole v. The Grafton Sch.*, 181 F.Supp.2d 475 (D. Md., 2002). See *also Anderson v. Memphis City Schs. Bd. of Educ.*, 75 F.Supp.2d 786 (W.D. Tenn., 1999).

30. See *Bronson v. Bd. of Educ.*, 550 F.Supp. 941 (S.D. Ohio, 1982) (persons from Appalachia not protected national origin).

31. See *Lewis v. State of Delaware Dep't of Pub. Instruction*, 948 F.Supp. 352 (D. Kan., 1997).

32. *Forsythe v. Bd. of Educ. of Unified Sch. Dist. No. 489*, 956 F.Supp. 927 (D. Kan., 1997).

33. *Tekula v. Bayport-Blue Point Sch. Dist.*, 295 F.Supp.2d 224 (E.D. N.Y., 2003).

34. *Gulino v. Board of Educ. of City Sch. Dist. of N.Y.*, 201 F.R.D. 326 (S.D. N.Y., 2001).

35. See, for example, *Blalock v. Dale County Bd. of Educ.*, 84 F.Supp.2d 1291 (M.D. Ala., 1999); *Hickman v. Gibson*, 2 F.Supp.2d 1481 (M.D. Ga., 1998); *Lakoski v. James*, 66 F.3d 751 (5th Cir., 1995).

36. *Fuhr v. Sch. Dist. of Hazel Park*, 131 F.Supp.2d 947 (E.D. Mich., 2001).

37. *Back v. Hastings on Hudson Union Free Sch. Dist.*, 365 F.3d 107 (2d Cir., 2004).

38. *Longariello v. Sch. Bd. of Monroe County*, 987 F.Supp. 1440 (S.D. Fla., 1997), affirmed, 161 F.3d 21 (11th Cir., 1998).

39. *Clark County School District v. Breeden (Clark County)*, 532 U.S. 268, 271 (2000).

40. *Succar v. Dade County Sch. Bd.*, 229 F.3d 1343 (11th Cir., 2000).

41. See *Corley v. Detroit Bd. of Educ.*, 681 N.W.2d 342 (Mich., 2004).

42. See *Johasson v. Lutheran Child and Family Servs.*, 115 F.3d 436 (7th Cir., 1997).

43. *Faragher v. City of Boca Raton*, 524 U.S. 775 (1998).

44. *Reinhold v. Commonwealth*, 151 F.3d 172 (4th Cir., 1998).

45. See *Watts v. Kroger Co.*, 170 F.3d 505 (5th Cir., 1999); *Watson v. Potter*, 2001 WL 1497773 (7th Cir., 1999).

46. *Ware v. Howard Univ.*, 816 F.Supp. 737 (D.D.C., 1993); *Marshall v. Shalala*, 16 F.Supp.2d 16 (D.D.C., 1998).

47. 29 U.S.C. § 623(f)(1).

48. 29 U.S.C. § 623(f)(3).

49. 29 U.S.C. § 623(f)(1).

50. 29 U.S.C. § 623(f)(2).

51. *Richane v. Fairport Cent. Sch. Dist.*, 179 F.Supp.2d 81 (W.D. N.Y., 2001).

52. See *Ranieri v. Highland Falls-Fort Montgomery Sch. Dist.*, 198 F.Supp.2d 542 (S.D. N.Y., 2002).

53. See *Spring v. Sheboygan Area Sch. Dist.*, 865 F.2d 883 (7th Cir., 1989).

54. *Johnson v. Easchester Union Free Sch. Dist.*, 211 F.Supp.2d 514 (S.D. N.Y., 2002).

55. *Equal Employment Opportunity Comm'n v. Francis W. Parker Sch.*, 41 F.3d 1073 (8th Cir., 1994), cert. denied, 515 U.S. 1142 (2005).

56. *General Dynamics Land Sys. v. Cline*, 540 U.S. 581 (2004).

57. See *Abrahamson v. Bd. of Educ. of Wappingers Falls Cent. Sch. Dist.*, 374 F.3d 66 (2d Cir., 2004); *Auerbach v. Bd. of Educ. of the Harborfields Cent. Sch. Dist. of Greenlawn*, 136 F.3d 104 (2d Cir., 1998).

58. *Ansonia Board of Education v. Philbrook*, 479 U.S. 60 (1986).

59. See *Bynum v. Fort Worth Indep. Sch. Dist.*, 41 F.Supp.2d 641 (N.D. Tex., 1999).

60. *Favero v. Huntsville Indep. Sch. Dist.*, 939 F.Supp. 1281 (S.D. Tex., 1996), affirmed, 110 F.3d 793 (5th Cir., 1997).

61. See *Helland South Bend Community Sch. Dist.*, 93 F.3d 327 (7th Cir., 1996).

62. See *Peloza v. Capistrano Unified Sch. Dist.*, 37 F.3d 517 (9th Cir., 1994); *LeVake v. Indep. Sch. Dist. No. 656*, 625 N.W.2d 502 (Minn. Ct. App., 2001).

63. *Sedalia v. Missouri Comm'n on Human Rights*, 843 S.W.2d 928 (Mo. Ct. App., 1992).

64. *Cowan v. Strafford R-VI School District*, 140 F.3d 1153 (8th Cir., 1998).

65. 42 U.S.C. § 2000-2(c)(1). See *Maguire v. Marquette Univ.*, 627 F.Supp. 1499 (E.D. Wis., 1986).

66. 42 U.S.C. § 2000e-2(e)(2). See *E.E.O.C. v. Mississippi College*, 626 F.2d 477 (5th Cir., 1980).

67. 42 U.S.C. § 20002-1. See *Corporation of the Presiding Bishop v. Amos*, 483 U.S. 327 (1987).

68. 42 U.S.C. § 12101 et seq.

69. 20 U.S.C. § 794.

70. Compare *Buckley v. Archdiocese of Rockville Centre*, 992 F.Supp. 586 (E.D. N.Y., 1998) (presence of publicly paid psychologist at religious school not sufficient to coverage under Title IX, another statute invoked only with the reception of federal aid).

71. 42 U.S.C. § 12112.

72. 29 U.S.C. § (8)(b); 42 U.S.C. § 12102.

73. See *Treiber v. Lindbergh Sch. Dist.*, 199 F.Supp.2d 949 (E.D. Mo., 2002).

74. See *Hooper v. St. Rose Parish*, 205 F.Supp.2d 926 (N.D. Ill., 2002).

75. 34 C.F.R. § 104.12(C); 42 U.S.C. § 12111(10).

76. 34 C.F.R. § 104.12(b); 42 U.S.C. § 12111(9).

77. 34 C.F.R. § 104,12(b); 42 U.S.C. § 12111(9).

78. See *Salmon v. Dade County Bd. of Educ.*, 4 F.Supp.2d 1157 (S.D. Fla., 1998).

79. 42 U.S.C. § 12113(d)(2).

80. 42 U.S.C. § 12114(a).

81. 42 U.S.C. § 12112(d)(4)(A).

82. See *Miller v. Champaign Community Unit Sch. Dist.*, 983 F.Supp. 1201 (C.D. Ill., 1997).

83. *Urofsky v. Gilmore*, 216 F.3d 401, 406–407 (4th Cir., 2000).

84. See *Pickering v. Bd. of Educ.*, 391 U.S. 563 (1968).

85. See *Zelmo v. Lincoln Intermediate Unit No. 12 Bd. of Directors*, 786 A.2d 1022 (Pa. Commw. Ct., 2001) (DUI arrest).

86. *Perry Education Association v. Perry Local Education Association*, 460 U.S. 37 (1983).

87. See *Hazelwood Sch. Dist. v. Kuhlmeier*, 484 U.S. 260 (1988).

88. See *Lacks v. Ferguson Reorganized Sch. Dist. R-2*, 147 F.3d 718 (8th Cir., 1998), cert. denied, 526 U.S. 1012 (1999); *Settle v. Dickson County School Board*, 53 F.3d 152 (6th Cir., 1995), cert. denied, 516 U.S. 989 (1995).

89. *Sivek v. Baljevic*, 758 A.2d 473 (Conn. Super. Ct., 1999).

90. *Cockrel v. Shelby County School District*, 270 F.3d 1036 (6th Cir., 2001), cert denied, 537 U.S. 813 (2002).

91. See, for example, *Alba v. Ansonia Bd. of Educ.*, 999 F.Supp. 687 (D. Conn., 1998) (non-tenured teacher's complaint about termination process); *Brewster v. Bd. of Educ.*, 149 F.3d 1010 (9th Cir., 1998) (accuracy of school attendance records); *Carey v. Aldine Indep. Sch. Dist.*, 996 F.Supp. 641 (S.D. Tex., 1998) (probationary teacher's complaints about working conditions); *Khuans v. Sch. Dist. 110*, 123 F.3d 648 (4th Cir., 1997) (complaints about being browbeaten by supervisor).

92. See, for example, *Harris v. Victoria Independent Sch. Dist.*, 168 F.3d 216 (5th Cir., 1999) (criticism of school improvement plan); *Settlegoode v. Portland Public Schools*, 362 F.3d 1118 (9th Cir., 2004) (criticism of lack of resources for physically disabled).

93. See *Farhat v. Jopke*, 370 F.3d 580 (6th Cir., 2004).

94. See *Mataraza v. Newburgh Enlarged City Sch. Dist.*, 294 F.Supp.2d 483 (S.D. N.Y., 1999).

95. See *Sharp v. Lindsey*, 285 F.3d 479 (6th Cir., 2002).

96. *Wigg v. Sioux Falls Sch. Dist.*, 382 F.3d 807 (8th Cir., 2004).

97. See *Bush v. Dassel-Cokato Bd. of Educ.*, 745 F.Supp.2d 562 (D. Minn., 1990).

98. See *Springdale Educ. Ass'n. v. Springdale Sch. Dist.*, 133 F.3d 649 (8th Cir., 1998); *Smith v. Bd. of Educ. of Sch. Dist. Fremont RE-1*, 83 P.3d 1157 (Colo. Ct. App., 2003).

99. *La Sota v. Town of Topsfield*, 979 F.Supp. 45 (D. Mass., 1997).

100. *Weaver v. Nebo School District*, 29 F.Supp.2d 1279 (D. Utah, 1998).

101. See *Weaver v. Nebo School District*, at 1285.

102. *O'Connor v. Ortega (Ortega)*, 480 U.S. 709 (1987).

103. *New Jersey v. T.L.O.*, 469 U.S. 325 (1985).

104. See *Shaul v. Cherry Valley-Springfield Cent. Sch. Dist.*, 363 F.3d 177 (2d Cir., 2004).

105. *Hearn v. Board of Public Education*, 191 F.3d 1321 (11th Cir., 1999).

106. *Knox County Education Association v. Knox County Board of Education*, 158 F.3d 361 (6th Cir., 1998).

107. See *Jefferson v. Jefferson County Pub. Sch. Sys.*, 360 F.3d 583 (6th Cir., 2004).

108. *Cleveland Board of Education v. Loudermill*, 470 U.S. 532 (1985).

109. See *Tweedale v. Fritz*, 987 F.Supp. 1126 (S.D. Ind., 1997).

110. See *Bd. of Educ. of City Sch. Dist. of City of N.Y. v. Mills*, 778 N.Y.S.2d 786 (N.Y. App. Div., 2004).

10

Student Rights

Patrick D. Pauken

In the landmark case of *Tinker v. Des Moines Independent Community School District*, the U.S. Supreme Court made the following often-quoted and groundbreaking statement: "It can hardly be argued that either students or teachers shed their constitutional rights to freedom of speech or expression at the schoolhouse gate."[1] Specifically, the majority in *Tinker* held that students may engage in personal, often controversial, speech on school grounds unless it materially disrupts or substantially interferes with the rights of others or the overall work of the schools. Yet the holding, highlighted by the "schoolhouse gate" statement above, is much deeper than simply the right of students to wear political symbols. *Tinker* opened the eyes and ears of public school leaders everywhere and reminded them that their decisions affecting the rights of students were subject to judicial scrutiny. It reminded them that public school students were citizens while at school and not devoid of the rights that citizens have outside of school. There were a few significant court decisions before 1969 involving the rights of students,[2] but from *Tinker* forward, the rights of public school students have been debated in courts with great regularity, in cases involving student due process, speech expressed in all forms and delivered through all types of media, discipline of student conduct committed both on and off school premises, search and seizure of student property, privacy in student records, and sexual or racial/ethnic harassment at the hands of peers and teachers.

As important as the development of students' rights has been to the administration of public schools, the rights and responsibilities of the school business officials and other educational leaders have not gone unnoticed. In fact, with every discussion of constitutional rights comes the necessary balance between the rights and responsibilities of individuals and of the organization or society as a whole. In recent decades, courts and legislatures, both state and federal, have been helpful and respectful toward the public school officials, particularly in situations involving vulgar speech, student conduct in school-sponsored events, drugs, weapons, violence, zero tolerance, and search and seizure. In other words, while the rights of students are highly regarded under the law, they are not without limits. This chapter discusses this balance of rights between school officials and students in the areas of student free speech, student discipline and due process, search and seizure, privacy and student records, and harassment.

FREEDOM OF EXPRESSION

Student Protests and the Disruption Standard

The landmark freedom of expression case for students in public schools is *Tinker v. Des Moines Independent Community School District*.[3] While future court cases limited the full effect of *Tinker*, the popular disruption standard adopted by *Tinker* and applied in situations involving personal speech of students (and staff, as well) remains well regarded. In *Tinker*, administrators suspended students for wearing black armbands to school in silent protest against the United States' involvement in the hostilities in Vietnam. The students and their parents had planned the protests for a while, and when school administrators found out, they drafted a policy forbidding the armbands. According to the policy, which all students and parents knew about in advance of its application, any student refusing to remove the armband would be suspended until he or she complied with the rule. The suspended students filed suit against the school board, claiming that the policy and subsequent suspensions violated their rights to free speech under the First Amendment. A federal trial court, relying on the administrators' stated fear of disturbance, held for the board and the Eighth Circuit affirmed the decision. The Supreme Court reversed the decision in ruling that public school administrators may not lawfully restrict the personal speech of students unless their speech substantially disrupts school operations, materially interferes with school discipline, or infringes on the rights of other students.

Tinker highlighted the necessary balance between the rights of students (who do not shed their constitutional rights at the schoolhouse gate) and the obligations of educators to maintain safe and orderly atmospheres for learning. But, importantly, the Court noted that administrative action that suppresses students' rights must be inspired by more than mere desire to avoid "the discomfort and unpleasantness that always accompany an unpopular viewpoint."[4] In fact, the Court took a page from the law of free speech in institutions of higher education, asserting that any word spoken in class that disagrees with the views of another has the potential to disturb. Even so, according to the *Tinker* Court, the American system must take that risk: "Schools may not be enclaves of totalitarianism. . . . Students may not be closed-circuit recipients of only that which the state chooses to communicate."[5] In effect, the defense of the school administration—fear of the riots and rallies so common on college campuses in the late 1960s—became powerful ammunition for the students' cause. Equally effective were two important facts in the case. First, officials had not restricted the wearing of other controversial symbols, including those associated with Nazism. Second, there was no evidence that the armbands led to any disruption or interference of school operation or the rights of others. Moreover, the protest did not offer any reasonable likelihood of such disruption.

Lewdness, Vulgarity, and the Inculcation of Fundamental Values

A different form of disruptive speech led the Supreme Court to make a statement not directly in furtherance of *Tinker*'s disruption standard, but instead in advancing a content-based restriction on student speech. In *Bethel School District No. 403 v. Fraser*,[6] a high school student, Matthew Fraser, delivered a speech at a school-sponsored assembly nominating a fellow student for elective office. More than 600 students, some of whom were as young as 14 years old, were required to attend the assembly or attend a study hall. During the speech, Fraser referred to his candidate in terms of a graphic sexual metaphor. Two of his teachers warned him in advance not to deliver the speech. During the speech, many students hooted and yelled while others made gestures relating to the words. The next day,

Fraser admitted to the assistant principal that he intended the sexual innuendo in the speech. He was suspended for three days and removed from consideration as a graduation speaker. A hearing officer determined that the speech fell within the school's "obscene language" rule and upheld the suspension.[7] Fraser brought suit alleging a violation of First Amendment free speech. Both the federal trial court and the Ninth Circuit ruled in favor of Fraser. The Supreme Court reversed in favor of the school officials.

The *Bethel* Court made a distinction between Fraser's vocal, vulgar speech and the silent political speech in *Tinker*, but did so not on the speech's effect but on its content. The Court explained that the First Amendment does not prevent school officials from deciding that permitting a student's lewd and vulgar speech would have undermined the school's basic educational mission. According to the Court, it is perfectly appropriate for a school to disassociate itself to make the point to students that lewd and vulgar conduct is wholly inconsistent with the fundamental values of public education. The role of public education, instead, wrote the Court, is the inculcation of fundamental values necessary to maintain a democratic political system. While tolerance of divergent political and religious views is necessary for this democracy, the Court thought that so is consideration for personal sensibilities of participants and audiences. Seemingly against the "schoolhouse gate" statement from *Tinker*, the *Bethel* Court specifically declared that the free speech rights of students on school premises and during school events are not coextensive with those of adults in other settings. The Court recognized the *in loco parentis* doctrine (that school officials act "in the place of the parents") and encouraged the protection of children from sexually explicit, indecent, or lewd speech.

In *Bethel* the Court noticeably did not simply apply *Tinker*'s disruption standard to hold that Fraser's speech was disruptive to the rights of others and the work of the school. Rather, the opinion implies that lewd and vulgar speech may be restricted in all forms, verbal and non-verbal, and in and out of school-sponsored events. *Bethel* is important not only for its substantive result but also for the school board's dedication. Having lost at the lower courts, the board continued to appeal, an expensive venture, but ultimately victorious and reflective now of one of the most important cases to affect curriculum and discipline in public schools.

Student Speech in School-Sponsored Activities

The last of the three major Supreme Court cases to affect student speech is *Hazelwood School District v. Kuhlmeier.*[8] In *Hazelwood*, high school students sued their school board and principal after he cut two pages of a school-sponsored newspaper to avoid the publication of two articles the principal deemed objectionable, invasive, and inappropriate. One article was on teenage pregnancy; it used false names, but the identities of the students profiled in the article were easily discoverable. The other article dealt with the effect of divorce on teenagers and mentioned a student's name and made some disparaging remarks about the student's father. There was no time to make changes to the articles or the paper's layout, so the principal cut two pages. The newspaper was published as part of a school course (Journalism II), but it had a large circulation that included families and other members of the community. A federal trial court ruled in favor of the school, but the Eighth Circuit reversed in favor of the students on the basis that the newspaper was a public forum. Applying the public forum analysis, the court applied *Tinker* and found no reasonable forecast of disruption. The Supreme Court, in another landmark decision, reversed in favor of the school.

The *Hazelwood* Court made three significant points. First, the Court held that the school-sponsored newspaper was not a public forum. According to the Court, the government does not create a public forum by inaction. School facilities may be deemed public forums only if the school has, by policy or practice, opened up the forum for indiscriminate use by the general public. That was not the case in *Hazelwood*. The newspaper was produced by students as part of a class, with full editorial authority in the hands of the teacher-advisor and principal. Second, the Court made the important statement that student speech in school-sponsored activities bears the imprimatur of the school. As a result, school officials may exercise greater control over such speech. This case and its implications are different from those of *Tinker*. *Tinker* demands tolerance for divergent student speech, while *Hazelwood* involves, instead, the promotion of particular school-sponsored speech. Third, and most substantively, the Court held that educators retain editorial control over the content and style of student speech in school-sponsored activities so long as their actions are reasonably related to legitimate pedagogical concerns.[9] Here, the Court was satisfied that the principal acted reasonably in removing the two articles, as the journalism curriculum, in part, concerned the treatment of sensitive controversial information.

Political and Other Expressive Activity and the Influence of Bethel and Hazelwood

Tinker retains much of its vitality, as analysis in student free speech cases is rarely complete without coverage of *Bethel* and *Hazelwood*. Some recent cases have a pure *Tinker* application, such as those involving more traditional personal, non-disruptive political speech of the type challenged in *Tinker*. Under those circumstances, students fare well.[10] In other circumstances, where the non-sponsored expressive activities are threatening or violent, school officials may step in and restrict them and/or punish speakers.[11] The Third Circuit recently held that age is a factor in free speech analyses, where elementary school students' speech, even in cases echoing *Tinker*, may be limited due to the age of the speaker and audience.[12]

Post-*Bethel* and *Hazelwood*, student speech in political activities has been scrutinized more closely than it may have been decades earlier. Much of the stricter analysis is due to the fact that student speech occurs in school-sponsored activities such as student council elections. However, the justifications for speech restrictions come not only from the speech's disruptive potential, but also from their content. For example, the Sixth Circuit, in *Poling v. Murphy*, held that civility in public speaking—the shared values of civilized social order—is a pedagogical concern in public schools.[13] The art of stating one's views without offense to others has a legitimate place in any school's curriculum. The Eighth Circuit made a similar ruling in *Henerey v. City of St. Charles School District*, when it upheld the disqualification of a student council candidate who affixed condoms to his campaign posters and ran as the "safe choice."[14]

Student Publications After Hazelwood: School-Sponsored and Underground

The public forum argument of *Hazelwood* extends from student-written articles to advertising policies for newspapers, yearbooks, and athletic programs. In *Planned Parenthood of Southern Nevada v. Clark County School District*, the Ninth Circuit upheld school officials' decision to deny advertisements from the well-known family planning organization on the basis that it did not serve the best interests of the school.[15] While, generally, a publisher is not normally viewed as endorsing the contents of its paid advertisements, schools stand in a different relationship with their publics. Here, the court agreed that rejecting the ads from Planned Parenthood was reasonable, in light of the board's desire to be viewpoint neutral, to avoid conflict with the state curriculum, and to consider the emotional maturity of the students. Similarly, the First Circuit held that the school officials were not liable for refusing to publish yearbook and newspaper ads promoting sexual abstinence under the school's unwritten policy against running ads for political or advocacy purposes.[16]

When controversial publications are not school sponsored, such as underground publications, courts approach the analysis a little differently. Courts permit educators to impose reasonable time, place, and manner restrictions against the distribution of non-sponsored literature.[17] In some instances, schools may claim a legitimate right to review student underground newspapers before their on-premises distribution. In *Bystrom v. Fridley High School Independent School District*,[18] the Eighth Circuit was of the opinion that the school's prior review policy, which prohibited material that was obscene to minors, libelous, pervasively indecent or vulgar, invasive of the privacy of others, dangerous to the health and safety of another person, disruptive of school activities, or against the law such as ads for alcohol was not impermissibly vague or overbroad.[19]

Dress Codes and School Uniforms

Tinker and *Bethel* give much judicial support to school district dress codes and uniform codes. It is, indeed, popular to challenge school restrictions on student dress, everything from hair length and earrings to political T-shirts, alleged gang symbols, and Confederate flags. Yet the defenses for restrictions on dress are many. First, some courts do not recognize a First Amendment right in what students choose to wear.[20] Second, most dress and grooming restrictions, with the exception of hair length and color, are only restrictive during school hours. Third, student dress codes are designed, in part, to instill school pride, school spirit, and a professional atmosphere for learning. Fourth, student safety and the maintenance of discipline are always concerns in the implementation and enforcement of dress codes.[21] Fifth, *Tinker* applies against all substantially disruptive and interfering speech, regardless of the medium. Prime recent examples include several cases involving restrictions on displaying the Confederate flag, particularly in school settings with a history of racial tension.[22]

Importantly, courts have held that school officials need not wait until there is full-fledged disruption or violence. A reasonable forecast of substantial disruption or interference with the rights of others or the work of the school will be enough. However, even with the propensity of courts to rule in favor of schools on dress code provisions, a *Tinker* application does require actual or reasonable likelihood of disruption.[23] In a recent case from Virginia, the Fourth Circuit thought that a dress code provision prohibiting clothing that depicts messages or pictures related to weapons was vague and overbroad.[24] Here officials attempted to prevent a student from wearing a T-shirt depicting words and images from the "shooting sports camp" he attended. The court noted that there was no evidence that this shirt or anything similar had ever caused any commotion or interference.

Most fascinating now are the applications of *Bethel* to student dress codes. Courts not only uphold dress restrictions on actual or reasonably forecasted disruption. They also support them in furtherance of a school's fundamental missions and inculcation of values. In *Boroff v. Van Wert City Board of Education*, a high school student was forbidden to wear "Marilyn Manson" T-shirts to school.[25] The shirt had a three-faced Jesus on the front with the words "See No Truth, Hear No Truth, Speak No Truth" and the word "BELIEVE" on the back with "LIE" highlighted. Officials applied a policy that prohibited clothing with "offensive illustrations, drug, alcohol, or tobacco slogans." Faced with the options of changing, turning the shirt inside-out, or going home, the student went home and returned to school wearing other Marilyn Manson shirts for the next three days. A federal trial court applied *Bethel* and ruled in favor of the school. On appeal, the student argued that the shirts were not vulgar or offensive, as *Bethel* requires. He also claimed that the shirts did not cause any disruption or the reasonable forecast thereof, as *Tinker* requires. The Sixth Circuit affirmed in favor of school officials who posited that some of Manson's lyrics and views were offensive to the school's basic educational mission. The court agreed that educators did not act manifestly outside the scope of their authority in determining that the student's conduct was inconsistent with the school's mission.

Free Speech in Cyberspace

It is widely held that *Tinker* applies most often in cases involving challenges to expressive conduct posted to the personal websites of students, even when such expression is directed to classmates and school personnel. In *Beussink v. Woodland R-IV School District*, for example, a student posted a home page that was critical of a high school, its teachers, and its administrators.[26] The criticism included crude and vulgar language, and invited readers to contact the school principal to communicate their opinions regarding the school. The home page was created at home on a home computer, not during school hours and not using school facilities or software. The student created a hyperlink from his home page to the school's, but there was not a corresponding link from the school to his home page. On a First Amendment challenge, the court applied *Tinker*. The court recognized the necessity of instilling and maintaining discipline and respect for school personnel, but found that the site did not disrupt school activities or the rights of others.[27] Naturally, when such websites do have a disruptive or harmful effect, such as causing physical and emotional injury to students and staff, restrictions my be upheld.[28] Unpleasant and upsetting speech on the Internet may have to be tolerated; violent or threatening speech, perhaps not.

STUDENT DISCIPLINE AND DUE PROCESS

The Basic Nature of the Protected Right: The Fourteenth Amendment

The Fourteenth Amendment reads in part that a state shall not "deprive any person of life, liberty, or property without due process of law; nor deny to any person within its jurisdiction the equal protection of the laws."[29] With respect to the disciplinary decisions school leaders make, each of the protected due process rights—life, liberty, and property—is important for policy-making and policy enforcing. Particularly applicable are the rights to property and liberty.[30] For students, the recognized property right under the Fourteenth Amendment is the right to public education generally. Property rights are most often implicated in cases involving suspension or expulsion, where the right to education must be balanced with the school's obligation to maintain a safe and orderly school environment. Liberty interests are a little more difficult to grasp concretely but are found, for purposes of student discipline, in the constitutional rights to speech, privacy, and freedom from bodily restraint such as corporal punishment, and in the student's good name, reputation, honor, and integrity.

Due process claims generally come in one of two forms. First, procedural due process challenges involve claims to the student's rights to notice and an opportunity to be heard. Most common in student discipline cases, students allege that school administrators failed to provide adequate notice of the applicable rules and/or the charges for violating them and failed to provide a fair opportunity to be heard. Suspension and expulsion, elaborated below, provide the best examples. Second, substantive due process holds that government action must be reasonable in content and application, and within the scope of governmental authority. For example, a student claiming a violation of substantive due process looks for an abuse of discretion on the part of the school officials, either in rule-making or in rule enforcing.

Rule-making

In practice, life, liberty, and property rights are likely most often implicated in the application of rules and regulations. However, due process concerns also arise in the making of rules. In most jurisdictions, state and local educational officials have broad statutory authority to adopt rules and regulations necessary for school governance, student discipline, and the health, safety, and welfare of all members of a school community. These laws range from general requirements that school boards make and enforce rules for all people who enter their premises, to specific rules involving suspension and expulsion, drugs, weapons, locker searches, and acts of student violence. Readers are encouraged to consult the state statutes in their jurisdictions. For example, Ohio's most general statutory law regarding rule-making states: "The board of education of a school district . . . shall make any rules that are necessary for its government and the government of its employees, pupils of its schools, and all other persons entering upon its school grounds or premises."[31] More specifically, though, are the statutes that require school boards to adopt "zero tolerance" policies. Ohio law, for example, declares that each school board must "adopt a policy of zero tolerance for violent, disruptive, or inappropriate behavior, including excessive truancy, and establish strategies to address such behavior that range from prevention to intervention."[32]

Turning to the rights of students, the rule-making authority of school officials is not without limits. First and foremost, rules and regulations must be reasonably clear and narrow.[33] Due process in student discipline does not begin with notice of infractions committed; it begins with notice of the rules themselves. This due process concern raises an interesting and tricky balance for policy-makers. On one hand, the rules and regulations must be clear enough so that students know what conduct is expected. On the other hand, the rules must be flexible enough to be sustainable and applicable in multiple situations. Schools, again, will get much of their guidance from state statutes.

In Ohio, for example, school boards are required "to adopt a policy regarding suspension, expulsion, removal, and permanent exclusion that specifies the types of misconduct for which a pupil may be suspended, expelled, or removed."[34] This seemingly harmless provision proved troublesome when officials suspended a student for five days for possession of two cigarettes in a coat pocket in his locker. In *Wilson v. South Central Local School District*,[35] an appellate court in Ohio struck down the five-day suspension, not because tobacco possession was not a violation of reasonable board policy, but because that particular infraction was not listed in the student code of conduct among the infractions for which a five-day suspension was warranted. In effect, the school board failed to comply with what the court found to be an unambiguous state statute. Admittedly, the school's code had a "very serious offenses" catch-all phrase that the school attempted to apply. Even so, the court held that, in addition to officials' failure to specify tobacco possession in that part of the code, the offense was not serious enough to warrant application of the "catch-all" provision. In addition, the court decided that the "very serious offenses" provision was potentially vague and that the state statute was designed to address such vagueness issues. Essentially, a case like *Wilson* wakes up policy-makers to the very real concern that rules must be explicit in infractions and penalties, with all the necessary cross-referencing for unequivocal application and compliance on the part of all the parties involved.

On the other end of the rule-making spectrum is the legitimate argument that school rules and regulations ought to be flexible enough to allow for broad, long-term application, particularly in unforeseen circumstances. The application of "old" law and policy to new situations is a frightening proposition in a world of constant change. How are school officials expected to respond to offenses for which students should be suspended or expelled but which are not specified clearly in the student code? For example, imagine the difficulty that school officials would have in applying a specific code of conduct provision on student harassment or violence if that provision defines harassment or violence in "face-to-face" terms only. Several years ago, for example, sexual harassment via email or instant messaging was largely unforeseen. Today, the perpetrators of these infractions do not have to be in the same physical setting as the victims.[36] Another example is the very real concern over plagiarism, cheating, and other forms of academic dishonesty in a technological age. Academic honesty provisions are clearly important and are only effective when they can keep pace with the academic infractions. Finally, imagine what might happen if educators adopt a legitimate, necessary, and specific prohibition on gang symbols in their schools, including symbols that might appear on student clothing or accessories,[37] only to have the gangs change their symbols in an effort to contravene clearly written policy. Situations such as these, with all due respect to the goodness of specific and fully cross-referenced policies, effectively take rule-making and rule-enforcing authority away from schools, place it in the hands of rule-breaking students, and keep school officials on the defensive. In addition, student discipline is part of the educational process, and therefore school district discretion and breadth of application are necessary.

Against the strong statement that rules must be written with absolute clarity are the statements of several courts that such rules need not carry with them the same specificity of criminal codes.[38] In other words, claims of unconstitutionality due to vagueness and overbreadth are not often successful. The vagueness doctrine holds that an enactment must define the prohibited conduct with sufficient definiteness such that ordinary individuals can understand just what conduct is prohibited and what conduct is permitted. The rule must also define the prohibited conduct in a manner discouraging arbitrary and discriminatory enforcement. In *Wiemerslage v. Maine Township High School District 207*,[39] for example, where high school administrators suspended students for loitering in an "off-limits" area immediately adjacent to the school, the students claimed that the rule was unconstitutionally vague. The Seventh Circuit disagreed, asserting that the rule was written with sufficient clarity that the students knew what was expected of them. The court consulted a dictionary and explained that the definition of the word "loitering" was sufficiently clear that people of common intelligence, especially those subject to the rule, could comply with it easily. Further, all parents and students at the high school were aware of the rule and the safety reasons for it.

The overbreadth doctrine relates to policies that may be too sweeping in coverage. Most often, overbreadth applies against overly broad policies that may have a deterrent or "chilling" effect on protected First Amendment expression. Against an allegation of overbreadth, schools must demonstrate that a challenged policy is narrowly tailored to meet a compelling governmental interest. This means that a school policy must be narrowly aimed at meeting school objectives such as health, safety, and welfare of students so as not to reach conduct that would otherwise be constitutionally protected.

RULE ENFORCEMENT AND PUNISHMENT

Exclusionary Discipline: Suspensions and Expulsions

Exclusionary discipline, usually in the form of suspensions and expulsions, is likely the most common and time-honored type of discipline that school officials impose on students who violate school policies and/or the law. Suspensions are limited exclusions of a specific period of time, usually not exceeding 10 days.[40] Ordinarily, building-level and district-level administrators have the authority to issue suspensions. Expulsions, on the other hand, are disciplinary removals of students for more than 10 days, often up to one year.[41] Typically, only superintendents and board members may issue expulsions. The length of the suspension or expulsion depends most often on the seriousness of the infraction. Not surprisingly, the more serious the infraction—such as bomb threats, weapon possession, and drug possession—the lengthier the exclusion. In most states today, the right to expel students for one year includes not only infractions involving guns, but also dealing with knives, other serious weapons, bomb threats, or incidents causing serious physical harm to persons or property. In some states, permanent exclusion is possible for students who are convicted of serious crimes.[42]

Traditionally, suspensions and expulsions prohibit the wrongdoing student from attending school for the length of the exclusion. However, several variations in exclusionary discipline exist today, as legislators, policy-makers, and school leaders address punitive and educational forms of discipline. For example, along with traditional suspension and expulsion, most schools offer some type of "in-school suspension" or alternative educational setting for students who have been removed from school for disciplinary purposes. The determination of whether an in-school or out-of-school suspension is to be imposed depends on a few important factors, including the seriousness of an infraction, a student's discipline record, whether the student has a disability,[43] and perhaps the student's age and grade level. In-school suspensions most often take place either in a specially designated room in a student's school or in a more long-term placement in an alternative school inside or outside a district. Just like traditional out-of-school suspensions, the length of in-school suspensions depends in large part on the seriousness of the infraction. In minor instances, an in-school "suspension" may amount to a brief cooling-off period in a separate room in the building, while more serious infractions could lead to temporary multiday reassignment within the building. Other, even more minor, exclusionary discipline measures include the withholding of privileges such as field trips or participation in extra-curricular activities.

Regardless of the form, length, and location of a student's suspension or expulsion, every imposition of student discipline demands that two very important questions be asked relative to the student's Fourteenth Amendment procedural due process rights of life, liberty, and property. First, does the Fourteenth Amendment due process clause apply? In other words, is a life, liberty, or property interest implicated by the school's disciplinary decision? Second, if the answer to the first question is "yes," then what process is due?

In their formal sense, the Supreme Court first asked these two questions in *Goss v. Lopez*.[44] In *Goss*, nine Columbus, Ohio, public school students were suspended for up to 10 days each after a variety of disturbances and student demonstrations throughout the district. According to state law at the time, students subject to suspension were not afforded the right to appeal and offer their side of a story. The students' parents were merely given a letter within 24 hours of the suspensions. Expelled students, on the other hand, were afforded the right to appeal. The students in *Goss* filed suit alleging that the statutes governing suspensions violated the Fourteenth Amendment due process clause. The Supreme Court agreed with the students.

In response to the first due process question, the Court held that both property and liberty rights are implicated in cases of suspensions of up to 10 days. According to the Court, children have a property right to a public education, secured by the state constitution's directive to the state legislature, requiring the legislature to establish a system of public education. The Court observed that the federal Constitution itself does not establish the property right to a public education, but instead protects it, found most often in state constitutions and compulsory attendance laws.[45] In addition, the Court noted a student's liberty interest in his or her good name, honor, integrity, and reputation. In other words, with respect to the liberty interest, a suspension (or expulsion) entered into the permanent record of a student could damage that student's prospects for higher education or employment post-graduation. Therefore, a school's decision to suspend (or expel) a student implicates a liberty interest as well. Importantly, the *Goss* Court held that the deprivation of life, liberty, or property must be more than de minimis in order to answer the first due process question in the affirmative. The Court considered that the deprivation of a student's right to attend school for up to two weeks was more than de minimis.

In response to the second due process question on the level of process that is due for suspensions of up to 10 days, the Court balanced three factors:[46]

1. A student's interests in life, liberty, and/or property. For suspensions, the issues are the property right to public education and the liberty interest in the student's good name, honor, and integrity.
2. The risk of erroneous deprivation of rights. This risk is obviously increased if only one side of the story is obtained. In cases of suspension and other exclusionary discipline, a student is deprived of the right to attend school, and his or her liberty interests are damaged. It

is important, in advance of such deprivation, to determine whether the imposition of such suspension or expulsion is warranted as not erroneous under the circumstances.

3. A school's interest in maintaining a safe, orderly educational atmosphere. This interest is undoubtedly high. Yet suspensions and expulsions are not just disciplinary; they ought to be educational, too. Without an opportunity to know the charges against him or her and without an opportunity to challenge them, the punished student learns nothing. Further, the Court decided that the costs associated with an informal hearing in advance of a suspension are not overly prohibitive.

Having chosen to provide a public education for the children of the state, the state cannot simply deprive that right without fundamentally fair procedures. With respect to a suspension of up to 10 days, the *Goss* Court reasoned that due process requires that students be given oral or written notice of the charges against them and, if they deny them, an explanation of the evidence against them and an opportunity for them to tell their side of the story.[47] The Court added that these procedures may be informal in cases of suspension, but must occur as soon as practicable after the infraction takes place. The Court declared that only in emergency circumstances where there is an immediate danger posed to students and staff may disciplinary removal occur before the due process associated with a suspension.

The answer to the second due process question varies, depending primarily on the severity of the deprivation of rights. The *Goss* Court was quick to comment that the procedures outlined in its opinion applied only to short-term suspensions. Unlike the informality of due process in suspension cases, in cases of long-term exclusions, the notice of charges and opportunity to be heard will be sufficiently more formal, perhaps including the right for the student and his or her parents to appear before the board of education, to be represented by counsel, to present evidence, and to question and cross-examine witnesses. Courts are silent on due process for in-school suspensions. In other words, whether an exclusion from the regular classroom, coupled with an assignment to an alternative educational setting, triggers the deprivation of due process rights is a largely unanswered question. On one hand, it can be argued that an exclusion from the regular student assignment, even if the new assignment is an in-school suspension classroom down the hall, is nonetheless still a deprivation of property and liberty rights worthy of some due process. On the other hand, it can be argued that the full right to public education in cases of in-school suspensions has not been deprived and, consequently, the deprivation is de minimis. For the procedural due process rights of students subjected to exclusionary discipline, readers are strongly encouraged to consult the statutes and regulations in their states.

Corporal Punishment

It is important to keep in mind that most states have outlawed corporal punishment in public schools. However, for those states that allow corporal punishment, the same two due process questions introduced in *Goss* apply. In *Ingraham v. Wright*,[48] the Supreme Court addressed these two questions and the procedural and substantive due process implications of corporal punishment. First, the Court held that corporal punishment implicated the student's liberty interest in the "freedom from bodily restraint." Moving to the second question, the Court was of the view that in cases of corporal punishment, no pre-deprivation due process was required. In other words, the Court did not think that school officials had to provide notice of the charges or an opportunity for students to tell their side of a story in advance of imposing corporal punishment. Post-deprivation remedies in the form of actions for monetary damages suffice to afford the student due process.

While the *Ingraham* Court did not necessarily praise the specific actions taken by the school officials in the case, it did discuss the state-based tradition associated with corporal punishment. The Court held that state law adequately protected students against whom corporal punishment is unlawfully or excessively imposed since it imposed tort liability on teachers and other educators who impose it unreasonably. According to the Court, pre-deprivation due process in cases of corporal punishment would unduly burden schools with time, money, and energy spent away from school activities and would damage the deterrent that the swift imposition of corporal punishment brings to students. Further, the Court posited that the instances of unreasonable infliction of corporal punishment are low enough that the common law tort remedies in state courts are sufficient to act as a deterrent for the school officials.

Even in jurisdictions where corporal punishment has been outlawed, it may still be lawful for teachers and administrators to use force or restraint in the course of reasonable discipline, for example in cases where a teacher attempts to break up a fight between students or attempts to restrain a dangerous student to avoid injury to the student, other students and staff, or property.[49]

Discipline of Off-Premises Conduct

One of the most significant recent practical developments in school administration is the prevalence of school policies and, often, associated state statutes authorizing the discipline of student conduct that occurs off-premises. Naturally, if the off-premises conduct is part of a school-sponsored event, say, a field trip or a sporting event at another school, a student code of conduct will apply along with other related rules and regulations.[50]

More complicated is the application of school policy to student conduct that occurs off premises and/or after hours but is not associated with school-sponsored activities. In some instances, state law allows school boards to adopt policies that punish students for acts committed against the person or property of school employees, regardless of where it occurs and regardless of whether those acts are connected to on-premises conduct or school-sponsored activities.[51] However, beyond those specifics, the legal permission to impose discipline for off-premises conduct is largely judicially untested. Educators have offered some successful defenses in the past, including the need and desire to ensure student safety after school and protect the property rights of homeowners who live near the school;[52] the exclusion of a student currently on trial for an off-premises after-hours felony committed against the mother of a classmate;[53] the general protection of the health, safety, and welfare of students;[54] and the expulsion of a student engaged in an off-campus sale of drugs that were later resold to another student at school.[55]

A final interesting speculation on the school's authority to discipline off-premises conduct is the legality of the so-called "24-7" rules adopted most often for student athletes and applied 365 days a year, rules that forbid students from drinking or smoking anytime and anywhere, and often from attending parties where alcohol and tobacco might be present, whether or not consumed. The argument on behalf of school officials is that such rules, as applied to student athletes, further the mission of the sport, team loyalty, and physical education in general. And while these rules are popular and most often supported by students and families, the argument from students against such rules is that they overstep the rule-making authority of schools and reach into the authority of families and/or law enforcement. In addition, 24-7 rules run the risk of inconsistent and discriminatory application.

Concluding Notes on Students' Rights and Student Discipline

Discretion in rule-making and enforcement is a wonderful thing and is, generally, well regarded by courts, statutes, and broader school communities. Yet it is also true that some applications of zero tolerance policies make for negative and embarrassing headlines publicizing the sexual harassment–based suspension of a six-year-old for kissing another six-year-old, the drug-possession charge to the middle-schooler with a cough drop, or the expulsion of a high school student who takes a gun away from a suicidal classmate. The best advice is to accept the discretion that has been offered and to use it well, not with formulaic establishment and enforcement of rules, but with a balance of clarity, flexibility, and reasonableness. In this respect, the Fifth Circuit stated: "Some degree of discretion must, of necessity, be left to . . . school officials to determine what forms of misbehavior should be sanctioned. Absent evidence that the broad wording [of school rules] is, in fact, being used to infringe on [constitutional] rights . . . we must assume that school officials are acting responsibly in applying the broad statutory command."[56]

With discretion in hand, school officials engaged in the business of implementing policy should be aware of their own liability risks. When students file suits alleging violations of constitutional rights, the defendants often include the school board as a whole, individual members, and other relevant administrators in their official and sometimes individual capacities. Sovereign immunity is a common and often successful defense in such cases. The deference and discretion to the important, required, and often controversial work of government officials gives the immunity defense its power. In defense of immunity, board members and other school officials must be given the leeway to perform their roles without fear of liability for every good faith action, even if that action is mistaken. Liability for every action that is violative of constitutional rights would unfairly impose on school decision-makers the burden of mistakes made in good faith in the course of exercising discretion within the bounds of their official duties. Liability in such cases would not lead to principled and fearless administration, but to intimidation. As a result, governmental officials are granted qualified immunity.

It is important, though, to recognize that immunity is qualified and not absolute. In *Wood v. Strickland*,[57] the Supreme Court held that school board members (and by implication, any other public school officials) are not immune from liability for damages under section 1983 of the Civil Rights Act if they knew or reasonably should have known that the action they took within the sphere of their official responsibilities would have violated the clearly established constitutional or statutory rights of students (or staff) affected, or if they took the action with the malicious intention to cause deprivation of constitutional rights or other injury to students (or staff).

SEARCH AND SEIZURE AND THE FOURTH AMENDMENT

The Basic Nature of the Protected Right

The Fourth Amendment reads, in part, that the "right of people to be secure in their persons, houses, papers, and effects, against unreasonable searches and seizures, shall not be violated." In similar form as the First and Fourteenth Amendments, the Fourth Amendment applies in public school settings and protects, in this instance, the privacy rights of students. Yet with the application of the Fourth Amendment comes balance of rights similar to the balance applied in circumstances involving free speech and due process: "Against the child's interest in privacy must be set the substantial interest of teachers and administrators in maintaining discipline in the classroom and on school grounds. Maintaining order in the classroom has never been easy, but in recent years, school disorder has often taken particularly ugly forms: drug use and violent crime in the schools have become major social problems."[58]

In the two decades since the Supreme Court decided *New Jersey v. T.L.O.*,[59] public concern over criminal activity among young people in schools has certainly not subsided. In return, courts and legislatures have been extremely deferential to the actions of school officials in response to drugs, weapons, and other contraband on school grounds and on student property. As vigilant as the legal system is in protecting the rights of citizens, young and old, the trend in search and seizure cases in public schools favors safety over privacy. As a result, in the two decades since *T.L.O.*, judicial protections of school policy and practice have gone from suspicion-based searches of a couple of students caught smoking in the bathroom to random, suspicionless urinalysis drug tests of any student involved in a competitive extra-curricular activity.

The Reasonable Suspicion Standard: *New Jersey v. T.L.O.*

In *T.L.O.*, a teacher discovered two students smoking in a school bathroom, in violation of a school rule. The teacher took the two girls to the school's assistant principal. One student admitted the violation, but the student known in the case as T.L.O. denied it. The assistant principal searched T.L.O.'s purse and discovered cigarettes and rolling papers, prompting him to search further, where he uncovered marijuana, a pipe, plastic bags, substantial amounts of money, an index-card list of students who owed T.L.O. money, and two letters that implicated T.L.O. in drug dealing. In a later criminal hearing, T.L.O. filed a motion to suppress the evidence, alleging that the search violated her Fourth Amendment rights. The juvenile court denied the motion and the appellate division affirmed. The supreme court of New Jersey reversed and held that the Fourth Amendment was applicable to searches conducted by school officials. The Supreme Court, in another balancing act, held in favor of the state and upheld the legality of the search. In doing so, the Court fashioned a unique and important legal standard governing school searches.

As a threshold question, the Court in *T.L.O.* held that the Fourth Amendment right against unreasonable searches applies in public school settings. Students, in fact, have some expectations of privacy in the personal effects they carry. And school officials are "state actors" for purposes of the Fourth Amendment. On balance, the Court understood the importance of maintaining a safe environment and doing so without unreasonable administrative burdens such as securing a warrant in advance of a search. As a result, the Court adopted a standard not of "probable cause," but of "reasonable suspicion" under the circumstances. According to the Court, evaluating the reasonableness of any search involves a twofold inquiry:

1. Was the search justified at its inception? A school official must have reasonable grounds for suspecting that the search will turn up some evidence that the student has violated or is violating the law or the rules of the school.
2. Was the search reasonably related in scope to the circumstances that justified the interference in the first place? The scope and sequence of the search must be reasonably related to the objectives of the search (the seriousness of the contraband sought) and not excessively intrusive in light of the age and sex of the student and the nature of the infraction.

Readers should not underestimate either prong of the test. Each has a significant contribution to make to the balance of rights, with the first prong emphasizing a school board's obligation to maintain safety and discipline and the second one respecting the privacy rights of students. *T.L.O.* actually involved two searches, the first for the cigarettes, where the teacher caught the two girls smoking in the bathroom, and the second for the marijuana, when the assistant principal found the rolling papers. The Court held that it was reasonable for the administrator to search a purse for cigarettes after a staff member caught the students smoking while the further search of the purse was reasonable after he discovered the rolling papers.

Individualized Suspicion

New Jersey v. T.L.O. did not answer all school search questions definitively. Even so, the reasonable suspicion standard remains well regarded and widely applied in school searches of nearly all forms and types. Many of the questions that remained after *T.L.O.* was decided have been resolved by state and federal courts. Among the applications are school searches of students' lockers, luggage, and cars, as well as dog-sniff searches, and the often controversial strip searches and random urinalysis drug tests.

The first primary unanswered question following *T.L.O.* was whether "individualized suspicion" was required for a determination of reasonableness. In other words, do school officials conducting a search need to have suspicion that a particular student or students possess contraband in violation of law or school policy? The answers to this question have varied. The trend indicates that individualized or particularized suspicion is not required in school searches. Examples should suffice at this point. In *Webb v. McCullough*,[60] the Sixth Circuit upheld the search of four students' hotel room and luggage after administrators and chaperones for a high school band trip to Hawaii heard rumors from hotel managers of alcohol among band members and their associated hotel rooms. While the facts were detailed and controversial, the question of the legality of the search was handled fairly cleanly by the court. The court held that there are exceptions to the individualized suspicion requirement when the privacy interests implicated by the search are minimal. The court rejected a pure application of the *T.L.O.* reasonableness standard, noting that the administrators were present not only as state actors, but also in loco parentis. This hybrid authority acts to reduce the expectation of privacy of students in hotel rooms secured through private funds. In fact, the supervisory responsibilities of school officials are increased in field-trip situations, particularly overnight trips. In *Webb*, the trip was voluntary; the greater range of activities produced greater need for supervision; and there was increased opportunity for students to get into trouble.[61] It is also worth recognizing that anyone with the authority to conduct searches on field trips, including volunteer chaperones, may be considered "state actors" who are subject to the Fourth Amendment.

Further eroding the individualized suspicion standard are cases involving suspicion-based "sweep" searches, where school administrators have reason to believe a law or school rule has been violated, but do not know specifically who may have acted. Nonetheless, searches may ensue. Recently, in light of events such as the school shootings at Columbine High School in Littleton, Colorado, in April 1999, and the terrorist attacks of September 11, 2001, courts have sided with the schools, largely on grounds of safety and security. In *Thompson v. Carthage School District*,[62] a school bus driver discovered fresh knife cuts on some of his bus seats and notified the school principal. The principal of the rural high school then ordered searches of all boys in grades 6–12. While the search did not produce a knife, educators expelled a student who possessed crack cocaine. The student challenged his expulsion as unlawful. A trial court agreed with the student on the individualized suspicion argument, but the Eighth Circuit disagreed. The court held that the search was justified at its inception and reasonable in scope in light of the rumors of weapons on the premises and the need to maintain student safety. Interestingly, part of the search here involved the use of a metal detector. Courts have widely supported searches with metal detectors in both random and non-random form and in both stationary and handheld varieties.[63] As a practical matter, handheld metal detectors should be used by educators of the same sex as those who are being searched.

Further Applications: Lockers, Dog Sniffs, Automobile Searches, and Strip Searches

Any controversy over the legality of student locker searches has subsided substantially. Many states have statutory provisions detailing the authority that schools have to search lockers, either randomly at any time or with individualized suspicion.[64] Locker searches are justified legally for two reasons. First, courts almost uniformly agree that the expectation of student privacy in lockers is extremely low, since lockers typically belong to schools and not students.[65] A low expectation of privacy makes the application of the second prong of *T.L.O.* relatively straightforward, especially in emergency circumstances or in cases involving serious and dangerous contraband, like drugs, weapons, or bombs. Second, it is strongly advised, and often required by statute, that school leaders declare the authority to conduct locker searches conspicuously in student codes of conduct and in policies posted on walls on or near the lockers.

A common form of locker searches in schools today involves the use of drug-sniffing dogs. While a certain measure of commotion tends to occur around random dog sniffs, courts have been kind to schools that conduct such searches, particularly when dogs are brought in to search lockers and, most especially, when students are not in the vicinity of the lockers or the dogs while the searches are taking place. The same suggestions apply here as apply in cases where schools conduct searches of lockers: educators should make sure the students and parents are aware that school policy allows for random searches of lockers by drug-sniffing dogs and reiterate that the lockers belong to schools, not students. In *Zamora v. Pomeroy*,[66] the Tenth Circuit upheld a sniff search of lockers on the notion that the lockers were, at best, jointly controlled by both the student and the school. Carrying the argument further, the Fifth Circuit, in *Horton v. Goose Creek Independent School District*,[67] decided that dog sniff searches of lockers are not searches for Fourth Amendment purposes. However, dog sniffs of items other than lockers raise more serious privacy concerns. Sniff searches of backpacks and cars in school parking lots have been upheld, despite the increased expectation of privacy that students may have in these items. Yet courts continue to balance the privacy right against the obligation to maintain safety and security. Dog sniffs of people are not recommended in any form, random or non-random.

Amid increased privacy concerns in the automobiles of students (and staff), it is legal to extend a school search conducted by school officials to cars in school parking lots, particularly when there is reasonable suspicion to conduct the search, usually for drugs or weapons.[68] Even so, questions remain with respect to the legality of random sweeping searches of cars undertaken by school officials. Similar questions remain as to whether automobile searches may extend to cars parked off school grounds. The best advice to offer school leaders is to involve the police in such searches if the matter is criminal in nature. See the brief discussion below.

Although highly intrusive and controversial for their legal and ethical implications, strip searches have been upheld in many cases in school settings. Using the *T.L.O.* reasonable suspicion standard, courts will weigh the seriousness of the infraction or the contraband when determining the legality of a strip search. For example, strip searches for drugs or weapons have been upheld,[69] while strip searches for allegedly stolen money have not.[70]

Involvement of Police in Searches

With violence, drugs, weapons, and even the threat of terrorism, the presence of police officers in schools is more common today than ever before. Naturally, their presence is, in part, educational for students. Even so, it stands to reason that, in the most serious of disciplinary matters, these officers would be consulted to play significant roles. Police participation in school searches can come in a number of ways.[71] First, if the police enter a school with a search warrant and request school officials to open a locker or desk, then the educators must respect the warrant and permit the search. Even so, educational leaders should make sure that student rights are well protected, including the minimization of embarrassment and privacy intrusion. Further, law enforcement officials must comply with the full Fourth Amendment, namely have a warrant and probable cause. Second, if police officers enter a school under similar circumstances, but without a warrant, then school officials may still permit the search, but need not comply with warrant and probable cause requirements. Third, if the school officials "direct" a search by merely requesting police assistance in a search, as in a case of drug trafficking in a parking lot, then the reasonable suspicion standard most likely applies. Finally, if police ask school officials to serve as their agents in uncovering criminal wrongdoing, then the determination as to which standard applies is a little trickier. Basically, the reasonable suspicion standard applies if school officials initiate a search, while the probable cause and warrant requirements apply if the police initiate a search.[72]

Random, Suspicionless Urinalysis Drug Tests

Two important Supreme Court cases over the past decade have upheld policies that require certain groups of students to submit to random, suspicionless urinalysis drug tests. In *Vernonia School District 77J v. Acton,*[73] the Court upheld a drug-testing policy that applied to all athletes in grades 7–12. Each targeted student was to submit to a test at the beginning of his or her respective sport's season and then randomly throughout that season. A same-sex monitor was present to guard against tampering. One positive test required a second test. A second positive resulted in required participation in a drug counseling program or suspension from all athletics for the remainder of the year and all of the next. In upholding the program against a Fourth Amendment challenge, the Court did not apply *T.L.O.* directly, but balanced the privacy rights of student athletes with the interests of schools in reducing and eliminating illegal drug use among students. According to the Court, the privacy rights of student athletes are minimal, as they engage in a voluntary activity and are subject to physical examinations, "communal undress" in locker rooms, and additional rules and regulations. Moreover, the Court was satisfied that the board had a strong governmental interest in maintaining a drug-free educational environment and the student athletes in *Vernonia* were widely known to be the center of the school's drug culture.

In *Board of Education of Independent School District No. 92 of Pottawatomie v. Earls*,[74] the Court addressed a similar policy, this one applicable to all students involved in competitive extra-curricular activities. These activities included Academic Team, Future Farmers of America, Future Homemakers of America, band, choir, cheerleading, and athletics. Under the policy, a drug test was mandatory before participation in the activity and random during participation. The policy was designed to detect only illegal drug use such as marijuana, cocaine, and amphetamines and not prescription drugs consumed for medical conditions. The policy required that a faculty monitor wait outside a closed stall and listen for the "normal sounds of urination." The monitor then poured the contents into two bottles for sealed delivery to a testing lab. The contents and results were kept strictly confidential, allowing access to only those school personnel with a legitimate need to know. The results were neither turned over to law enforcement nor did they lead to disciplinary or academic penalties. After the first positive test, educators contacted parents for a meeting. A student was permitted to continue participation if he or she showed proof of attendance at drug counseling and submitted to a second drug test. On the second positive, a student was removed from extracurricular activities for 14 days. On the third positive, a student was removed for the remainder of the year, or 88 days, whichever was longer.

Several students challenged the policy. After a federal trial court ruled in favor of the board, the Tenth Circuit reversed in favor of the students, noting that educators failed to identify a drug problem among a sufficient number of the students who would have been subject to the policy. The Supreme Court reversed again and upheld the policy. The majority applied the three-part test from *Vernonia* in validating the policy. First, it considered the nature of the privacy interest and held that the students' privacy interests are limited in school settings, where the school acts in furtherance of the students' health and safety. The Court rejected the students' argument that non-athletic activities do not require or entail the same elements of "communal undress" as the athletic activities at issue in *Vernonia*. The Court, instead, held that the argument was not dispositive. In any event, students in non-athletic activities may well experience occasional off-campus travel and communal undress. Further, the Court acknowledged that participating students voluntarily subject themselves to additional rules and regulations in much the same way that athletes do.

In *Earls*, all students who were subject to the policy, as applied, had to abide by rules of the state's activities' association. Under the Court's analysis, voluntary submission to rules in addition to those required of non-participating students diminishes the expectation of privacy of students to a level permitting a drug-testing policy.

Second, the Court considered the character of the intrusion. The Court agreed with the board that the intrusion was minimal. Focusing less on the inherent privacy interest and more on the policy's procedures, the Court praised the board for its attention to detail. According to the Court, the testing procedures and the uses of the results are both minimally intrusive. Ultimately, the Court characterized the privacy intrusion as "negligible."

Third, the Court addressed the nature and immediacy of the governmental concern. The Court again favored the board and its obligation to help prevent drug use by students. Insofar as problems with drug use had "hardly abated" since *Vernonia*, the Court saw no reason to deny the nature and the immediacy of the board's concerns. Further, and importantly, the Court held that the reasonableness of a suspicionless drug-testing policy does not depend on any particularized or pervasive drug-use problem among the members of the targeted population. The Court thus upheld the policy. While the *T.L.O.* reasonable suspicion test still carries weight, it is possible that the three-part test in *Earls* will guide school search litigation beyond drug-testing cases.

FAMILY EDUCATIONAL RIGHTS AND PRIVACY ACT (FERPA)

Under the Family Educational Rights and Privacy Act (FERPA), school officials may not disclose the contents of students' educational records, other than "directory information," without prior written consent from parents.[75] Under FERPA, an "educational record" includes those records, files, documents, and other materials which contain information directly related to students and are maintained by educational agencies or institutions or by persons acting for such agencies or institutions. Examples include academic and behavioral performance records, standardized tests, psychological examinations, health information, and special education evaluation and placement records. Exceptions to "educational records" include private notes and memos written by instructional, supervisory, and administrative personnel and kept separate from student files. Parents have access to their children's educational records. However, students get this right when they turn 18. With this right to access educational records comes the opportunity for a hearing to challenge content and to provide corrections.

The non-disclosure provision of FERPA is important but not without its exceptions. Among the exceptions are the following, meaning that disclosure is permitted to the people or agencies without advanced written parental consent: people with legitimate educational interests (teachers, counselors, administrators), other schools (where students plan to enroll), federal or state audits (for financial support), applications for student financial aid, accrediting agencies during accreditation process, health or safety emergencies, data necessary for standardized test validation, judicial order or subpoena, juvenile justice system, and national security.

Two Supreme Court cases addressed important FERPA issues. In *Owasso Independent School District v. Falvo*,[76] the Court held that peer grading, where teachers have students trade papers and grade each other's work, does not violate the privacy rights protected by FERPA. The Court ruled that teachers do not "maintain" students' grades on individual assignments as "education records" under FERPA until final grades are recorded in grade books or in the office of a central registrar. In addition, the Court noted that students engaged in peer grading are not acting on behalf of the school. Peer grading was well protected by the Court and was hailed as much a part of the assignment as the content of the assignment itself. *Gonzaga University v. Doe*[77] is more fundamental and speaks to the enforcement rights of FERPA. In *Gonzaga*, a college student filed a Section 1983 suit against his university after he discovered that its teacher certification specialist relayed allegations of his sexual misconduct to the state agency responsible for teacher certification. The student alleged a violation of FERPA, claiming that the university employee released private information without prior written consent. The supreme court of Washington held that FERPA does not provide for a private cause of action, but noted that FERPA's non-disclosure provision allows for a section 1983 action. However, the Supreme Court rejected all claims, ruling that the student could not sue his private university for damages under section 1983 to enforce FERPA because his sole remedy was to complain to the federal Department of Education, since it had enforcement powers under the act.

HARASSMENT

Title IX and Sexual Harassment

Under the law, there are two types of sexual harassment. First, with quid pro quo harassment, a person explicitly or implicitly grants or withholds benefits as a result of the other person's willingness or refusal to submit to the first person's unwelcome sexual advances, requests for sexual favors, or other verbal, non-verbal, or physical conduct of a sexual nature. These benefits may include, but are not limited to, hiring, promotion, salary, grades, or participation in educational activities or programs. The critical point is not whether the submission by the victim was made voluntarily, but rather whether the conduct one submitted to was unwanted. Second, hostile-environment sexual harassment is sexually harassing conduct, including unwelcome sexual advances, requests for sexual favors, and other verbal, non-verbal, or physical conduct of a sexual nature, by an employee, a student, or a third party that is sufficiently severe, persistent, or pervasive to limit the victim's ability to participate in or benefit from an education program or activity, or to create a hostile or abusive educational environment. Severity can be measured in as few as one incident. The victims need not be intentional, nor must there be only one harasser and one victim. The critical point is not whether the harasser's behavior is deliberate or simply has the effect of creating an offensive atmosphere; it is the outcome. The conduct has to be motivated by the victim's sex. Further, same-sex sexual harassment claims are plentiful as well,[78] and courts have begun to recognize formal claims for discrimination on the basis of sexual orientation.[79]

A student's rights in cases of sexual harassment are best addressed through Title IX of the Education Amendments of 1972. Title IX provides that "no person in the United States shall, on the basis of sex, be excluded from the participation in, be denied the benefits of, or be subjected to discrimination under any education program or activity receiving Federal financial assistance."[80] The Supreme Court initially found that a student could proceed with a sexual harassment claim under Title IX in *Franklin v. Gwinette County Public Schools.*[81] In two more recent landmark cases, the Court outlined the legal principles governing sexual harassment claims. The factual settings are different, but the legal tests for school board liability are identical. In *Gebser v. Lago Vista Independent School District,*[82] the Court reasoned that a school board can be liable in a private right action under Title IX for the damages that result from employee-to-student sexual harassment if a school official who, at minimum, has the authority to institute corrective measures on the district's behalf has actual knowledge of the harassing conduct and is deliberately indifferent to it. Similarly, in *Davis v. Monroe County Board of Education,*[83] the Court held that Title IX liability for student-to-student sexual harassment exists only where school officials have actual knowledge of harassment and are deliberately indifferent to it. *Davis* involved a fifth-grade student who suffered over five months of verbal and physical sexual harassment at the hands of a classmate. After nearly all of the alleged incidents, the student and/or her mother notified the teacher and/or the principal. Disciplinary response was promised, but none was forthcoming. The only response was that the students' desks were separated in one of the victim's classes. The student's academic work began to suffer and, after several months of abuse, she wrote a suicide note.

There is no question that the liability standards adopted in *Gebser* and *Davis* are substantial alerts to the policy-making and policy enforcing duties of school boards. Yet, litigation has not subsided since these decisions. Questions of what it means to have "actual knowledge" of harassment and who has to have the knowledge for board liability to kick in have been plentiful. The safe side of the argument states that anyone in an official capacity, including teachers, with actual knowledge of harassment is under a duty to act. While a teacher may not typically have the direct ability to stop the harassment or suspend or expel a perpetrator, common sense may dictate that the teacher's acting on behalf of the alleged victim is most appropriate under the circumstances and certainly not deliberately indifferent.

It is true that the prospect of liability under Title IX for even small acts of harassment, especially peer-to-peer harassment in hormonally charged middle and high schools, is fear inducing for even the most reasonable school official. However, it can be argued rather comfortably that "deliberate indifference" is not a tough standard for a school district to meet.

Basically, the best practical advice is to be vigilant and consistent in the enforcement of harassment codes. When the alleged harassment is minor, react with lesser forms of punishment, such as the temporary loss of privilege, or a break in the lesson for a "teachable moment" on harassment policy. When alleged harassment is more serious, some care for the victim is in order, such as meetings with a counselor and swift and clear discipline for the perpetrators, in the form of suspensions or expulsions. Merely talking to harassers after repeated incidents of student-to-student harassment will not be enough.[84]

Title VI and Racial/Ethnic Harassment

While there has not been a Supreme Court opinion to this effect, it is plausible that a claim for "racial or ethnic harassment," filed under Title VI (a statute similar to Title IX in words and spirit), may find some success. One case highlights this possibility. In *Monteiro v. Tempe Union High School District*,[85] the Ninth Circuit held for the school board in a claim by students and parents asking that controversial stories and books, like *The Adventures of Huckleberry Finn* and "A Rose for Emily," be removed from high school courses. The court deferred to the school board for the development of curriculum, but noted that schools should be careful in its delivery. The court thought that since the students presented a claim for hostile-environment racial harassment, their claim should have been allowed to proceed to trial. The court adopted the standard adopted in *Gebser*, that a board is liable when officials are deliberately indifferent to its students' right to a learning environment free from racial hostility and discrimination.

CONCLUSION

At the outset of this chapter, the notion of students' rights was presented as a balance between two important but often competing interests. On one hand, students have interests in free expression in personal and academic ventures; due process rights to life, liberty, and property; privacy rights in person, property, and student records; and freedom from harassment at the hands of both school personnel and peers. On the other hand, educational leaders, including school business officials, have interests in protecting the rights of personnel and students while maintaining safe, secure atmospheres conducive to learning. Clearly, the search for the appropriate balance in schools has been an expensive and long-standing journey. Overall, courts and legislatures favor the tough work of school officials and, in terms of the students' rights discussed above, have largely deferred to the daily decisions made by educators. In other words, school officials should be pleased at the respect they receive from courts, legislatures, and other policy-making bodies. At the same time, student rights are not without their respectful weight, as courts have not shied away from taking cases that check the authority of educators who overstep their bounds. It is true that students have rights. It is similarly true that school officials have rights.

Finally, it remains true that these rights have their limits. It is all about balance and the relationships that school officials build and maintain with their students and staff. Cases such as *Tinker, Goss*, and *T.L.O.* have their age. Even so, they remain good laws today, even if some of the rights of students have been "shed at the schoolhouse gate" in the rightful name of safety, security, and curricular authority.

NOTES

1. *Tinker v. Des Moines Independent Community Sch. Dist.*, 393 U.S. 503, 506 (1969).
2. See, for example, *Meyer v. Nebraska*, 262 U.S. 390 (1923); and *Pierce v. Society of Sisters*, 268 U.S. 510 (1925); *West Virginia State Bd. of Educ. v. Barnette*, 319 U.S. 624 (1943) (a public school may not mandate the daily recitation of the Pledge of Allegiance); *Brown v. Board of Educ.*, 347 U.S. 483 (1954) (racial segregation in public schools violates the Fourteenth Amendment equal protection clause).
3. *Tinker v. Des Moines Independent Community Sch. Dist.*, 393 U.S. 503 (1969).
4. *Tinker v. Des Moines Independent Community Sch. Dist.*, at 509.
5. *Tinker v. Des Moines Independent Community Sch. Dist.*, at 511.
6. *Bethel Sch. Dist. No. 403 v. Fraser*, 478 U.S. 675 (1986).
7. The school's rule stated: "Conduct which materially and substantially interferes with the educational process is prohibited, including the use of obscene, profane language or gestures."

8. *Hazelwood Sch. Dist. v. Kuhlmeier*, 484 U.S. 260 (1988).

9. See also *Romano v. Harrington*, 725 F.Supp. 687 (E.D. N.Y., 1989), distinguishing *Hazelwood* on the ground that school officials have greater authority over a newspaper written for a class than they do for a purely extra-curricular, albeit school-funded, newspaper; striking down the removal of a teacher-advisor to the paper after he allowed an article opposing the federal holiday celebrating the life and work of Martin Luther King Jr.

10. See, for example, *Chandler v. McMinnville Sch. Dist.*, 978 F.2d 524 (9th Cir., 1992), permitting students to wear buttons reading "I'm not listening" and "Do scabs bleed" to the classes of replacement teachers during a strike.

11. *Boucher v. School Bd. of Sch. Dist. of Greenfield*, 134 F.3d 821 (7th Cir., 1998) (expulsion of a student who wrote an article for an underground publication that described how to hack into the school's computers); *Lavine v. Blaine Sch. Dist.*, 257 F.3d 981 (9th Cir., 2001) (expulsion of a student who wrote a lengthy poem called "Last Words" detailing the shooting deaths of 28 people in a school setting and the ultimate suicide of the shooter), and *S.G. v. Sayreville Bd. of Educ.*, 333 F.3d 417 (3d Cir., 2003) (suspension of a kindergartner for saying "I'm going to shoot you" to a classmate).

12. *Walker-Seraano v. Leonard*, 325 F.3d 412 (3d Cir., 2003).

13. *Poling v. Murphy*, 872 F.2d 757 (6th Cir., 1989).

14. *Henerey v. City of St. Charles Sch. Dist.*, 200 F.3d 1128 (8th Cir., 1999).

15. *Planned Parenthood of Southern Nevada v. Clark County Sch. Dist.*, 941 F.2d 817 (9th Cir., 1991).

16. *Yeo v. Town of Lexington*, 131 F.3d 241 (1st Cir., 1997).

17. *Hemry v. School Bd.*, 760 F.Supp. 856 (D. Colo., 1991).

18. *Bystrom v. Fridley High School Independent Sch. Dist.*, 822 F.2d 747 (8th Cir., 1987).

19. But see *Burch v. Barker*, 861 F.2d 1149 (9th Cir., 1988), striking down a prior review policy that required submission and approval of all material to be distributed in school.

20. *Karr v. Schmidt*, 460 F.2d 609 (5th Cir., 1972); and *Olesen v. Board of Educ.*, 676 F.Supp. 820 (N.D. Ill., 1987).

21. *Bivens v. Albuquerque Public Sch.*, 899 F.Supp. 556 (D. N.M., 1995), holding that a dress code provision prohibiting the wearing of sagging pants was not discriminatory against race or ethnicity, but was enacted in furtherance of student safety and applicable to all students.

22. *Phillips v. Anderson County Sch. Dist.*, 987 F.Supp. 488 (D. S.C., 1997); and *West v. Derby Unified Sch. Dist.*, 206 F.3d 1358 (10th Cir., 2000).

23. See *Castorina v. Madison County Sch. Bd.*, 246 F.3d 536 (6th Cir., 2001) (ruling that T-shirts that, in part, had an image of the Confederate flag were

nondisruptive), and *Sypniewski v. Warren Hills Reg'l Bd. of Educ.*, 307 F.3d 243 (3d Cir., 2002) (permitting students to wear T-shirts containing depictions of Jeff Foxworthy's "redneck" humor).

24. *Newsom v. Albemarle County Sch. Bd.*, 354 F.3d 249 (4th Cir., 2003).

25. *Boroff v. Van Wert City Bd. of Educ.*, 220 F.3d 465 (6th Cir., 2000).

26. *Beussink v. Woodland R-IV Sch. Dist.*, 30 F.Supp.2d 1175 (E.D. Mo., 1998).

27. See also *Flaherty v. Keystone Oaks Sch. Dist.*, 247 F.Supp.2d 698 (W.D. Pa., 2003); *Coy v. Board of Educ.*, 205 F.Supp.2d 791 (N.D. Ohio, 2002); *Mahaffey v. Aldrich*, 236 F.Supp.2d 779 (E.D. Mich., 2002); and *Killion v. Franklin Reg'l Sch. Dist.*, 136 F.Supp.2d 446 (W.D. Pa., 2001).

28. *J.S. v. Bethlehem Area Sch. Dist.*, 807 A.2d 847 (Pa., 2002).

29. Note that the Fifth Amendment also protects a person's rights to life, liberty, and property. However, since decisions made by public school officials are almost invariably authorized by state statutory and regulatory law, it is the Fourteenth Amendment that applies most often in school settings.

30. A student's interest in life is certainly important, but cases involving governmental deprivation of life are rare in public school settings. See, for example, *Waechter v. School Dist. No. 14-030*, 773 F.Supp. 1005 (W.D. Mich., 1991).

31. Ohio Rev. Code Ann. § 3313.20(A). See also Mo. Rev. Stat. § 171.011; Okla. Stat. tit. 70 § 6-114; and Vt. Stat. Ann. tit. 16 § 1161a.

32. Ohio Rev. Code Ann. § 3313.534.

33. *Soglin v. Kaufman*, 418 F.2d 163 (7th Cir., 1969).

34. Ohio Rev. Code Ann. § 3313.661(A).

35. *Wilson v. South Central Local Sch. Dist.*, 669 N.E.2d 277 (Ohio Ct. App., 1995).

36. For a full discussion on student violence in a technological age, see P. T. K. Daniel and P. D. Pauken, "The Electronic Media and School Violence: Lessons Learned and Issues Presented," *Education Law Report* 164 (2002).

37. See, for example, *Olesen v. Board of Educ.*.

38. See, for example, *Esteban v. Central Mo. State College*, 415 F.2d 1077 (8th Cir., 1969); and *Wiemerslage v. Maine Twp. High Sch. Dist. 207*, 29 F.3d 1149 (7th Cir., 1994).

39. *Wiemerslage v. Maine Township High Sch. Dist. 207*.

40. See, for example, Ohio Rev. Code Ann. § 3313.66(A). Ohio's statute on suspensions is typical of statutory provisions from other states. But readers are encouraged to consult the laws in their jurisdictions.

41. See, for example, Ohio Rev. Code Ann. § 3313.66(B).

42. In Ohio, if a student age 16 or older is convicted of one or more of several certain listed offenses, the superintendent may file for an additional expulsion of

80 days or may file for permanent exclusion from school. Among the listed offenses are homicide, drug-related crimes, and other certain felonies. See Ohio Rev. Code Ann. 3313.66(F).

43. The general due process concerns discussed in this chapter apply to all students, regardless of disability status. However, the Individuals With Disabilities Education Act and the Individuals With Disabilities Education Improvement Act of 2004 outline specific due process rights and procedures for children with disabilities. For a more complete discussion of discipline of children with disabilities, please see the chapter on students with disabilities.

44. *Goss v. Lopez*, 419 U.S. 565 (1975).

45. It is typical for a student's due process rights to be found in compulsory education statutes. But they may also be found in other state statutes, in student codes of conduct, and in other school district policies and practices.

46. *Matthews v. Eldridge*, 424 U.S. 319 (1976).

47. Note that, in some states, the notice must be in writing only. See, for example, Ohio Rev. Code Ann. § 3313.66(A).

48. *Ingraham v. Wright*, 430 U.S. 651 (1977).

49. See, for example, Ohio Rev. Code Ann. § 3319.41.

50. See, for example, Ohio Rev. Code Ann. § 3313.661(A).

51. See, for example, Ohio Rev. Code Ann. § 3313.661(A).

52. *Wiemerslage v. Maine Twp. High Sch. Dist. 207*, 824 F.Supp. 136 (N.D. Ill., 1993), affirmed, 29 F.3d 1149 (7th Cir., 1994).

53. *Pollnow v. Glennon*, 594 F.Supp. 220 (S.D. N.Y., 1984).

54. *Pollnow v. Glennon.*

55. *Giles v. Brookville Area Sch. Dist.*, 669 A.2d 1079 (Pa. Commw. Ct., 1995).

56. *Jenkins v. Louisiana State Bd. of Educ.*, 506 F.2d 992, 1004 (5th Cir., 1975), quoting *Murray v. West Baton Rouge Parish Sch. Bd.*, 472 F.2d 438, 442 (5th Cir., 1973).

57. *Wood v. Strickland*, 420 U.S. 308 (1975). In addition, it is important to recall that plaintiffs often rely on section 1983 of the Civil Rights Act, 42 U.S.C. § 1983, in suits alleging violations of constitutional rights by state actors.

58. *New Jersey v. T.L.O.*, 469 U.S. 325, 339 (1985).

59. *New Jersey v. T.L.O.*

60. *Webb v. McCullough*, 828 F.2d 1151 (6th Cir., 1987). The facts in *Webb* are extremely detailed, partially disputed, and in addition to the search, involve physical altercations between an administrator and a student. Insofar as officials found alcohol in an unoccupied adjacent room, four students were sent home early, with stand-by tickets from Hawaii to Chattanooga, Tennessee, and little money for meals. Substantive and procedural due process complaints followed, along with battery and other intentional tort claims.

61. See also *Desilets v. Clearview Regional Bd. of Educ.*, 627 A.2d 667 (N.J. Super. Ct. App. Div., 1993), upholding an across-the-board search of all students' carry-on luggage.

62. *Thompson v. Carthage Sch. Dist.*, 87 F.3d 979 (8th Cir., 1996).

63. See, for example, *People v. Dukes*, 580 N.Y.S.2d 850 (N.Y. Crim. Ct., 1992); *People v. Pruitt*, 662 N.E.2d 540 (Ill. App. Ct., 1996).

64. See, for example, Ohio Rev. Code Ann. § 3313.20(B).

65. See *Commonwealth v. Carey*, 554 N.E.2d 1199 (Mass., 1990); *Isiah B. v. Wisconsin*, 500 N.W.2d 637 (Wis., 1993); *Zamora v. Pomeroy*, 639 F.2d 662 (10th Cir., 1981). But see *Iowa v. Jones*, 666 N.W.2d 142 (Iowa, 2003), determining that since a student has an expectation of privacy in the contents of his locker, such a search was unreasonable.

66. *Zamora v. Pomeroy*.

67. *Horton v. Goose Creek Independent Sch. Dist.*, 690 F.2d 470 (5th Cir., 1982). A year after *Horton*, in a non-school-related case, the Supreme Court ruled that dog sniffs of personal property are limited in intrusiveness and are not considered searches. See *United States v. Place*, 462 U.S. 696 (1983).

68. See, for example, *Illinois v. Williams*, 791 N.E.2d 608 (2003); and *State v. Slattery*, 787 P.2d 932 (Wash., 1990).

69. See, for example, *Williams v. Ellington*, 936 F.2d 881 (6th Cir., 1991) (upholding a strip search of a female high school student for a vial of an illegal drug); and *Cornfield v. Consolidated High Sch. Dist. No. 230*, 991 F.2d 1316 (7th Cir., 1993) (upholding a fully nude search of a student suspected of "crotching" drugs).

70. See, for example, *State v. Mark Anthony B.*, 433 S.E.2d 41 (W. Va., 1993); and *Oliver v. McClung*, 919 F.Supp. 1206 (N.D. Ind., 1995). But see *Jenkins v. Talladega City Bd. of Educ.*, 95 F.3d 1036 (11th Cir., 1996), vacated rehearing, en banc, 115 F.3d 821 (11th Cir., 1997) (while not fully addressing the strip search of two eight-year-old girls for seven dollars, holding that a teacher and counselor were immune from liability because there was no clearly established law in the jurisdiction declaring strip searches illegal under the circumstances).

71. For a more complete discussion, see David Sperry, Philip T. K. Daniel, Dixie S. Huefner, and E. Gordon Gee, *The Law and Public Schools: A Compendium* (Norwood, Mass.: Christopher-Gordon Publishers, 1998).

72. See *Commonwealth v. Lawrence*, 792 N.E.2d 109 (Mass., 2003).

73. *Vernonia Sch. Dist. 77J v. Acton*, 515 U.S. 646 (1995).

74. *Board of Education of Independent Sch. Dist. No. 92 of Pottawatomie v. Earls*, 536 U.S. 822 (2002).

75. 20 U.S.C. § 1232g.

76. *Owasso Independent Sch. Dist. v. Falvo*, 534 U.S. 426 (2002).

77. *Gonzaga University v. Doe*, 536 U.S. 273 (2002).

78. *P.H. v. Sch. Dist. of Kansas City*, 265 F.3d 653 (8th Cir., 2001).

79. *Flores v. Morgan Hill Unified Sch. Dist.*, 324 F.3d 1130 (9th Cir., 2003), filed under the equal protection clause of the Fourteenth Amendment rather than Title IX.

80. 20 U.S.C. § 1681.

81. *Franklin v. Gwinette County Public Schools*, 503 U.S. 60 (1992).

82. *Gebser v. Lago Vista Independent Sch. Dist.*, 524 U.S. 274 (1998).

83. *Davis v. Monroe County Bd. of Educ.*, 526 U.S. 629 (1999).

84. *Vance v. Spencer County Pub. Sch. Dist.*, 231 F.3d 253 (6th Cir., 2000).

85. *Monteiro v. Tempe Union High Sch. Dist.*, 158 F.3d 1022 (9th Cir., 1998).

11

Special Education and Students With Disabilities

Allan G. Osborne Jr.

In 1975 the U.S. Congress passed landmark legislation, then known as the Education for All Handicapped Children Act, designed to provide the nation's students with disabilities with unprecedented access to educational services. Now known as the Individuals With Disabilities Education Act (IDEA),[1] the law called for school systems to offer each child with disabilities an appropriate education in the least restrictive environment. The law also provided qualified students and their parents with due process rights, including the right to contest school board decisions regarding the provision of a free appropriate public education (FAPE). Consequently, since the enactment of the law in 1975, literally thousands of lawsuits have been filed challenging the actions of school boards.

The IDEA has undergone three major amendments since its original enactment in 1975. Two important amendments, passed in 1986, added clauses to allow parents who prevail in a proceeding against a school board to recover their legal costs as long as certain conditions are met,[2] and to extend the law's protections to children ages three to five.[3] The latter amendment also established grants for states to provide services to infants with disabilities from birth to age three. Another significant amendment, passed in 1990, gave the law its present title while abrogating states' Eleventh Amendment immunity.[4] That amendment also added a requirement for transition planning and introduced the requirement for school boards to provide assistive technology devices and services. Extensive changes to the IDEA came in 1997 when, after much debate, Congress reauthorized the special education law.[5] Among other provisions, the 1997 amendment spelled out elaborate procedures for disciplining special education students and clarified a school board's obligation to provide special education services to students voluntarily enrolled in private schools.

The latest IDEA amendment is entitled the Individuals With Disabilities Education Improvement Act of 2004.[6] The major substantive changes in the IDEA resulting from this reauthorization include the following: new criteria for identifying students as learning disabled; language that will bring the requirements for personnel to be highly qualified in line with the No Child Left Behind Act; expansion of the definition of parent; provisions for paperwork reduction; changes to individualized education program (IEP) requirements; a new statute of limitations for requesting a hearing; and changes to disciplinary provisions.

The IDEA is not the sole law governing the delivery of special education services in the schools. Section 504 of the Rehabilitation Act (section 504)[7] and the Americans With Disabilities Act (ADA)[8] also provide students with disabilities with additional protections. Section 504 prohibits discrimination against individuals with disabilities by recipients of federal funds. The ADA expands section 504's discrimination prohibition to the private sector but includes provisions applicable to public entities. In addition all states currently have laws governing the provision of special education.

Legal disputes between parents and school officials are very costly, and the cost is not just in dollars. Indirect costs in terms of the diversion of resources, the toll it takes on school personnel, and most importantly, the breakdown in the relationship between the parents and the school have a profound impact on the fiscal resources of a school district. The most efficient means of dealing with a legal dispute is to prevent it from occurring in the first place. A careful analysis of the thousands of suits that have arisen since the passage of the IDEA shows that many can be avoided. Many lawsuits, particularly those where the school board is the losing party, can be prevented through better knowledge of special education law.

The purpose of this chapter is to present information on legal issues that are relevant for school business officials. It is impossible in this brief chapter to cover all of the myriad provisions of the IDEA, section 504, and the ADA. Thus, only the major procedural and substantive provisions of these laws will be discussed. The chapter covers issues that, as the ones most related to the day to day provision of special education and related services, have a substantial financial impact on school boards.

FREE APPROPRIATE PUBLIC EDUCATION

The IDEA requires school boards to provide students with disabilities with an appropriate education but provides little guidance in terms of what constitutes appropriate. The IDEA's regulations indicate that an appropriate education consists of special education and related services and is provided in conformance with an IEP.[9] However, a precise definition of the term appropriate cannot be found in either the statute itself or its implementing regulations. Accordingly, one must turn to court decisions for further guidance as to what legally constitutes an appropriate education.

In *Board of Education of the Hendrick Hudson Central School District v. Rowley*,[10] the Supreme Court enunciated a minimal definition of an appropriate education. *Rowley* arose when the parents of a kindergarten student with a hearing impairment contested the school board's denial of their request to provide the child with a sign language interpreter. Lower courts previously ordered the school board to provide the requested interpreter, asserting that an appropriate education was one that allowed the student to achieve at a level commensurate with that of her non-disabled peers. On the other hand, the Supreme Court, seeing that the student was achieving passing marks and advancing from grade to grade without the sign language interpreter, reversed. The high Court maintained that an appropriate education is one that is formulated in conformance with all of the IDEA's procedures and is designed to provide the student with some educational benefit. Inasmuch as the student in *Rowley* was receiving some educational benefit without the sign language interpreter, the Court held that the school board was not required to provide the interpreter even though the student might achieve at a higher level with those services.

Rowley set a minimum standard for what constitutes an appropriate education. Individual states may set higher standards. In fact, courts in North Carolina, New Jersey, Massachusetts, Michigan, Missouri, and California have held that those states have higher standards of appropriateness.[11] In some of these decisions the courts specifically ruled that the higher state standard replaced the federal standard because one of the requirements of the IDEA is that special education programs must meet "the standards of the state educational agency."[12]

Over the years the *Rowley* standard has been refined further. Courts have argued that the *some educational benefit* criteria requires more than just minimal or trivial benefits.[13] Other courts have stated that the educational benefit must be meaningful[14] or appreciable.[15] One court wrote that the gains made by a student must be measurable to meet the *Rowley* criteria.[16] A student's potential should be taken into consideration when determining whether or not an educational benefit is meaningful.[17]

It is unfeasible to offer an exact definition of an appropriate education, since special education and related services must be provided on an individualized basis. What is appropriate for one child may not be appropriate for another, but the courts have given school practitioners, parents, and attorneys some guidelines. *Rowley* stated that a program must confer some meaningful educational benefit. A program is meaningful if it is reasonably expected to result in progress toward the goals and objectives of the student's IEP. Yet, when it comes to questions of methodology, the courts defer to school officials as long as proposed methods are generally accepted in the educational community. Courts have consistently ruled that parents do not have the right to dictate methodology.[18]

LEAST RESTRICTIVE ENVIRONMENT

The IDEA states that a student with disabilities must be educated in the least restrictive environment. The law specifically states that removal of students with disabilities from the general educational setting may occur only when the nature or severity of the disability is such that education in regular classes with the use of supplementary aids and services cannot be achieved satisfactorily.[19] In recent years this provision has spawned a fair amount of debate as a result of the inclusion movement. Inclusion is the practice of educating students with disabilities within the general education environment. Inclusion may be full or partial. In spite of the congressional preference for inclusion, students may be removed from the general education environment, if necessary, to provide specialized services.

In several high-profile cases, federal appeals courts have directed school boards to place students with moderate to severe cognitive disabilities in regular education classes rather than segregated special education classrooms.[20] In these decisions the courts have pointed out that there are several factors that school boards must consider when determining the least restrictive environment for a given student. The Ninth Circuit concisely summarized those factors: the educational benefits of placement in a regular classroom; the nonacademic benefits of such a placement; the effect the student would have on the teacher and other students in the class; and the costs of an inclusionary placement.[21] In applying these factors, courts must perform a balancing act. Some courts have ascertained that it is appropriate to sacrifice a degree of academic benefit for the sake of increased social benefit.[22]

Ingrained in these decisions is the axiom that school boards must make all reasonable efforts to place students with disabilities in an inclusionary setting by providing them with supplementary aids and services to ensure success. But this does not mean that all students with disabilities must be placed in regular education classes. Courts approve segregated settings when the school board is able to demonstrate that the student cannot function in a regular education setting, or will not benefit from placement in such a setting, even with supplementary aids and services. For example, the Ninth Circuit reasoned that an off-campus alternative program was the least restrictive environment for a disruptive and assaultive student because his own behavior prevented him from learning.[23] The court also noted that the student's behavior significantly impaired the education of the other students in the regular education setting. In a separate case, that same court approved a private school placement for a student who had a history of not doing well in regular education programs, after concluding that mainstreaming, which had resulted in total failure for the student, was not appropriate.[24] The bottom line is that an inclusionary placement should be the placement of choice and a segregated placement should be considered only when an inclusionary placement has failed in spite of the school board's best efforts[25] or there is overwhelming evidence that such a placement is not feasible.[26]

PLACEMENTS IN PRIVATE OR RESIDENTIAL SCHOOLS

Irrespective of the IDEA's preference for placing students in the least restrictive environment, such a placement is not feasible for all students. The IDEA requires school boards to offer a continuum of placement alternatives to meet the special education needs of students with disabilities.[27] A private school placement may be required when a school system simply does not have an appropriate placement available. This may occur in situations where the student has a low-incidence type of disability and there are not enough students with the same type of disability within the district to warrant development of a program. Courts recognize that school boards, particularly in smaller districts, cannot afford to develop specialized programs for a small number of students and must look outside the district for placements.

Residential placements may be necessary when the student's disabilities require 24-hour per day programming or consistency between the school and home environments. Usually, students in this situation are those with severe, profound, or multiple disabilities. Residential placements may also be required for students with significant behavior disorders[28] or those who require total immersion in an educational environment to progress.[29]

When a residential placement is required solely for educational reasons, its costs must be fully borne by the school boards, which cannot require parents to contribute toward the placement costs. Conversely, when the placement is needed for other than educational reasons, such as medical or social concerns, the school board is responsible for paying for only the educational component of the residential placement.[30] In these circumstances the school board may enter into a cost-share agreement with other agencies. Even so, a school board can be held responsible for all costs associated with a residential placement if the student's educational, medical, social, and emotional needs are so intimately intertwined that they cannot be treated separately.[31] Thus, it is very important for school boards to seek out other agencies to cost-share residential placements for students whose needs are complex.

EXTENDED SCHOOL YEAR PROGRAMS

When students with disabilities need an educational program that extends beyond the traditional school year, it must be provided. In several early decisions, federal appeals courts decreed that extended school year programs must be an available option, and that a school board's refusal to consider such programs violates the IDEA.[32] An extended school year program is commonly required when a student's regression and the time it takes to recoup lost skills interferes with overall progress toward the attainment of the goals and objectives of the student's IEP.[33] The regression the student suffers must be greater than the regression that normally occurs during a school vacation. When the regression is minimal, an extended school year program is not required.[34]

RELATED SERVICES

The IDEA requires school boards to provide related, or supportive, services to students with disabilities when those services are needed to assist the students in benefiting from their special education programs.[35] The IDEA specifically lists developmental, supportive, or corrective services, such as transportation, speech-language pathology, audiology, interpreting services, psychological services, physical therapy, occupational therapy, recreation (including therapeutic recreation), social-work services, school nurse services, counseling services (including rehabilitation counseling), orientation and mobility services, medical services (for diagnostic or evaluative purposes only), and early identification and assessment as related services.[36] Surgically implanted medical devices are specifically excluded.[37]

The only limitations placed on what could be a related service are that medical services (unless they are specifically for diagnostic or evaluative purposes) and surgically implanted devices are exempted. For that reason the IDEA's list of related services is not exhaustive and could include other services that are needed to help a student with disabilities to benefit from special education. For example, services such as artistic and cultural programs, or art, music, and dance therapy, could be related services. Related services may be provided by persons of varying professional backgrounds with a variety of occupational titles. Although related services are often considered auxiliary services, their importance cannot be minimized. By their very definition, related services are provided to ensure that the student with disabilities benefits from his or her total special education program. Thus, related services can be the critical element that determines whether or not the child will receive a FAPE from a proposed IEP.

Related services must be provided only to students who are receiving special education services. Under the IDEA's definitions, a child is disabled only when the child requires special education and related services.[38] Inasmuch as related services must be provided only when necessary for a child to benefit from special education, a school board is not required to provide related services when the child is not receiving special education.[39] However, it should be noted that many related services qualify as accommodations under section 504 and may need to be provided under that act to students who have disabilities but do qualify for special education under the IDEA.

One of the most controversial topics under the umbrella of related services involves the distinction between medical and school health services. In 1984, in *Irving Independent School District v. Tatro*, the Supreme Court held that a service, such as catheterization that can be performed by a school nurse or trained layperson, is a required related service under the IDEA.[40] Obviously, procedures that, by law, must be performed by a licensed physician would be exempted medical services. Thus, psychiatric therapy would not be a related service because a psychiatrist is a licensed physician. Many students with significant medical needs require round-the-clock nursing services. This type of service falls somewhere on the continuum between school health services and medical services. However, in *Cedar Rapids Community School District v. Garret F.*, the Court further stipulated that full-time nursing services are a required related service, not an exempted medical service.[41]

ASSISTIVE TECHNOLOGY DEVICES AND SERVICES

Another potentially costly service is the provision of assistive technology devices or services. In the 1990 IDEA amendments, definitions of assistive technology devices and services were added. An assistive technology device is any item or piece of equipment that is used to increase, maintain, or improve the functional capabilities of individuals with disabilities.[42] These devices may include commercially available, modified, or customized equipment. However, surgically implanted medical devices are specifically excluded from the definition of an assistive technology device.[13] An assistive technology service is designed to assist an individual in the selection, acquisition, or use of an assistive technology device.[44] It includes an evaluation of the individual's needs, provision of the assistive technology device, training in its use, coordination of other services with assistive technology, and maintenance and repair of the device. These services are required when it is necessary for a child to receive an appropriate education under the *Rowley* standard. They also allow many students with disabilities to benefit from education in less restrictive settings.

DISCIPLINE

Arguably the most controversial legal issue in special education concerns the imposition of disciplinary sanctions on students with disabilities. This is a very delicate issue, as it pits the duty of school administrators to maintain order, discipline, and a safe school environment against a special education student's rights to receive a FAPE in the least restrictive environment. While most will agree that the authority of school officials to maintain discipline should not be frustrated; at the same time a student should not be denied the rights accorded by the IDEA if the student's misconduct is caused by the student's disability.

School officials may impose disciplinary sanctions on special education students as long as they follow procedures that do not deprive the students of their rights. School administrators may use normal disciplinary sanctions, including suspensions, with special education students by following usual procedures and providing customary due process.[45] School administrators do face some restrictions when they want to mete out more drastic punishments, such as an expulsion, or wish to change the student's placement for disciplinary reasons. Basically, in these situations the due process procedures in the IDEA replace the normal due process protections.

A long line of case law ordains that a student with disabilities cannot be expelled for misconduct that is related to the student's disability but can be expelled if there is no relationship between the misconduct and disability.[46] The 2004 IDEA amendments clarify that any misconduct that was caused by or had a direct and substantial relationship to the student's disability establishes the necessary nexus to prohibit an expulsion.[47] Previously, in *Honig v. Doe*,[48] the Supreme Court supported the prohibition of expelling students for disability-related misconduct, but stated that special education students may be suspended for up to 10 days. During that cooling-off period, school personnel may attempt to negotiate an alternative placement with the student's parents. If they are unsuccessful, and can show that the student is truly dangerous, they may obtain a court injunction or administrative order to exclude the student from school.[49] The IDEA requires school officials to conduct a functional behavioral assessment and develop a behavior intervention plan to address the student's misconduct within 10 days of taking disciplinary action.[50]

The 1997 IDEA amendments added a provision to allow school officials to transfer a student who is found in possession of a weapon or drugs to an alternative educational setting for a period of up to 45 days.[51] The 2004 amendments added an additional clause to permit a similar transfer of any student who inflicts serious bodily harm.[52] This may be done even over the objections of a student's parents. The IDEA requires school boards to continue to provide educational services to special education students who have been properly expelled for conduct unrelated to their disabilities.[53]

In an illustrative case involving a student who was prone to impulsive, unpredictable, and aggressive behavior that included biting, hitting, kicking, poking, throwing objects, and overturning furniture, the Eighth Circuit had to balance the right of the student to receive a FAPE against the responsibility of school officials to maintain a safe and orderly environment for all students.[54] In approving the student's removal from her current educational placement, the court stated that removal may occur when the school board can show that a student presents a danger even when all reasonable efforts have been made to minimize the likelihood that the student will injure herself or others.[55]

MEDIATION

Even with a school board's best efforts, legal conflicts will arise. The IDEA requires states to establish procedures to allow parties to resolve disputes via a mediation process.[56] Mediation is voluntary on the part of those involved in the dispute and cannot be used to delay or deny an administrative due process hearing. Mediation is an excellent means of resolving conflicts in a non-adversarial manner.

The most important benefit of mediation is that it can help salvage the relationship between the parent and school officials. However, for mediation to be successful, each party must be willing to compromise. School officials must be willing to listen to any reasonable proposals advanced by the parents and should be prepared to make counter-proposals.

ADMINISTRATIVE DUE PROCESS HEARINGS

Under the IDEA, states must establish a means for an impartial due process hearing for the resolution of disputes between the parents and the school board.[57] States are free to establish either a one- or two-tiered system of administrative due process hearings. In a one-tiered system, the hearing is provided by the state. In a two-tiered system, the initial hearing is provided at the local level with provision for an appeal at the state level. A hearing may be held for any matter related to the provision of a FAPE.

Which party, the school board or parents, bears the burden of proof in an administrative due process hearing is unsettled. Several courts have ruled that the school board bears the burden of showing that its IEP and recommended placement are appropriate.[58] However, other courts have held that the party challenging the IEP, generally the parents, must bear the burden of proof.[59] The issue is important because, in a close case, the determination of which party must bear the burden of proof may very well affect which party is victorious. At this writing, the issue is before the Supreme Court.[60]

COURT ACTION

The IDEA gives the losing party in an administrative hearing the right to bring a civil action in any federal or state court of competent jurisdiction.[61] The courts are empowered to grant whatever relief they determine is appropriate. When a dispute reaches the court level, the court will receive and review the administrative record; however, the parties, with the court's permission, may be allowed to present additional evidence. The courts have placed some limitation on what additional evidence is acceptable. Generally, courts will not hear evidence that could have been introduced at the administrative level but was not.[62] On the other hand, new evidence, or evidence that was not available previously, will be admitted.[63]

Which party bears the burden of proof at the court level varies according to jurisdiction and the particular circumstances of the case. For example, some jurisdictions require the party challenging the administrative decision to bear the burden of proof.[64] However, in many situations the burden may be on the school board to prove, by a preponderance of the evidence, that its proposed IEP is appropriate.[65] Yet other courts place the burden of proof on the party seeking a change in the IEP.[66]

DAMAGES

To date there has not been a successful lawsuit for educational malpractice in special education. Thus far, courts have not imposed punitive damages on school officials for failing to provide a FAPE. Similarly, general damages awards for "pain and suffering" have not been prevalent. However, recent litigation indicates that this could change. In several recent lawsuits, courts have indicated that monetary damages may be available under other statutes, such as section 504[67] or section 1983 of the Civil Rights Act of 1871,[68] if the parents can show that school officials intentionally discriminated against the student, egregiously disregarded the student's rights, or violated the IDEA.[69] The operative word here is *intentional*. If school officials act in good faith, but their efforts fall short of the statutory requirements, they will be immune from damages.

TUITION REIMBURSEMENT

Often parents who are dissatisfied with the school board's educational placement unilaterally enroll their child in a private school and later seek to recover tuition expenses. The Supreme Court, in *Burlington School Committee v. Department of Education, Commonwealth of Massachusetts*, said that parents are entitled to tuition reimbursement if they can show that the school board failed to offer an appropriate placement and that their chosen placement is appropriate.[70] The Court reasoned that a reimbursement award simply requires the school board to retroactively pay the costs it should have been paying all along. Subsequently, in *Florence County School District Four v. Carter*,[71] the Court added that parents can also be awarded tuition reimbursement even when their chosen placement is not in a state-approved facility as long as it provides an otherwise appropriate education. Conversely, when parents make unilateral placements, they do so at their own financial risk because they are not entitled to be reimbursed if the school board can show that it offered, and can provide, an appropriate educational placement. In order for parents to be reimbursed, they must provide the school board with proper notice of their dissatisfaction with the IEP.[72]

Parents may also be reimbursed for unilaterally obtained related services if they can show that the school board failed to provide the needed services. For example, courts have frequently ordered school boards to reimburse parents for the costs of counseling or psychotherapy after the parents succeeded in showing that these services were necessary for the child to benefit from special education.[73]

COMPENSATORY SERVICES

A tuition reimbursement award is granted only when a parent incurs the expenses of privately obtaining alternate educational services for the child. It is of little use to parents who are unable to obtain such services because they cannot afford to pay the costs up front. When parents cannot afford to take the financial risk of making a unilateral placement, their child may remain in an inappropriate placement for some time while the dispute winds its way through administrative due process hearings and judicial proceedings. Under these circumstances, a court may award additional educational services along with prospective relief to compensate the child for the loss of appropriate educational services. Compensatory services are provided during a time period when the student would not normally receive services, such as during the summer months or after the student's eligibility for services has ended.

When determining whether an award of compensatory educational services is justified, most courts apply a rationale similar to that used in tuition reimbursement cases. Several courts have said that compensatory services, like reimbursement, simply compensate the student for the school board's failure to provide an appropriate placement. The logic behind compensatory educational services awards is that an appropriate remedy should not be available only to those students whose parents can afford to provide them with an alternate educational placement while litigation is pending.[74] Compensatory services normally are provided for a time period equal to the time the student was denied services.[75] Services may be granted even after the student has passed the ceiling age for eligibility under the IDEA.[76]

As is the case with tuition reimbursement, awards of compensatory educational services are granted only when it has been determined that the school board failed to provide an appropriate placement.[77]

ATTORNEYS' FEES

The costs of litigation can be very high, for parents as well as school boards. Many parents, after successfully bringing a lawsuit against the school board, believe that they should be reimbursed for their legal expenses. From the parents' point of view, they achieve a hollow victory when they prevail in their dispute with the school board but are left with burdensome legal bills. Congress agreed and amended the IDEA in 1986 with the Handicapped Children's Protection Act (HCPA).[78] This amendment now gives courts the power to grant an award of reasonable attorneys' fees to parents who prevail against the school board in any action or proceeding brought pursuant to the IDEA. An award is to be based on the prevailing rates in the community in which the case arises. Under the HCPA, the courts may determine what is a reasonable amount of time an attorney should have spent preparing and arguing the case in terms of the issues litigated. The award may be limited if the school board makes a settlement offer more than 10 days before the proceedings began that is equal to or more favorable than the final relief obtained. A court may reduce a fee award if it finds that the parents unreasonably protracted the dispute,[79] the attorney's billed hourly rate is excessive,[80] or the time billed and legal services furnished are excessive in light of the issues litigated.[81]

The Supreme Court's decision in a 2002 non-education case, *Buckhannon Board and Care Home v. West Virginia Department of Health and Human Resources*,[82] generated a new line of attorneys' fees litigation under the IDEA. In *Buckhannon* the Court struck down the catalyst theory as a means for recovering attorneys' fees by holding that to be reimbursed for legal expenses a plaintiff must either receive an enforceable judgment on the merits or a court-ordered consent decree. Many courts have applied *Buckhannon* to IDEA suits to deny fees to parents who have settled their disputes with school boards via settlement agreements.[83]

ANTI-DISCRIMINATION LAWS

As noted, in addition to the IDEA, students with disabilities have rights under, and are protected by, two other significant pieces of federal legislation. The first, section 504 of the Rehabilitation Act, provides that "No otherwise qualified individual with a disability . . . shall, solely by reason of her or his disability, be excluded from participation in, be denied the benefits of, or be subjected to discrimination under any program or activity receiving Federal financial assistance."[84] The second law, the ADA, was passed in 1990 to provide "a comprehensive national mandate for the elimination of discrimination against individuals with disabilities."[85] It effectively extends the protections of section 504 to the private sector but has implications for public entities, such as schools.

Although most students with disabilities are covered by the IDEA, section 504, and the ADA, some may be protected only by the latter two statutes. Inasmuch as a student must require special education services to fall under the auspices of the IDEA, a student with disabilities who does not need special education services would be protected only by section 504 and the ADA. One court has held that section 504 does not require affirmative efforts to overcome the student's disability but only prohibits discrimination on the basis of the disability.[86]

Section 504 and the ADA both require school boards to provide reasonable accommodations to students with disabilities. This may involve modest accommodations, such as allowing the student to be accompanied in school by a service dog[87] or providing basic health services that would allow a medically fragile student to be present in the classroom.[88] Accommodations that are unduly costly, create an excessive monitoring burden, expose others to excessive risk, or fundamentally alter the nature of a program generally are not required.[89]

CONCLUSION

Federal laws guaranteeing students with disabilities a FAPE and prohibiting discrimination on the basis of the disability have provided these students with unprecedented access to the public schools. Implementing these

laws has not been without controversy, however. As a result of disputes between parents and school board officials, thousands of lawsuits have been
filed in the past two decades, making this one of the most explosive areas
of school law.

Litigation is costly, not only in terms of dollars, but also in the expenditure of human capital. It is far better to devote available resources to the
education of children than to litigation. School officials who understand
the law are in a much better position to make legally correct decisions and
thus avoid costly litigation. In this respect, there is no substitute for adequate legal and procedural training of those involved in the special education process. In the long run, the cost of this training will result in much
greater savings.

NOTES

1. 20 U.S.C. § 1400 et seq. Each reauthorization replaces the former version
in the United States Code, sometimes requiring a reordering and renumbering of
sections. The latest version, the Individuals With Disabilities Education Improvement Act of 2004, has an effective date of July 1, 2005, for most of its provisions. Since the reauthorization has yet to be codified, the codification of the
1997 reauthorization is used for all citations in this chapter. However, to provide
the most up-to-date citations at this writing, section numbers of the 2004 statute
follow in brackets.

2. The Handicapped Children's Protection Act of 1986, P.L. 99-372, 100 Stat.
796 (1986).

3. The Education of the Handicapped Amendments of 1986, P.L. 99-457, 100
Stat. 1145 (1986).

4. The Individuals With Disabilities Education Act of 1990, P.L. 101-476,
104 Stat. 1103 (1990).

5. The Individuals With Disabilities Education Act Amendments of 1997,
P.L. 105-17, 111 Stat. 37 (1997).

6. P.L. 108-446, 118 Stat. 2647 (2004). [Hereinafter cited as IDEIA 2004.]

7. 29 U.S.C. § 794.

8. 42 U.S.C. § 12101 et seq.

9. 34 C.F.R. § 300.13.

10. *Board of Educ. of the Hendrick Hudson Central Sch. Dist. v. Rowley*, 458
U.S. 176 (1982).

11. Allan Osborne and Charles Russo, *Special Education and the Law* (Thousand Oaks, Calif.: Corwin, 2003).

12. 20 U.S.C. § 1401(8)(B). [IDEIA 2004 § 602(9)(B)].

13. *Carter v. Florence County Sch. Dist. Four,* 950 F.2d 156 (4th Cir., 1991), affirmed on other grounds sub nom. *Florence County Sch. Dist. Four v. Carter,* 510 U.S. 7 (1993); *Hall v. Vance County Bd. of Educ.,* 774 F.2d 629 (4th Cir., 1985).

14. *Polk v. Susquehanna Intermediate Unit 16,* 853 F.2d 171 (3d Cir., 1988); *Bd. of Educ. of East Windsor Regional Sch. Dist. v. Diamond,* 808 F.2d 987 (3d Cir., 1986).

15. *Chris C. v. Gwinnett County Sch. Dist.,* 780 F.Supp. 804 (N.D. Ga., 1991).

16. *J.S.K. v. Hendry County Sch. Bd.,* 941 F.2d 1563 (11th Cir. 1991).

17. *Deal ex rel. Deal v. Hamilton County Dep't of Educ.,* 392 F.3d 840 (6th Cir., 2004).

18. See for example, *Watson ex rel. Watson v. Kingston City Sch. Dist.,* 325 F.Supp.2d 141 (N.D. N.Y., 2004); *Johnson ex rel. Johnson v. Olathe Dist. Schs. Unified Sch. Dist. No. 233,* 316 F.Supp.2d 960 (D. Kan., 2003); *J.P. ex rel. Popson v. West Clark Community Schs.,* 230 F.Supp.2d 910 (S.D. Ind., 2002).

19. 20 U.S.C. § 1412(a)(5).

20. See, for example, *L.B. and J.B. ex rel. K.B. v. Nebo Sch. Dist.,* 379 F.3d 966 (10th Cir., 2004); *Sacramento City Unified Sch. Dist. Bd. of Educ. v. Rachel H.,* 14 F.3d 1398 (9th Cir., 1994); *Oberti v. Bd. of Educ. of the Borough of Clementon Sch. Dist.,* 995 F.2d 1204 (3d Cir., 1993).

21. Id. *Sacramento City Unified Sch. Dist. Bd. of Educ. v. Rachel H.*

22. Allan Osborne and Philip DiMattia, "The IDEA's Least Restrictive Environment Mandate: Legal Implications," *Exceptional Children* 61 (1994).

23. *Clyde K. v. Puyallup Sch. Dist. No. 3,* 35 F.3d 1396 (9th Cir., 1994).

24. *Capistrano Unified Sch. Dist. v. Wartenberg,* 59 F.3d 884 (9th Cir., 1995).

25. *Bd. of Educ. of Frederick County v. I.S. by Summers,* 325 F. Supp.2d 565 (D. Md., 2004).

26. *Sch. Dist. of Wisconsin Dells v. Z.S.,* 184 F.Supp.2d 860 (W.D. Wis., 2001); *Doe v. Arlington County Sch. Bd.,* 41 F.Supp.2d 599 (E.D. Va., 1999).

27. 34 C.F.R. § 300.551(a).

28. *S.C. ex rel. C.C. v. Deptford Township Bd. of Educ.,* 248 F.Supp.2d 368 (D. N.J., 2003); *Indep. Sch. Dist. No. 284 v. A.C.,* 258 F.3d 769 (8th Cir., 2001).

29. *Mohawk Trail Regional Sch. Dist. v. Shawn D.,* 35 F.Supp.2d 34 (D. Mass., 1999).

30. *State of Wisconsin v. Randall H.,* 653 N.W.2d 503 (Wis., 2002); *McKenzie v. Jefferson,* 1983 EHLR 554:338 (D.D.C., 1983).

31. *North v. District of Columbia Bd. of Educ.*, 471 F.Supp. 136 (D.D.C., 1979).

32. Osborne and Russo, *Special Education and the Law*.

33. *M. M. v. Sch. Dist. of Greenville County*, 303 F.3d 523 (4th Cir., 2002); *Armstrong v. Kline*, 476 F.Supp. 583 (E.D. Pa., 1979), rem'd sub nom. *Battle v. Commonwealth of Pennsylvania*, 629 F.2d 269 (3d Cir., 1980), on rem'd 513 F.Supp. 425 (E.D. Pa., 1981).

34. *Kenton County Sch. Dist. v. Hunt*, 384 F.3d 269 (6th Cir., 2004); *Todd v. Duneland Sch. Corp.*, 299 F.3d 899 (7th Cir., 2002); *Anderson v. Thompson*, 658 F.2d 1205 (7th Cir., 1981).

35. 20 U.S.C. § 1401(22). [IDEIA 2004 § 602(26)].

36. IDEIA 2004 § 602(26)(A).

37. IDEIA 2004 § 602(26)(B).

38. 20 U.S.C. § 1401(3)(A)(ii). [IDEIA 2004 § 602(3)(A)(ii)].

39. *Irving Indep. Sch. Dist. v. Tatro*, 468 U.S. 883 (1984).

40. *Irving Indep. Sch. Dist. v. Tatro*.

41. *Cedar Rapids Community Sch. Dist. v. Garret F.*, 526 U.S. 66 (1999). For an in-depth discussion of this opinion, see Allan Osborne, "Supreme Court Rules That Schools Must Provide Full-time Nursing Services for Medically Fragile Students," *Education Law Report* 136 (1999).

42. 20 U.S.C. § 1401(1). [IDEIA 2004 § 602(1)(A)].

43. IDEIA 2004 § 602(1)(B).

44. 20 U.S.C. § 1401(2). [IDEIA 2004 § 602(2)].

45. *Goss v. Lopez*, 419 U.S. 565 (1975). IDEIA 2004 § 615(k)(1)(B) also provides explicit authority for the removal of a student with disabilities for up to 10 school days.

46. Allan Osborne, *Disciplinary Options for Students With Disabilities* (Dayton, Ohio: Education Law Association, 1997).

47. IDEIA 2004 § 615(k)(1)(E)(i).

48. *Honig v. Doe*, 484 U.S. 305 (1988).

49. 20 U.S.C. § 1415(k)(2). [IDEIA 2004 § 615(k)(3)(B)].

50. 20 U.S.C. § 1415(k)(1)(B). [IDEIA 2004 § (k)(1)(F)].

51. 20 U.S.C. § 1415(k)(1)(A). [IDEIA 2004 § 615(K)(1)(G)].

52. IDEIA 2004 § 615(k)(1)(G)(iii).

53. 20 U.S.C. § 1412(a)(1)(A). [IDEIA 2004 § 612(a)(1)(A)].

54. *Light v. Parkway C-2 Sch. Dist.*, 41 F.3d 1223 (8th Cir., 1994).

55. See also *Roslyn Union Free Sch. Dist. v. Geffrey W.*, 740 N.Y.S.2d 451 (N.Y. App. Div., 2002).

56. 20 U.S.C. § 1415(e). [IDEIA 2004 § 615(e)].

57. 20 U.S.C. § 1415(f). [IDEIA 2004 § 615(f)(1)(A)].

58. See, for example, *Walczak v. Florida Union Free Sch. Dist.*, 142 F.3d 119 (2d Cir., 1998).

59. See, for example, *Cordrey v. Euckert*, 917 F.2d 1460 (6th Cir., 1990).

60. *Schaffer v. Weast*, 2005 WL 405756 (U.S.).

61. 20 U.S.C. § 1415(i)(2). [IDEIA 2004 § 615(i)(2)].

62. *Board of Educ. of Paxton-Buckley-Loda Unit Sch. Dist. No. 10 v. Jeff S.*, 184 F.Supp.2d 790 (C.D. Ill., 2002).

63. *Konkel v. Elmbrook Sch. Dist.*, 348 F.Supp.2d 1018 (E.D. Wis., 2004).

64. See for example, *Dong v. Bd. of Educ.*, 197 F.3d 793 (6th Cir., 1999).

65. See for example, *Oberti v. Bd. of Educ. of the Borough of Clementon Sch. Dist.*, 995 F.2d 1204 (3d Cir., 1993).

66. *Elida Local Sch. Dist. Bd. of Educ. v. Erickson*, 252 F.Supp.2d 476 (N.D. Ohio, 2003).

67. 29 U.S.C. § 794.

68. 42 U.S.C. § 1983.

69. See for example *Walker v. District of Columbia*, 969 F.Supp. 794 (D.D.C., 1997); *Whitehead v. Sch. Bd. for Hillsborough County*, 918 F.Supp. 1515 (M.D. Fla., 1996); *W.B. v. Matula*, 67 F.3d 484 (3d Cir., 1995).

70. *Burlington Sch. Comm. v. Dep't of Educ., Commonwealth of Massachusetts*, 471 U.S. 359 (1985).

71. *Florence County Sch. Dist. Four v. Carter*, 510 U.S. 7 (1993).

72. 20 U.S.C. § 1412(a)(10(C)(iii). [IDEIA 2004 § 612(a)(10)(C)(iii)]. See also *Schoenback v. District of Columbia*, 308 F.Supp.2d 71 (D.D.C., 2004).

73. *Straube v. Florida Union Free Sch. Dist.*, 801 F.Supp. 1164 (S.D. N.Y., 1992); *Gary A. v. New Trier High Sch. Dist. No. 203*, 796 F.2d 940 (7th Cir., 1986).

74. *Manchester Sch. Dist. v. Christopher B.*, 807 F.Supp. 860 (D. N.H., 1992); *Todd D. v. Andrews*, 933 F.2d 1576 (11th Cir., 1991); *Lester H. v. Gilhool*, 916 F.2d 865 (3d Cir., 1990).

75. See, for example, *Valerie J. v. Derry Coop. Sch. Dist.*, 771 F.Supp. 483 (D. N.H., 1991).

76. *Pihl v. Massachusetts Dep't of Educ.*, 9 F.3d 184 (1st Cir., 1993).

77. For a recent case, see *Diatta v. District of Columbia*, 319 F.Supp.2d 57 (D.D.C., 2004).

78. P.L. 99-372, 100 Stat. 796 (1986). [IDEIA 2004 § 615(i)(3)].

79. *Howie v. Tippecanoe Sch. Corp.*,734 F.Supp. 1485 (N.D. Ind., 1990).

80. *Beard v. Teska*, 31 F.3d 942 (10th Cir., 1994).

81. *Hall v. Detroit Pub. Schs.*, 823 F.Supp. 1377 (E.D. Mich., 1993).

82. *Buckhannon Board and Care Home v. West Virginia Department of Health and Human Resources*, 532 U.S. 598 (2001).

83. See *Doe v. Boston*, 358 F.3d 20 (1st Cir. 2004); *T.D. v. LaGrange Sch. Dist. No. 102*, 349 F.3d 469 (7th Cir., 2003). But see *Noyes v. Grossmont Union High Sch. Dist.*, 331 F.Supp.2d 1233 (S.D. Cal., 2004).

84. 29 U.S.C. § 794.

85. 42 U.S.C. § 12101(b)(2).

86. *Lyons v. Smith*, 829 F.Supp. 414 (D.D.C., 1993).

87. *Sullivan v. Vallejo City Unified Sch. Dist.*, 731 F.Supp. 947 (E.D. Cal., 1990).

88. *Irving Indep. Sch. Dist. v. Tatro*, 468 U.S. (1984).

89. *Eva N. v. Brock*, 741 F.Supp. 626 (E.D. Ky., 1990); *Kohl v. Woodhaven Learning Center*, 865 F.2d 930 (8th Cir., 1989).

12

Religion in Public Schools

Ralph D. Mawdsley

During the past 20 years, the Supreme Court has decided far more cases involving religion in schools than any other area. School business officials, like other administrative personnel in pubic education, need to be aware of the changing and emerging legal status of the law. This chapter acquaints business officials with key areas of concern and how courts have addressed questions involving religion in the schools.

RIGHTS OF PARENTS TO MAKE DECISIONS FOR THEIR CHILDREN

The earliest Supreme Court cases involving religious issues and public schools, *Myers v. Nebraska*[1] and *Pierce v. Society of Sisters*,[2] addressed the rights of parents to make educational decisions for their children. In both cases, the Court invalidated post–World War I state statutes that exerted considerable control over non-public schools by criminalizing the teaching of subjects in a language other than English (*Myers*) and prohibiting student attendance at other than public schools (*Pierce*). In both cases the Court injected into the national legal vocabulary the notion that parents had the right to make choices for their children. Under the liberty clause of the Fourteenth Amendment, the Court twice ruled that the parental right to direct the education of their children superseded that of state legislatures to prohibit non-public schools from carrying out their religious missions. The Court thus held in *Myers* that charging a teacher in Nebraska who read the Bible in German with a crime interfered with parents' right to choose a school where religion is taught. Likewise, prohibiting the existence of all non-public (including religious) schools in *Pierce* prevented parents in Oregon from having a choice of a school where their children could be taught.

Pierce is probably best known for the often quoted comment: "The child is not the mere creature of the state; those who nurture him and direct his destiny have the right, coupled with the high duty, to recognize and prepare him for additional obligations."[3] However, the *Pierce* Court also observed: "No question is raised concerning the power of the state reasonably to regulate all schools, to inspect, supervise and examine them, their teachers and pupils; to require that all children of proper age attend some school, that teachers shall be of good moral character and patriotic disposition, that certain studies plainly essential to good citizenship must be taught, and that nothing be taught which is manifestly inimical to the public welfare."[4]

These two cases, especially *Pierce*, are extraordinary by today's standards. After *Pierce*, the emphasis shifted from legislating non-public schools out of existence to regulating them. Forty-seven years after *Pierce*, in *Yoder v. Wisconsin*,[5] the Court considered whether Wisconsin's compulsory attendance law that required all children to attend school until age 16 could be applied to the Amish, whose children attended school through eighth grade but refused to attend public high schools. In a remarkable case, the Court found that applying the compulsory attendance law to the Amish violated both the liberty clause's right of parents to make educational choices for their children and the First Amendment's protection of free exercise of religion. The Court engaged in a lengthy discussion of the Amish approach to education that included eight years of formal education and additional years of vocational training on their farms. Insofar as the only choice for Amish parents, if they were required to follow Wisconsin's mechanical enforcement of its 16-year-old compulsory attendance regulation, was to send their children to public high schools, the Court reasoned that large numbers of children would likely leave the Amish farms, thus destroying 300 years of religious tradition. The most important outcome of *Yoder* was its tripartite, burden-shifting test under the free exercise clause: education in a religious school must be based on a sincerely held religious conviction; the state's regulation substantially burdens those religious convictions; and if a parent/school has produced evidence of the first two, then a state then must demonstrate a compelling interest to justify the burden to religious beliefs.

Yoder did not produce any immediate dramatic changes in state regulation of non-public (especially religious) schools. Beginning in the 1970s and 1980s, many churches started religious schools and claimed *Yoder* as a precedent for not adhering to state regulations, such as required state approval, curriculum requirements, and teacher certification. However, courts generally limited *Yoder* only to Amish educational settings, thereby upholding state regulations under a reasonableness test.[6] In 1990, the Court further limited the effectiveness of the free exercise clause by holding in a non-education case, *Employment Division v. State*,[7] that free exercise could no longer be a defense to neutral, generally applicable laws/regulations.

By the 1990s, though, the rapid increase in religious schools, and especially home schooling, led to political solutions by state legislatures for the conflicts between these schools and state regulators. In many cases, objected-to regulations such as teacher certification requirements were eliminated.[8]

Although free exercise has been relegated to a lesser role with regard to religious claims, free exercise in conjunction with the right to direct the education of one's children still has vitality in two important areas: requests by students in non-public schools and home schools to participate in public school academic courses or extra-curricular activities, and adverse employment actions involving public school personnel who send their children to religious schools. Generally, non-public and home schooled student requests to take public school courses have been successful only where state law permits dual enrollment so that public school districts receive partial state subsidy and where the schools have room in the courses.[9]

Requests to participate in extra-curricular activities are more complicated because public schools must conform to state athletic association rules that, generally, prohibit non-public school participation in public school activities. Courts usually have found little reason to interfere in athletic association rules because these activities are only extra-curricular in nature.[10] Yet courts have responded vigorously to adverse employment actions against public school personnel who have their children in religious

schools. In *Barrow v. Greenville Independent School District*,[11] the Fifth
Circuit held that a teacher in Texas whose superintendent denied her a job
as an assistant principal because she enrolled her children in a private
school had a claim against the superintendent for violating her right to educate her children in a private school. Similarly, in *Barrett v. Steubenville
City Schools*,[12] the Sixth Circuit affirmed that since a superintendent in
Ohio repeatedly denied an elementary teacher a job because his child attended a religious school, the teacher was entitled to a trial as to whether
this action violated his liberty clause right to rear his child. Both courts
found the law so well established regarding parent choice of the venue for
their children's education that the superintendents were denied qualified
immunity for their actions in denying the positions.[13]

ACCESS BY COMMUNITY GROUPS TO PUBLIC SCHOOLS

Public school boards are not required to open their facilities for community organizations. However, once boards open their schools to groups,
they create what is known as a limited public forum under the free speech
clause. A limited public forum means that officials can designate not only
the uses of their facilities but also which organizations can use the facilities. However, this designation applies only as long as it does not violate
the federal Constitution. To the extent that designations are based on the
viewpoints of organizations, the free speech clause is invoked. Over the
past 12 years, the Supreme Court has rendered two important judgments
balancing the rights of boards to control access to their facilities by community organization and the rights of the organizations to not be discriminated against due to their religious viewpoints.

   In the landmark case *Lamb's Chapel v. Center Moriches Union Free
School District*,[14] the Supreme Court protected, under the free speech
clause, a church in New York's after-school access to a public school au-
ditorium for the purpose of showing a religious film series.[15] The film series in this case involved a Christian approach to child rearing and family
values.[16] Evidence revealed that the board permitted a variety of other
uses that touched on child rearing, among which were a lecture by a psychologist, a New Age religious group, and various scout groups. In a
unanimous decision, the Court reasoned that once the board permitted

secular views of a subject (in this case, child rearing and family values), its refusal to permit a religious perspective constituted impermissible viewpoint discrimination under the free speech clause. Having determined that the church's access was protected under the free speech clause, the Court explained that the board was not permitted, under the establishment clause, to separate itself from all religious uses. The Court observed that the group's presence could not be reasonably interpreted as endorsing religion in violation of the establishment clause[17] since the meetings occurred in the evenings between 7 and 10 p.m.[18]

Lamb's Chapel addressed a set of facts that presented little risk of an inappropriate connection between the school and the religious beliefs of the church. The film series occurred in the evenings when pupils who attended the school were not likely to be present.[19] However, what if a community religious organization requested the right to meet in an elementary school building immediately after school?

Eight years after *Lamb's Chapel*, in *Good News Club v. Milford Central Schools*,[20] a divided Court[21] ruled that an evangelical organization, a Good News Club, could use elementary school facilities in New York immediately after school. As in *Lamb's Chapel*, the Court found that school officials permitted secular groups such as the Girl and Boy Scouts and 4-H[22] to meet immediately after school in the building. In ordering officials to permit the Good News Club to meet after school, the Court held that the Scouts, 4-H Club, and Good News Club all shared a common subject matter, namely character and moral development. According to the Court, to deny the Good News Club the opportunity to present its religious viewpoint regarding that subject matter constituted impermissible viewpoint discrimination under the free speech clause. Worth noting though is that, although the Good News Club had the same right of access as other youth groups, elementary students were permitted to attend the religious club only if they had signed parental consent forms. In essence, parent permission became a kind of circuit breaker to negate the claim that public school personnel might influence children to participate in the religious club in violation of the establishment clause.

The free speech clause prohibits other kinds of discrimination against religious uses. In *Bronx Household of Faith v. Board of Education of City of New York*,[23] a church in New York sued to be permitted to rent school facilities on Sunday for its worship services. In reversing an earlier judgment against the church, the Second Circuit followed the reasoning in *Good News*. Insofar as the board opened its facilities to "the teaching of moral values" by permitting scout meetings in its buildings, the court held that even a "quintessentially religious" use that included "prayer, the singing of Christian songs, and communion" could not be prohibited.[24] Similar to the rationale in *Lamb's Chapel*, the court decided that the church services presented no establishment clause problems where they took place on Sunday mornings when schoolchildren and employees would be present.[25] Yet, as part of its establishment clause analysis, the court also cautioned that the school employees and students could not attend the services. Thus, the court injected some uncertainty as to whether attendance at the church services by students or employees might have altered its establishment clause analysis.

In terms of charging rental rates for use of school facilities, school boards cannot discriminate against religious users. In *Fairfax Covenant Church v. Fairfax County School Board*,[26] the Fourth Circuit invalidated a Virginia school board's ordinance that provided: "Churches/religious organizations servicing Fairfax County citizens may be granted use of a school for as many as five years. . . . Church/religious groups may be authorized the usage after five years of use at increasing rental rates until the full commercial rates become effective in the ninth year of use."[27] The court maintained that the board lacked a compelling interest in setting differential rates for school property so that churches paid more than nonreligious groups. The board had thought that extended religious use of its facilities could have been characterized as "domination" as suggested in dicta in *Widmar v. Vincent*,[28] wherein the Court implied an establishment clause violation where a religious group comes to dominate a forum. In *Fairfax Covenant*, the circuit court could not discover any support for the notion that low rates and extended use by churches would create such religious domination. Thus, absent neutral, generally applicable rules that limit uses of school facilities, school boards cannot prohibit long-term use by religious groups.

Other kinds of access issues have emerged involving community members and use of school premises. In *Daugherty v. Vanguard Charter School Academy*,[29] a federal trial court in Michigan upheld a Moms Prayer Group to use the Parents' Room for 90 minutes once a week where other parent groups were permitted to use the room. In addition, the court found no establishment clause violation in the school's policy of sending religious literature home with students at the end of the school day along with non-religious materials.

A number of federal courts have prohibited public schools from permitting community groups to insert religious materials in materials distributed to students at the end of the school day. The Sixth Circuit, in *Rusk v. Clearview Local Schools*,[30] upheld a school board policy that required teachers to include religious materials in packets distributed to students at the end of the school day where non-religious materials were permitted. The court determined not only that sending religious materials home did not send a message favoring religion in violation of the establishment clause, but that refusal to send home the religious materials might cause students to "conclude that the school disapproves religion."[31] Other federal circuit courts reached similar results to *Rusk* and required that, if schools send home the materials of secular community organizations, they cannot refuse to send home the materials of religious organizations.[32]

The message from the discussion above is that school boards cannot choose to treat community religious groups or materials differently from their secular counterparts. At the same time, boards can restrict religious uses as long as they do so by means of neutral, generally applicable rules. The most obvious neutral rule would be prohibiting all community use of school buildings, although such a draconian measure would not do much to generate community support for public schools. Short of closing school facilities to all community uses, boards can create neutral rules that apply to all community groups. For example, boards could limit the number of times a community group can use school facilities per month or per year. School boards could also require all uses on a first come, first serve basis or limit community use only to certain school buildings. What boards cannot do is single out religious uses for different treatment.

A new genre of cases has developed relying on school boards' control over curriculum to justify restriction of religious expression. In *Bannon v. School District of Palm Beach County*,[33] the Eleventh Circuit addressed a Florida principal's policy of permitting students, as part of a beautification project, to decorate temporary panels located in the school while long-term renovations occurred. After a student representing a religious club was given permission to paint messages on the panels, the principal expressed surprise that the message conveyed was religious in nature and directed that certain religious words be painted over. The principal likened the religious words to "profanity, gang symbols, and satanic symbols" that he had removed from other panels. In upholding the principal's action and denying the student's free speech claim, the court determined that the beautification project constituted school-sponsored speech and fell within school board control over curriculum under *Hazelwood School District v. Kuhlmeier*.[34] In *Hazelwood*, the Supreme Court held that school officials needed only a reasonable basis for restricting student expression in matters relating to school curriculum and upheld a school principal's decision to excise two pages from a school newspaper prepared as part of a journalism course. In *Bannon*, the court decided that since the panels were a curricular activity and school sponsored, the principal's reasonable concern about student reaction to the religious messages on them represented a reasonable basis for requiring their deletion.

Similarly, in *Fleming v. Jefferson County School District R-1*,[35] the Tenth Circuit held that a tile painting and installation project that was established by the school board as part of reconstruction of the school after the multiple fatal shootings at Columbine High School was school-sponsored speech over which officials could exercise editorial control. As a result, the court permitted officials to remove tiles with religious messages, in effect upholding guidelines established by them and communicated to plaintiffs before their tiles were painted with religious symbols and messages, namely that there could be no references to the attack, to the date of the attack, April 20, 1999, or 4/20/99, no names or initials of students, no Columbine ribbons, no religious symbols, and nothing obscene or offensive.

PRAYER AT SCHOOL EVENTS

Following World War II, a number of religious practices in public schools came under assault from the Supreme Court. In 1948 the Court, in *McCollum v. Board of Education*,[36] found in violation of the establishment clause an Illinois school board practice of permitting clergy on school premises during the school day to provide religious instruction to students who had parental consent. Yet four years later, the Court, in *Zorach v. Clauson*,[37] upheld a public release-time program that permitted students in New York to be excused from the public school to attend religious classes off campus.

In 1962, in *Engle v. Vitale*,[38] the Court invalidated a state-created prayer that was recited in public schools in New York. The following year, in *School District of Abington Township v. Schemmp*,[39] the Court struck down the practice of Bible reading over school intercoms in Maryland and Pennsylvania involving verses from the King James Bible. In 1968 in *Epperson v. Arkansas*,[40] the Court struck down an Arkansas state statute that prohibited the teaching of evolution in public schools because it amounted to the legislative furthering of a religious point of view. Another 17 years intervened before the Court, in *Wallace v. Jaffree*,[41] invalidated another state law, this time one that authorized, during school time for students, moments of silence for "meditation and prayer in Alabama"; the Court found the reference to prayer an endorsement of religion. Two years later, in 1987, in *Edwards v. Aguillard*,[42] the Court struck down a Louisiana state balanced-treatment law that permitted the teaching of evolution only if scientific creationism was also taught. In 1992 the Supreme Court, in *Lee v. Weisman*,[43] invalidated the use of prayer at graduation organized and coordinated by a high school principal in Rhode Island. The prayer in this case was by a member of the local clergy selected by the principal from a revolving list of available persons. In finding the prayer a violation of the establishment clause, a majority was of the opinion that if persons in attendance at the graduation felt pressured to stand during the prayer, then such pressure amounted to an unconstitutional "psychological coercion."

The message from this history of Supreme Court decisions was that the establishment clause prohibited religious activities in public schools or at public school activities where government entities or officials such as state legislatures, school boards, and school administrators were involved. What the cases did not address was whether school prayer and religious activities might be permissible if student initiated and student led. In *Santa Fe Independent School District v. Doe*,[44] the Court provided some direction in this area by invalidating a Texas school board policy that permitted students to vote whether another student would deliver a "message" before a football game. Even though the word "prayer" did not appear in the policy, the Court relied on the board's past practice of permitting religious involvement in the public schools to invalidate it despite the fact that it had never been implemented.

Following *Lee v. Weisman*, two federal appellate courts upheld student-initiated and student-led prayer at graduation where school officials had no control over the content. In *Jones v. Clear Creek Independent School District*,[45] the Fifth Circuit upheld a school board resolution in Texas that permitted a volunteer from the senior class to deliver a non-sectarian, non-proselytizing invocation at graduation. The court found that senior class choice of another student to deliver the prayer was sufficient to take this case outside the purview of *Lee v. Weisman*. Similarly, in *Chandler v. Seligman*,[46] the Eleventh Circuit lifted an injunction by a district court enjoining enforcement of an Alabama statute that permitted non-sectarian, non-proselytizing, student-initiated prayer at school-related events. The court thought that the injunction was overbroad to the extent that it equated all student religious speech in any public context with state speech. As the court observed, so long as the prayer is genuinely student-initiated endorsement of religion, and not the product of any school policy which actively or surreptitiously encourages the speech, "the speech is private . . . [and] is constitutionally protected."[47] In effect, this element of student free speech was sufficient to overcome scrutiny under *Santa Fe*. On the other hand, the Third and Ninth Circuits invalidated school board policies permitting student-initiated and student-led prayer at graduation, finding such prayer at a school-sponsored graduation event to be a violation of the establishment clause, although not a violation of student free speech.[48]

STUDENT SPEECH WITHIN PUBLIC SCHOOLS

In 1984 Congress enacted the Equal Access Act (EAA)[49] in response to rulings that upheld the right of public school systems to deny student Bible clubs the opportunity to meet on school premises on the same basis as other student groups. The EAA prohibited public school boards that had created "limited open fora" from engaging in discrimination in "religious, political, philosophical, or other speech content." A limited open forum was declared to exist whenever one or more non-curriculum-related student groups meets on school premises during non-instructional time. While EAA does not define what constitutes non-curriculum-related student groups, it does define non-instructional time as that which is "set aside by the school before actual classroom instruction begins or after actual classroom instruction ends." In order to assure that students have a fair opportunity to conduct meetings under a school's limited open forum, meetings: must be voluntary and student initiated; cannot be government sponsored; can be attended by government employees only in a non-participatory capacity; cannot materially or substantially interfere with the educational activities of the school; and cannot be directed, conducted, or regularly attended by non-school persons.

The immediate and dramatic impact of the EAA was that student religious groups that were denied access to public school facilities in the past now had statutory authority to claim the same access rights as other non-curriculum-related student groups.[50] In *Westside Community Schools v. Mergens*,[51] the Supreme Court upheld the EAA against an establishment clause challenge from Nebraska. More important though, the Court prohibited schools from using fanciful and gerrymandered connections between academic courses and student clubs so as to avoid compliance with the EAA. For example, a chess club could not be curriculum related to logic or mathematics classes nor could the surfing club be so related to a physical education class. The presence of just one non-curriculum-related club is sufficient to invoke access rights under the EAA.

Subsequent interpretations of the EAA have extended the protection under the statute to gay-rights student groups.[52] In addition, courts have extended the term "non-instructional time" not just to meeting times before or after school, but also to any meeting time during the school day. Thus, in *Ceniceros v. Board of Trustees of Dan Diego School District*,[53] the Ninth Circuit held that the lunch period during the school day when students were free to leave campus constituted non-instructional time as long as other student groups were permitted to meet. Five years later, in *Prince v. Jacoby*,[54] in a second case from California, the same circuit held that a morning student/staff activity period also constituted a non-instructional time even though attendance was taken. As long as students had an option to meet with student clubs during this time period, religious clubs could not be excluded. In addition, the Ninth Circuit held that the EAA extended to providing the religious club equal access to funding, the yearbook, the public address system, and bulletin boards.

What has been the most extraordinary effect of EAA, though, has resulted from the interaction of the statute with free speech rights. In *Hsu v. Roslyn Union Free School District*,[55] the Second Circuit balanced a school board in New York's policy prohibiting discrimination in a wide range of areas including religion against a prospective religious student club's free speech claim. The principal had refused to permit a religious club to meet because a provision of the club's constitution that its president, vice president, and song leader be "Christians" was viewed as violating the school board's non-discrimination policy. In upholding the club's provision, the court found that the religious requirement was necessary to preserve the expressive rights of the club. In *Prince v. Jacoby*, the Ninth Circuit ruled that, in addition to items covered under the EAA, free speech required that the religious club have equal access to items that could not properly be included under the act. Thus, the club was entitled to a number of other items available to other student groups that had to be provided to the religious club under the free speech clause. Included among these items were being permitted to meet during the student/staff time and having access to school supplies, vehicles, and audio/visual equipment on the same basis as other student groups. Likewise, in *Donovan v. Punxsutawney Area School Board*,[56] the Third Circuit held that refusal of school officials in Pennsylvania to permit a religious club to meet during an activity period when attendance was taken and where other student groups were permitted to meet constituted viewpoint discrimination in violation of free speech. Even though the student in *Donovan* had graduated by the time the case reached the Third Circuit, the court held that she still was entitled to damages and attorney fees for the violation of her free speech rights.

The right of individual students to express their views on school premises or at school events is not as clear as is expression for student religious groups. Students enjoy a right to private expression as long as their speech does not represent a substantial and material likelihood of disruption under *Tinker v. Des Moines Independent School District*,[57] but this right can also be restricted where student expression might be interpreted as school endorsement of religious views. Thus, in *Cole v. Oroville Union High School District*,[58] the Ninth Circuit upheld denial of injunctive relief for two students in California who sought to deliver what the school principal considered a proselytizing prayer and a proselytizing valedictory speech at graduation. The court observed that, because the school maintained control over all aspects of the graduation ceremony, the students' proselytizing comments might be viewed as those of the school district. However, in *Westfield High School L.I.F.E. Club v. City of Westfield*,[59] the federal trial court in Massachusetts issued a preliminary injunction against a high school principal's effort to enforce a policy prohibiting distribution of "non-school curriculum or activity related literature of any kind to other students on school grounds."[60] In enjoining the principal from enforcing the rule against a student's distribution of candy canes with a clearly proselytizing message,[61] the court reflected that such "private, school-tolerated speech" can be controlled by the school only "to the extent it substantially disrupts or materially interferes with the school's disciplinary concerns."[62] The Third Circuit reached a compromise position in *Walz v. Egg Harbor Township Board of Education*.[63] The court upheld a school accommodation that permitted a student in New Jersey to distribute pencils with religious messages during non-instructional time, such as in the hallways and at lunch, but not during class time. However, the court suggested that the school's permitting the student to distribute his pencils in the hallways and at lunch may not be required under free speech.

GOVERNMENT ASSISTANCE TO RELIGIOUS SCHOOLS

The Supreme Court has an almost 60-year history of addressing government assistance to religious schools under the establishment clause. In the earliest case, *Everson v. Board of Education*,[64] in 1947, the Court upheld a New Jersey statute that provided reimbursement for parents of students in both public and religious schools who paid bus fares for their children to attend school. The Court relied on a legal fiction, the child benefit doctrine, to find that beneficiaries of the transportation reimbursement were not the schools, but instead the students who were provided a means of transportation to their schools. Similarly, 21 years later, the Court, in *Board of Education v. Allen*,[65] used the same child benefit doctrine to uphold a New York law that required public school boards to loan textbooks to non-public schools for secular subjects.

However, beginning in 1971, the Court during the next 12 years rendered a series of cases largely invalidating a number of state efforts to provide assistance to non-public schools. Since approximately 90% of non-public schools were (and still are) religious, any effort to aid non-public schools was challenged under the establishment clause. The singular most important case in this 12-year series of cases was *Lemon v. Kurtzman*[66] in 1971, which addressed a Rhode Island statute providing teacher salary supplements for

teachers teaching secular subjects, as well as providing textbooks and instructional materials used in the teaching of secular subjects. Other than the
loaning of textbooks, the Supreme Court invalidated all other forms of assistance. In analyzing the constitutionality of the statute in this case, the
Court fabricated its well-known tripartite *Lemon* test. Any government assistance violates the Constitution if it violates one or more of the three tests:
fails to have a secular purpose; advances or inhibits religion; or involves
government in an excessive entanglement with religion.

Subsequent to *Lemon*, the Court struck down the following state efforts:
New York's provision of maintenance and repair grants for schools and tuition credits for parents;[67] New York's reimbursement to non-public schools
for tests that included teacher prepared tests;[68] Pennsylvania's reimbursement to parents of tuition paid to non-public schools;[69] Pennsylvania's loaning of instructional materials and providing auxiliary services such as psychological testing, counseling, and hearing and vision;[70] and Ohio's loaning
of instructional materials, but upholding reimbursement of standardized
testing materials and the provision of on-site diagnostic services.[71]

A change began in 1983 in *Mueller v. Allen*,[72] where the Court upheld
a Minnesota statute permitting a $500 and $700 state tax deduction for
students in public or non-public elementary and secondary schools. Even
though the parents of non-public students were far more likely to claim
the full benefit of the tax deductions, the Supreme Court found the state
statute constitutional under the establishment clause; the benefit (deduction) was facially applicable to parents of both public and non-public students, and in any case, the benefit to non-public school parents resulted
from their choice, not the government's choice, to enroll their children in
non-public schools. Ten years after *Mueller*, the Court, in *Zobrest v.
Catalina Foothills School District*,[73] held that the provision of on-site
IDEA services at a religious school in Arizona did not violate the establishment clause, again relying on the concepts that the benefit went to the
student, not the school, and that the student's presence in the religious
school was the result of parent choice. Four years after *Zobrest*, the Court,
in *Agostini v. Felton*,[74] upheld the provision of Title I services on-site in
religious schools in New York, following the reasoning in *Zobrest*.
In reaching its conclusion, the Court in *Agostini* reversed its decision in
Aguilar v. Felton[75] 12 years earlier holding that providing Title I services
in religious schools violated the establishment clause.

Three years after *Agostini*, the Court, in *Mitchell v. Helms*,[76] in 2000, upheld the provision of Chapter 2 instructional materials on-site in religious schools in Louisiana; a plurality reversed a pair of the Court's decisions from more than two decades earlier, *Meek v. Pittenger* and *Wolman v. Walter*, which held that providing such instructional materials violated the establishment clause. Writing for the majority in *Mitchell*, Justice Thomas explained that no violation of the establishment clause occurred as long as materials being loaned to religious schools were equally available to public schools, the materials loaned were neutral in content, and the presence of students in the religious schools was the result of parent choice. Finally, two years after *Mitchell v. Helms*, the Court, in *Zelman v. Simmons-Harris*,[77] upheld the Cleveland Voucher Program. The Court found the voucher program to contain common elements upheld in earlier decisions: the program permitted voucher funds to be spent on a number of public and non-public educational options, and any benefit to religious schools was the result of parent choice in sending their children to religious schools.

CEREMONIAL RELIGION

Two issues in need of Supreme Court resolution are the presence of the Ten Commandments on school premises and "under God" in the Pledge of Allegiance. Over 20 years ago, the Supreme Court, in *Stone v. Graham*,[78] held that a Kentucky statute requiring the posting of the Ten Commandments in each public school in the state violated the establishment clause under the *Lemon* test because it lacked a secular purpose and because it had the effect of advancing religion by encouraging students to read them. The fact that the copies of the Ten Commandments were paid for by private funds was irrelevant. Whether the Ten Commandments might fare better if they are placed among other secular historical documents presents an argument parallel to *Lynch v. Donnelly*,[79] where the Supreme Court upheld display of a publicly owned crèche among a variety of other secular symbols.

In *Elk Grove Unified School District v. Newdow*,[80] the Supreme Court avoided deciding whether the words "under God" in the Pledge of Allegiance violated the establishment clause. The Court limited its judgment to finding that the plaintiff lacked standing to challenge California's requirement of a teacher-led Pledge of Allegiance. This case has been refiled and will most likely wind its way back to the Supreme Court. While some argue that the words "under God" should be permissible under the establishment clause as a kind of ceremonial deism, others argue that the name of a deity can never properly be considered ceremonial in nature. In effect, some persons espousing this latter argument would prefer that "under God" be deleted altogether rather than be diluted to a meaningless ceremonialism.

CONCLUSION

For 60 years, courts have engaged in a vibrant debate regarding the appropriate balance between protecting free exercise of religion while prohibiting government endorsement of particular religious perspectives. More recently, the Supreme Court has injected religious speech as a fully protected subset of free speech into the equation. In the ebb and flow of judicial opinions, the free exercise clause has become less of a force in protecting religious beliefs, but the gap appears to be more than filled by the free speech clause. The establishment clause, once a formidable force in restricting government assistance to religious schools, has been reduced to a more manageable obstruction only where government actions are not neutral and cannot be justified under the aegis of parent choice.

NOTES

1. *Myers v. Nebraska*, 262 U.S. 390 (1923).
2. *Pierce v. Society of Sisters*, 268 U.S. 510 (1925).
3. *Pierce v. Society of Sisters*, at 535.
4. *Pierce v. Society of Sisters*, at 534.
5. *Yoder v. Wisconsin*, 406 U.S. 205 (1972).
6. See, for example, *New Life Baptist Church Acad. v. East Longmeadow*, 885 F.2d 940 (1st Cir., 1989); *State v. Shaver*, 294 N.W.2d 883 (N.D., 1980).
7. *Employment Division v. State*, 494 U.S. 872 (1990).
8. See, for example, Minn. Stat. Ann. § 120A-22 (9) (10) (11).
9. Compare *Snyder v. Charlotte Sch. Dist.*, 365 N.W.2d 151 (Mich., 1984) with *Swanson v. Guthrie Independent. Sch. Dist.*, 135 F.3d 694 (10th Cir., 1998).

10. See *Thomas v. Allegany County Bd. of Educ.*, 443 A.2d 622 (Md. Ct. Spec. App., 1982).

11. *Barrow v. Greenville Independent Sch. Dist.*, 332 F.3d 844 (5th Cir., 2003).

12. *Barrett v. Steubenville City Schools*, 388 F.3d 967 (6th Cir., 2004).

13. See *Barrett v. Steubenville City Schools*, at 972–974.

14. *Lamb's Chapel v. Center Moriches Union Free Sch. Dist.*, 508 U.S. 384 (1993).

15. *Lamb's Chapel v. Center Moriches Union Free Sch. Dist.*, at 388, fn. 3.

16. *Lamb's Chapel v. Center Moriches Union Free Sch. Dist.*, at 391, fn. 5.

17. See *Widmar v. Vincent*, 454 U.S. 263 (1981).

18. See *Lamb's Chapel v. Center Moriches Union Free Sch. Dist.*, 959 F.2d 381, 384 (2d Cir., 1992).

19. *Lamb's Chapel v. Center Moriches Union Free Sch. Dist.*, 508 U.S. at 395.

20. *Good News Club v. Milford Central Schools*, 533 U.S. 98 (2001) [*Education Law Report* 154 (2001), 45].

21. Voting for the majority on the merits were Chief Justice Rehnquist and Justices Scalia, O'Connor, Kennedy, and Thomas. Justice Breyer concurred on procedural grounds.

22. *Good News Club v. Milford Central Schools*, at 108.

23. *Bronx Household of Faith v. Board of Educ. of City of New York*, 331 F.3d 342 (2d Cir., 2003).

24. *Bronx Household of Faith v. Board of Educ. of City of New York*, at 353, 354.

25. *Bronx Household of Faith v. Board of Educ. of City of New York*, at 356.

26. *Fairfax Covenant Church v. Fairfax County School Board*, 17 F.3d 703 (4th Cir., 1994).

27. *Fairfax Covenant Church v. Fairfax County School Board*, at 705.

28. *Widmar v. Vincent*, 454 U.S. 263 (1981).

29. *Daugherty v. Vanguard Charter School Academy*, 116 F.Supp.2d 897 (W.D. Mich., 2000).

30. *Rusk v. Clearview Local Schools*, 379 F.3d 418 (6th Cir., 2004).

31. *Rusk v. Clearview Local Schools*, at 423.

32. See *Child Evangelism of Maryland v. Montgomery County Pub. Schs.*, 373 F.3d 589 (4th Cir., 2004); *Hills v. Scottsdale Unified Sch. Dist.*, 329 F.3d 1044 (9th Cir., 2003).

33. *Bannon v. Sch. Dist. of Palm Beach County*, 387 F.3d 1208 (11th Cir., 2004).

34. *Hazelwood Sch. Dist. v. Kuhlmeier*, 484 U.S. 260, 273 (1988).

35. *Fleming v. Jefferson County Sch. Dist. R-1*, 298 F.3d 918, 930 (10th Cir., 2002).

36. *McCollum v. Board of Educ.*, 333 U.S. 203 (1948).

37. *Zorach v. Clauson*, 343 U.S. 306 (1952).

38. *Engle v. Vitale*, 370 U.S. 421 (1962).

39. *Sch. Dist. of Abington Township v. Schemmp*, 374 U.S. 203 (1963).

40. *Epperson v. Arkansas*, 393 U.S. 97 (1968).

41. *Wallace v. Jaffree*, 472 U.S. 38 (1985).

42. *Edwards v. Aguillard*, 482 U.S. 578 (1987).

43. *Lee v. Weisman*, 505 U.S. 577 (1992).

44. *Santa Fe Independent Sch. Dist. v. Doe*, 530 U.S. 290 (2000).

45. *Jones v. Clear Creek Independent Sch. Dist.*, 977 F.2d 963 (5th Cir., 1992).

46. *Chandler v. Seligman*, 230 F.3d 1313 (11th Cir., 2000).

47. *Chandler v. Seligman*, at 1317.

48. *Am. Civil Liberties Union of New Jersey v. Black Horse Pike Reg'l Bd. of Educ.*, 84 F.3d 1471 (3d Cir., 1995); *Cole v. Oroville Union High Sch. Dist.*, 228 F.3d 1092 (9th Cir., 2000); *Lassonde v. Pleasanton Unified Sch. Dist.*, 320 F.3d 979 (9th Cir., 2003).

49. 20 U.S.C. § 4071.

50. See *Lubbock Civil Liberties Union v. Lubbock Indep. Sch. Dist.*, 669 F.2d 1038 (5th Cir., 1982); *Brandon v. Guilderland Bd. of Educ.*, 635 F.2d 971 (2d Cir., 1980).

51. *Westside Community Schools v. Mergens*, 496 U.S. 226 (1990).

52. See *East High Sch. Prism Club v. Seidel*, 95 F.Supp.2d 1239 (D. Utah, 2000).

53. *Ceniceros v. Board of Trustees of Dan Diego Sch. Dist.*, 106 F.3d 878 (9th Cir., 1997).

54. *Prince v. Jacoby*, 303 F.3d 1074 (9th Cir., 2002).

55. *Hsu v. Roslyn Union Free Sch. Dist.*, 85 F.3d 839 (2d Cir., 1996).

56. *Donovan v. Punxsutawney Area School Board*, 336 F.3d 211 (3d Cir., 2003).

57. *Tinker v. Des Moines Independent Sch. Dist.*, 393 U.S. 503, 509 (1969).

58. *Cole v. Oroville Union High Sch. Dist.*, 228 F.3d 1092 (9th Cir., 2000), cert. denied sub nom., *Niemeyer v. Oroville Union High Sch. Dist.*, 532 U.S. 905 (2001).

59. *Westfield High School L.I.F.E. Club v. City of Westfield*, 249 F.Supp.2d 98 (D. Mass., 2003).

60. *Westfield High School L.I.F.E. Club v. City of Westfield*, at 104.

61. *Westfield High School L.I.F.E. Club v. City of Westfield*, at 104, 105.

62. *Westfield High School L.I.F.E. Club v. City of Westfield*, at 114, note 13.

63. *Walz v. Egg Harbor Township Board of Educ.*, 342 F.3d 271, 280 (3d Cir., 2003).

64. *Everson v. Board of Educ.*, 330 U.S. 1 (1947).
65. *Board of Educ. v. Allen*, 392 U.S. 236 (1968).
66. *Lemon v. Kurtzman*, 403 U.S. 602 (1971).
67. *Committee v. Nyquist*, 413 U.S. 756 (1973).
68. *Levitt v. Committee*, 413 U.S. 472 (1973).
69. *Sloan v. Lemon*, 413 U.S. 825 (1973).
70. *Meek v. Pittenger*, 421 U.S. 349 (1975).
71. *Wolman v. Walter*, 433 U.S. 229 (1977).
72. *Mueller v. Allen*, 463 U.S. 388 (1983).
73. *Zobrest v. Catalina Foothills Sch. Dist.*, 509 U.S. 1 (1993).
74. *Agostini v. Felton*, 521 U.S. 203 (1997).
75. *Aguilar v. Felton*, 473 U.S. 402 (1985).
76. *Mitchell v. Helms*, 530 U.S. 793 (2000).
77. *Zelman v. Simmons-Harris*, 536 U.S. 639 (2002).
78. *Stone v. Graham*, 449 U.S. 39 (1980).
79. *Lynch v. Donnelly*, 465 U.S. 668 (1984).
80. *Elk Grove Unified Sch. Dist. v. Newdow*, 124 S.Ct. 2301 (2004).

About the Editor and Contributors

Frank Brown, Ph.D., is the Cary C. Boshamer Distinguished Professor of Education and dean emeritus, School of Education, University of North Carolina at Chapel Hill, and a review officer for the State of North Carolina. He earned his Ph.D. at the University of California at Berkeley in policy, planning, and administration. A regular presenter at the annual conferences of the Education Law Association and the American Educational Research Association, Dr. Brown has spoken and written extensively on issues involving school law, policy studies, local school administration, and higher education administration. He is also a member of the editorial board of *School Business Affairs* published by the Association of School Business Officials.

Bradley Colwell, J.D., Ph.D., professor of education law and department chair, has been at Southern Illinois University, Carbondale, since 1996. He earned both his Ph.D. and J.D. from the University of Illinois at Urbana-Champaign. He teaches classes in Illinois school law, professional negotiations, school finance, and the politics of education. Dr. Colwell is active in scholarly research and public service to elementary and secondary education. His research agenda includes issues involving Fourth Amendment search/seizure, home schooling, and institutional accountability. He is co-editor of the *School Law Reporter*, the primary journal for the Education Law Association, and was elected to the ELA board of directors in 2002.

Timothy J. Ilg, Ph.D., is an associate professor in the Department of Educational Leadership at the University of Dayton in Dayton, Ohio. His research interests include distance learning and the impact of Catholic high schools on urban children. Dr. Ilg also has 30 years of experience in public education, including 23 years in a large urban school district. He currently coordinates his department's online masters and principal licensure programs and assists the KnowledgeWorks Foundation in the creation of small urban high schools and early college high schools associated with local universities.

Donald R. Johnson, Ed.D., is deputy assistant executive director of the Illinois Association of School Business Officials, and associate professor emeritus, Northern Illinois University, DeKalb. Prior to these positions, Dr. Johnson was employed as a superintendent or business manager, in local school districts and regional offices of education. He has been a regular contributor to and a former editorial board member of *School Business Affairs*.

Ralph D. Mawdsley, Ph.D., J.D., a professor in the Department of Counseling, Administration, Supervision, and Adult Learning at Cleveland State University, is a past president of the Education Law Association and a regular presenter at the annual ELA conference, as well as at numerous national and international law and education conferences. In addition to past practical experience that includes serving as a private school superintendent, university legal counsel, and a vice president of human resources, he is the sole author or co-author of a number of books on the subject of education and law and serves as co-editor of the Education Law Into Practice section of the *Education Law Reporter*. Dr. Mawdsley currently teaches courses in school law, special education law, and sports law.

Timothy E. Morse, Ed.D., is an assistant director of special education overseeing curriculum and instruction matters for the Harrison County School District, Gulfport, Mississippi, and director of the district's assistive technology resource team. He is also an adjunct assistant professor of special education at the University of Southern Mississippi, where he teaches preservice special education teacher preparation courses. Dr. Morse publishes on issues pertaining to technology applications in schools and special education, as well as on curriculum, instruction, and administrative issues pertaining to special education.

Allan G. Osborne Jr., Ed.D., is the principal of the Snug Harbor Community School in Quincy, Massachusetts. He has authored numerous articles, monographs, and textbooks on special education law. A past president of the Education Law Association, he is a frequent presenter at ELA conferences and writes the Students With Disabilities chapter of the *Yearbook of Education Law* published by ELA. Dr. Osborne is on the Editorial Advisory Committee of *West's Education Law Reporter* and is co-editor of the Education Law Into Practice section of that journal.

Patrick D. Pauken, J.D., Ph.D., is an associate professor of educational administration and leadership studies at Bowling Green State University, where he teaches school law, special education law, and moral and ethical leadership. He has presented and published in various areas of ethics and school law, including school violence, technology and cyberspace, copyright law, religion and public school curriculum, special education, and higher education. Dr. Pauken earned his law degree and Ph.D. from Ohio State University and is a member of the Ohio Bar.

C. Daniel Raisch, Ph.D., is an associate professor in educational administration and associate dean of the School of Education and Allied Professions at the University of Dayton. Dr. Raisch teaches education law, school administration, and school finance. Prior to joining the faculty at the University of Dayton, he was a superintendent in two Ohio schools for 18 years, taught in public school for five years, and held other school administrative positions for seven years. In addition, Dr. Raisch has made numerous presentations to teachers and administrators relating to education law.

Charles J. Russo, J.D., Ed.D., is the Panzer Chair in Education and an adjunct professor of law at the University of Dayton. In addition to being a past president of the Education Law Association, he is vice chair of the editorial board of *School Business Affairs* and a member of the Legal Affairs Committee. He is also on a variety of other editorial boards and is editor-in-chief of *Education and Urban Society*. A regular presenter at the annual conferences of ELA and ASBO, Dr. Russo has written and spoken extensively on a variety of legal issues in journals and conferences in the United States and overseas.

Philip E. Tieman, Ph.D., is the administrator in residence, Department of Educational Leadership, at the University of Dayton School of Education and Allied Professions. He earned his Ph.D. at Ohio State University and has taught at Ohio State and lectured at universities in New Jersey and New York. Dr. Tieman has served as a superintendent of schools, principal, and teacher in New Jersey, New York, and Ohio. His specific areas of interest are leadership development, public school politics and policy, the superintendency, school finance and business management, labor relations, dispute resolution programs, and the development of administrative internships.